D0271424

VIEW FROM THE BOYS

PEOPLE, PLANS AND PROBLEMS SERIES

General editor: Professor J. B. Mays
                   Department of Sociology
                   University of Liverpool

published

The Family in Transition   F. George Kay
It's Past, Present and Future Patterns

Friend of the Family   Patrick Goldring
The Story of the Family Service Units

From School to Work   Kenneth Roberts
A Study of the Youth Employment Service

A New Bill of Rights for Britain   Frank Stacey

Planning and Human Need   Philip Heywood

Violence in Human Society   John Gunn

The Character Training Industry
Kenneth Roberts, Graham E. White
and Howard J. Parker
Adventure-Training Schemes in Britain

Pressure Groups   Bridget Pym

in preparation

Penal Reform   Merfyn Turner

The Sociology of Race   Gideon Ben-Tovim

View from The Boys is an associated volume in this series

VIEW FROM
THE BOYS

A Sociology of Down-Town Adolescents

HOWARD J. PARKER

*Formerly Research Worker, now Lecturer in
Department of Sociology, University of Liverpool*

DAVID & CHARLES
NEWTON ABBOT   LONDON
NORTH POMFRET (VT)   VANCOUVER

0 7153 6456 1

Set in 11 on 13 point Baskerville
and printed in Great Britain by
Latimer Trend & Company Ltd Plymouth
for David & Charles (Holdings) Limited
South Devon House Newton Abbot Devon

Published in the United States of America
by David & Charles Inc North Pomfret
Vermont 05053 USA

Published in Canada by Douglas David &
Charles Limited 3645 McKechnie Drive
West Vancouver BC

Contents

	Preface	7
	Introduction	11
1	Roundhouse	21
2	Delinquency on the Move	45
3	Catseye Kings for a While	62
4	A Question of Style	117
5	The Authority Conspiracy	157
6	On the Edge of Society	195
	Final Words	208
	Glossary	212
	Appendix: The Fieldwork Approach	214
	Notes and References	225
	Acknowledgements	234
	Index	235

'Why should we have to rob money off the fuckin' business classes, what's toffee-nose done for it, he hasn't worked. Distribution of wealth is fuckin' scandalous. You know the aristocrats that are loaded, where did he get it from? From his father and his father, it probably boils down, boy, that he fought a fuckin' peasant for a bit of land. So you says OK I'll fight you for it and he says, "But that's not cricket old boy, not cricket." ' (*Streak*)

Preface

The research sociologist ought, perhaps, to have his own identity problems about who he is, who he serves and by what right he functions. Such dilemmas lie at the heart of sociology. The sociologist who becomes involved in investigating social phenomena that are also officially designated 'problems' and subjects of public concern suffers all the more. On juvenile delinquency, if the sociologist states the 'obvious' he is accused of wasting his time and other people's money; if, however, his thesis goes against conventional wisdom he is likely to find his work refuted and rejected as misinformed or biased.

Such a concern of course assumes a readership, which may appear pretentious in itself. Yet without such an assumption I would have found the motivation and personal justification for a project such as the one described in this book hard to come by. Obviously an important section of my hypothetical readership is made up of fellow sociologists, both colleagues and students. Yet their reaction to this book, whilst it may turn out to be painfully deflating, is not really problematic. When talking with social scientists about delinquency at the relevant conferences and seminars, one is often preaching to the converted. Here I have tried quite consciously to write for another potential audience, small but influential, that concerns me sufficiently to want to 'catch' them before they look at the pages ahead. There is a large trade in adolescence and delinquency, and many people are employed to care for, educate, find jobs for and control the down-town, and indeed all, adolescents. Most of those so employed are respected members of the community, whether they be local government officials, magistrates, policemen, probation officers, social workers, youth workers or school teachers. The integrity of these people should, in the main, not be doubted. It is their daily task to hold opinions and make decisions which determine the fate of the urban adolescent, especially if he should break the law.

Of late, I have increasingly found myself talking to, sitting around the conference table with, and writing to these 'professionals'. (That too I believe to be a meaningful role for the sociologist.) Despite their official titles, congeniality and obvious 'concern' about delinquency, these local decision-makers often seem to be extremely distant from the characters about whom they hold forth. This is not so much a criticism of them as of society's communication and power structures.

It is to these people that this book should have something to say. My hope is that some may mellow and melt a little, denounce some misleading stereotypes and open a little wider to the other side. My fear is that they will instead recoil in self-defence. The down-town adolescent in the privacy of his own world has his own opinions and holds his own informal conferences about those who decide his fate. The systematic recording of such views and their interpretation make up an important part of this book. A good deal of what the boys say will be of little immediate comfort to people who have official dealings with them. Some may get upset. I ask the angry and offended not to bristle and retreat, however, but to battle on beyond apparent insult in search of the meaning behind the down-town adolescents' views.

This study is not, nor does it claim to be, anything approaching a definitive statement about delinquency. It is an exploratory and groping affair. The participant observer who knocks around with a group of adolescents can only look in some corners. He can say little for instance about the significance of the home or parental failure—such limitations are in the very nature of the study. It is the great social and physical distance between the city adolescent and those concerned with his behaviour which leads to vast over-generalisation, inaccurate and insensitive stereotyping and misrepresentation of who he is and in what sense he is a problem. I hope that this book may provide an additional perspective, perhaps a missing link, which will at least help humanise the down-town adolescent.

Introduction

He was very friendly, this natural-gas man who'd come to convert me. We were getting on fine talking about all sorts of things, football and the price of stand tickets, inflation, and how things generally seemed to be 'going down the nick'. With this in mind the gas man assured me that, 'You can't leave your car in town for a couple of minutes nowadays without someone breaking into it. I left mine down there the other week and had it done in, windows smashed, radio wrenched out, the lot. They're a right shower of bums down there, never done an honest day's work in their lives.' Concerned that my dismantled gas fire would never be put together again, I made some neutral comment and went back to writing this book about the 'shower of bums' in question.

The gas man was what some people call 'respectable working class'. He lived in a 'nice' house on a new council estate 'well out' of the city, but still had his Liverpool accent. And here he was condemning his proletarian contemporaries who lived down in the city proper. He was calling them no-good layabouts and robbers, just as the wealthy businessman was when he took his Rover 2000 TC car to the Lord Mayor to show him the extensive damage done by repeated attacks from 'vandals'. By speaking to the local press and lobbying city MPs, this businessman, as reported in the *Liverpool Echo*, aimed 'to start a survey of people who had their cars damaged in the city as I believe it is a far bigger problem than a few people are letting on'.

The gas man and the Rover-owning businessman remind us of the need to define carefully what we mean by 'Us' and 'Them': this dichotomy means more than simply 'middle class' and 'working class'. When some down-town adolescents talk about 'Them' they don't simply mean 'middle-class' people but include all outsiders who 'think they're better than us'. 'Them' could include the gas man with his well-paid skilled manual job, his newish car, centrally heated, gardened council house and his conviction not to 'live down there no more'.

Using the Registrar General's classification of the employed population, we see he divides them into 5 social classes one below another. The businessman would come in Class I or II with his fellow managers, directors and professionals. The gas man would find himself in Class III with clerks, typists, and other skilled manual workers. Although such a break down of social class by occupation is very crude it does give some indication of where the subjects of this book, The Boys from Roundhouse, are situated in terms of occupation and subsequent wealth in relation to society as a whole. Roundhouse men are most often in Class IV and V; in occupational terms they are relegated to the bottom of the pile.

Many people would also regard living 'down town' as another symptom of being at the bottom. As far as The Boys are concerned, living 'down town' in the main means little more than living in flats close to Liverpool's city centre. In connotative terms and in outsiders' eyes, however, living down town often means belonging to one of those neighbourhoods made up of dilapidated, obsolete, tenement blocks common to the inner area of Liverpool and other large cities. Roundhouse is one such area, looked on unfavourably by most who scurry past.

The down-town adolescents have a bad reputation. Whilst they must share this general reputation with their youthful, inner-city and 'new estate' neighbours, The Boys from Round-

house are, like all their contemporaries, not in fact the *same*.
Neighbourhoods simply aren't the same. Roundhouse still, like
other down-town neighbourhoods, has its own integrity, history
and identity. The Boys are more than stereotyped down-town
adolescents: they are from Roundhouse, and for them and their
story this is important. Although in no way a miniature community study, Chapter 1 considers some aspects of Roundhouse's identity and the constraints on youngsters growing up
in the neighbourhood. Delinquent action always takes place in
a context in which actors find meaning. Roundhouse is a vital
part of that context.

The Boys (see Figure 3, p 65) have now grown up. They are
a social network of late adolescents who, as the dominant peer
group at their own age level, have reached manhood together,
having lived in Roundhouse all their lives. Nearly all The
Boys, during their adolescence, have behaved—many of them
regularly—in a way which has brought them the label 'severely
delinquent'. Much of this book is about their delinquent activities. However, since it aims towards presenting The Boys' view
of such behaviour, what follows contrasts starkly with the outsider's view. Certainly with the owners of vandalised cars already mentioned, and with large sections of the general population with enough investment in society actually to own a car
that can be vandalised, The Boys are unpopular. This sometimes
delinquent social group is seen by outsiders as part of that pool
of delinquents usually classed as the cause of vandalism, hooli-
ganism and mugging; they are the riff-raff, the yobs and the
bums. This well-established 'bottom of the pile' can be seen
standing around corners, walking around town as if they owned
it, propping up the bars of a certain class of pubs throughout
opening hours. They're probably long-haired, almost certainly
scruffy and invariably ill-mannered.

Such is the stereotype, and few people have the time, inclina-
tion or opportunity to go beyond it. Often sociologists are
accused of being naïve even to try. Certainly they are frequently
condemned for having their heads in the clouds and nothing

better to do than preach 'understanding' for the deviant. Wait, one hears it said, until it's their turn to have their car stolen or get their tiny academic minds split open and their wallets snatched. Yet it's all relative. Not long ago a tutor in criminology asked his class of future social workers if any of them had met a real juvenile delinquent. The attitude behind such an objectifying comment is not uncommon in the world of social science. When it comes down to it, most of the academics and researchers, whom society inadvertently selects to study its chosen social problems, are distant from and unappreciative of the adolescent who sometimes commits specific delinquent acts. The student of deviance often never meets his *subjects* of study, only his *objects* of study. For by visiting the deviants in prison, borstal and other human zoos, or by cornering them in classrooms and youth clubs to answer questionnaires and write essays, the sociologist misses meeting them as people and seeing them in their 'normal society'.

This study has several limitations and is open to much criticism, yet I believe it was worth undertaking because it visits relatively unexplored territory for sociologists, social workers, school teachers and 'Them' generally. By seeing The Boys as subjects and as 'natural' people in their own normal social world, it aims to be 'appreciative'. This over-used term comes from a leading sociological light, David Matza, who has headed a theoretical if not empirical search-party into 'naturalism'. Matza's demand is for a constant effort by the sociologist to remain true to the phenomenon he is studying—to tell it like it really is. Within this frame of reference a sociology of a sometimes delinquent group of down-town adolescents must focus on what the members of that network perceive and believe and how they act. Yet if we are not careful such appreciation will lead us into believing that anything they themselves do not say or do is unimportant to our comprehension. This would be a mistake. Thus whilst the book is concerned almost wholly with The Boys' views, it also points out, in my terms, that what the network say they do and what they actually do are not always synonymous. It tries to explain behaviour The Boys themselves cannot always articulate to *anybody*, and it points out where their views are parochial in their comprehension of the situation. The Boys are neither romanticised nor condemned. The message is 'stay cool'.

To adopt such an ambitious stance for a study leads one into heavily booby-trapped terrains, for it demands a method of research—participant observation—which despite encouraging academic noises is rarely attempted and even less frequently successfully completed. Although I discuss my fieldwork approach in some detail in the Appendix a few points should be made now. Firstly, I did not pick Roundhouse or its largest identifiable male adolescent group as a subject of study. Although Roundhouse is regarded as a 'high-delinquency area' and The Boys' delinquent careers* are seen as highly problematic by the relevant agencies, these were not the prime reasons why the fieldwork took place where it did.

It was whilst working as a residential dog's-body 'go and play with the kids' community-youth worker at a country holiday centre for Liverpool 'street kids', Sandhills, that I first encountered The Boys, who were only about sixteen years old at the time. Although I was twenty-two years gone there was little difference in our appearance. Initially I became involved with Roundhouse kids of all ages and both sexes. They came and stayed at Sandhills for weekends, in their holidays and whenever they could. We went on camping holidays and day trips, had parties, discos and arguments. It was only because I got on with and enjoyed being with The Boys and The Girls that this study evolved. My acceptance into the network would have been highly unlikely if my credentials hadn't been checked in the highly favourable atmosphere of Sandhills. I could not have become a regular face in Roundhouse without the Sandhills introduction, nor would I have tried.

* 'Career' is used loosely in this book and is in no way implying a determinism or predisposition to delinquency. The Boys' delinquency, as we shall see, is far from rigid, inevitable, or totally predictable.

By the time I came down town I was established as OK—
that is, amongst other things, boozy, suitably dressed and un-
groomed, playing football well enough to survive and badly
enough to be funny, 'knowing the score' about theft behaviour
and sexual exploits. Once accepted locally by a few of The
Boys I was able to take on the role of a relatively quiet 'OK'
outsider who for several reasons was hanging around. Since I
had been vetted by reliable sources I was able to move slowly
into a wider acceptance until I could join any combination of
the network when I had time. There were intensive periods
when I spent all my waking hours with combinations of The
Boys, other periods when I only spent some evenings and
weekends. Never did I disappear for more than a week except
when I was actually out of the area with some of the network.
Rarely did I spend less than 10 hours in any one week with the
core of the group.

I am still a regular at Roundhouse and hope to continue to
be, for I enjoy the friendship I like to think I have there. Such
friendship has been the basis of the whole study, being friends
with the few has allowed acquaintanceship with many, and so
on. To some, talking about friendship in relation to social
research may seem misplaced. Perhaps to those who have
attempted a depth-participant observation study such sentiments will seem less irrelevant. All I can say is that *this* study
would not have survived without such reciprocity.

Secondly this study is based largely on words, on what people
say to each other, and for this reason extensive dialogue is used.
Except where indicated as 'taped' (T), all the conversations in
the book are reconstructed from memory. I mention this point
now because my own ability to recall vividly lengthy conversations has come as a pleasant surprise personally but may be
viewed, understandably, with scepticism by the reader. Two
factors have helped reliable reconstruction. Firstly most conversations included as 'themes' occur regularly and repetitively,
and I usually had more than one chance to grasp significance
and meaning. Further the 'third man', the observer, listening

into normal conversation, say in a pub or club, can concentrate on certain aspects of the evening's dialogue. Many was the time I came home late at night with just a few sentences ringing in my ears demanding to be written down and pondered before I could sleep. However, for readers concerned with methodology in particular it is perhaps wise to read the Appendix before the book and hopefully alleviate some questions about research method.

Another methodological problem in writing up fieldwork has involved the thorny topic of anonymity. Few real names are used in the book and the identity of The Boys is heavily disguised. Further, I have indulged in a selective distortion of the area and the censorship of events. I don't, however, think these disguises distort the picture unduly or undermine the significance of locality. The area itself is more difficult to disguise, but its identification by a few local Sherlock Holmeses is hopefully of little consequence. Roundhouse is no freak area with a dreadful reputation in a law-abiding city. It is just one neighbourhood of walk-up tenement blocks, one of a dozen in downtown Liverpool alone. In terms of outsiders' definition, society's concern, and Authority's surveillance it is just one not very special grey spot on a big black map. Anonymity is important mainly because Roundhouse should not be made something more than it is by being picked for the spotlight.

Moving on to the content of the book, Chapter 2 deals with some Roundhouse youths who, as The Boys' juniors, are at present involved in the 'processes' of growing up in the neighbourhood. By looking briefly at the delinquent activities these kids are involved in two themes are furthered. Firstly, some insight into The Boys' earlier adolescence can be gained, since in many ways they shared the same contingencies of childhood as their successors are doing. The innovatory nature of much delinquency is also illustrated. Delinquent traditions are not simply passed on, initiative and innovation often *transform* former styles. After this chapter, The Boys take over the stage. The study looks at three years of their adolescence. For most of

B

the network Year One was their first post-school year. Information about this period was not gained from direct observation but from taped interview and directed and incidental conversations which occurred in Year Two. Years Two and Three involved the meat of the fieldwork period, with six months at Sandhills and the remainder in the city. Each year commences in the spring.

Chapter 3 deals with a description and analysis of the *context* in which The Boys became heavily involved in delinquent action, stealing car radios, 'catseyes', to the extent that they christened themselves the 'Catseye Kings'. The problem-solving and choice-making involved in delinquency is often lost sight of: this chapter attempts to analyse more fully than is normal the nature of delinquent choice. Chapter 5 considers The Boys' view of Authority—all those involved in the prosecution process, as illustrated through their contest with such officials during the catseye business. These two chapters present a glimmering of the real complexity of the processes involved in the down-town adolescents' delinquent careers. Indeed who is delinquent, why, when and how often are questions which, even after sustained observation, can only be answered tentatively.

Chapter 4 takes a different track and considers other aspects of The Boys' style. Like many other people's, the down-town adolescent's average week is mundane, routine and sometimes boring. Some months, over the two years, The Boys were 'hanging around', at other times they were employed in manual work. It is from these extensive nothing-doing periods that The Boys sometimes break out and search for the good times. The style of their break out is part of the subject-matter of this fourth chapter. Hence nights-out-down-town and all that they involve become the focus of our attention, since it is during such action-packed periods that The Boys are most vibrant, spontaneous and witty, and perhaps to the outsider or onlooker most aggressive and irresponsible.

Chapter 6 considers The Boys' position in society. It asks

where they stand in relation to the dominant ideology and why, looking briefly at the less punitive dealings they have had with the wider society.

Finally while The Boys' particular expressive style and delinquent solutions are unique to themselves, and distinctive even in their own city, they should merely be placed in part of a wider category of deviant solutions. Most publicity and advertised public concern goes to the muggers and chibbers; The Boys are rarely involved in such offences (which in itself will be a revelation to many). Their delinquency is mundane and everyday. It is rarely colourful and indeed not always considered very 'clever' by The Boys themselves. Actual delinquent styles, as this book suggests, vary over time and place and are related to age, opportunity, contingency and personal experience. Having said this I am convinced that whilst local factors influence specific styles, the general responses of 'unskilled' working-class urban adolescents out on the edge of society are related to much wider structural constraints and causal factors which are part of a more important dialectic only touched by this book. Before this etiology is fully accepted a million communication hurdles must be removed. Thus if I could wish one thing for this book it is that it dispels just a few of the prejudices, stereotypes and myths which refuse to admit choice, rationality, initiative and normality to much of that behaviour most often called juvenile delinquency.

1 Roundhouse

Everybody's heard of Roundhouse, it's always been known.

Liverpool, what does it mean to the outsider—football, strikes, a peculiar accent as if everybody's got a clothes-peg on their nose, The Beatles, a famous port, a working-class conurbation? Like that of any exciting city, Liverpool's meaning changes the deeper one gets immersed into its heart. Drive into the city through the great socio-economic arcs of urban decay and renewal and you'll reach that heart or what's left of it—the Inner City.

To live in the Inner City is to live down town. To live in the inner areas is to be part of an extensive chess game which planners and redevelopers are playing with whole neighbourhoods. Recent moves are evident as new housing sprouts up adjacent to the old, but it is still the new which is the eyesore amongst the grey homogeneity of urban decay. As in a chess game the players aim to empty the board; if present strategies prevail the inner population could eventually fall from 230,000 to 80,000.

Yet there are signs that 'the people' will not allow 'them' to decide their fates for ever. As yet they are only murmuring with tenants' associations, community councils and newsletters. Nowadays to live down town is to be in the way; if you don't move out to Cantril Farm or Netherley or other faraway estates they'll build around you, through you, talk about what to do with you, action-project you and give you a fair rent increase. If you don't expect things to improve then life is tolerable, and life is tolerable for most down towners because they don't even think they have an authentic right to decide their future. The political awareness promised by the grassroots community development, growing slowly through the City, is not yet a real force and unless and until it becomes one the chess game will continue; the pawns must go where they are put.

As far as 'them', those in charge, are concerned, the Inner City has presented itself as 'a problem' for decades—the local press of the 1930s and 1950s carried much the same sort of commentary about these 'problems' as it does today. Crime, Vandalism, Deprivation have long been topics of concern and to-day's city fathers likewise form steering groups and committees to decide what should be done, as is their custom and duty. The City Planning Department makes frequent recommendations, surveys of social malaise are published,[1] a Community Development Project is set up, the Department of the Environment finances a four-year action project. There is concern amongst 'them', that cannot be doubted, yet to many down-towners it seems far away, bureaucratic and totally unaware of how it really is. The slogans protest 'Demolish the houses not the people'.

From time to time specific areas hit the headlines, as in The Liverpool 8 'riots' of 1972, but generally there are so many 'notorious' 'problem' down-town neighbourhoods that no one area stands out as special. None has undergone the intense 'labelling process' that for instance Easterhouse in Glasgow was subjected to.[2] It is the Inner City as a whole that has 'had its heart torn out by the planners', is 'deprived', suffering from 'social malaise', from high crime rates and widespread delinquency.

Bricks and Mortar
Roundhouse is one well-known down-town neighbourhood

which stands close to the city centre. Like the wrinkled film star clutching her press cuttings tightly to her bosom, Roundhouse too has seen better days. The *Liverpool Review* in May 1890 described the Stockbridge Abattoir as 'Liverpool's Great Slaughterhouse'. The abattoir had come under renewed criticism for alleged 'insanitary conditions'. This type of criticism and the obsolescence of the buildings led to plans for building a new abattoir on a different site. By 1920 these plans were being executed and The Corporation was considering what to put in place of the slaughterhouse. The growing concern about slum clearance during this decade and a Housing Act in 1930 saw the start of a costly 5-year programme 'to do away with slums'. The early thirties saw many areas declared insanitary and earmarked for re-development. In 1931 the *Evening Express* reported that Liverpool Corporation Finance Committee had decided to recommend the City Council to allocate for housing purposes 'the Stockbridge Abattoir site now closed down'. The site was cleared for the construction of tenement blocks to provide residence for those tenants moved from a nearby clearance area where 'back to back' housing of some 100 years standing had been condemned. Long before the new tenements were completed the residents from the clearance area were reported by the *Liverpool Post and Mercury* as telling a housing inquiry 'they had lived in the area for periods up to thirty-five years, were perfectly satisfied with them, always enjoyed good health both themselves and their children, and were not anxious to move into tenements'.

However, true to bureaucratic form, four years late the 'proud', 'reluctant', residents moved up the hill into the new corporation tenements. The family names bear great resemblance to those on the Housing Department's books today. These tenants were seen as rather privileged at the time as the new Roundhouse complex was of 'striking modernistic design'. The new Minister of Health performed the opening ceremony and pointed out that these new tenements were built to 'emancipate people from the slums'.[3] At the same ceremony the chairman of the Housing Committee was reported to note that 'The buildings might be regarded as modernistic in conception, but though little had been spent on external adornment, no effort had been spared to maintain and even improve the old standard of equipment and amenities which had always been associated with the housing efforts of the Liverpool Corporation.'

In passing it must be pointed out that this very same old standard of equipment and amenities is still associated with the housing efforts of the Liverpool Corporation, and will be till the modernisation programme agreed in 1968 actually materialises. It seems hard to believe that once upon a time the walk-up tenement blocks could be praised for their Viennese grace and considerable amenities.

'On the south side the frontage to Bleak Street is recessed in the centre forming a court yard and garden approached through a large archway. In the centre of the horse-shoe shape thus formed the playgrounds with gymnasium equipment are placed. The buildings are of five storeys constructed of brick and reinforced concrete. The brick balconies are a special feature, especially those to which direct access is made from the flats and which are highly valued by the fortunate tenants of those particular flats.'[4]

There were many photographs taken illustrating this 'show piece' of the late thirties. At the time the 'Gardens' epithet given to many of the tenements was not inappropriate as trees and shrubbery were visible, though the planners' talk of a 'magnificent quadrant enclosing a sunken public garden' was somewhat misplaced. What never appeared in the area were the shops, clinic and other 'amenity buildings' originally planned. The redevelopment of an adjacent area, planned shortly afterwards, likewise never materialised, postponed by the War and not revived.

In terms of housing and general physical and environmental conditions Roundhouse has declined steadily to the present day, as have the several other walk-up flat complexes throughout the

Inner City. Architecturally they are obsolete. In 1948 and intermittently through to a special report in 1970 the Corporation looked at modernisation proposals, especially the installation of lifts, an idea now finally dismissed.[5] In the 1950s the 'gardens' disappeared, due to vandalism and neglect, and the whole courtyard area was tarmaced. Even a Housing Manager admitted that 'Tarmac is a supreme example of dealing with things in an ad hoc manner. It is the Corporation's message to the tenants—we've finished with you now, we give up.'

It was not till the 1960s that the air-raid shelters in the courtyard were removed, and then only after continued pressure from local councillors. Housing conditions were so bad in the mid-sixties that with the organising power of a newly formed community group a rent strike, of over a month, was executed with some success. These bad conditions were highlighted by the building, in the mid-fifties, of two- and three-storey maisonettes and flats 'edging' the area, hiding the physical decay from the outside. With more tenants rejecting flats, especially high-rise, in Liverpool, these newer maisonettes gave the local population increasing evidence that their dwellings were not up to standard. Although the rent strike did bring improvements to plumbing, electrical fittings and glazing, it brought little more.

The Housing and Planning departments are not unaware of this gradual decay and obsolescence, and various reports have called for intensive action, though without much consequence. A major document was produced in 1967. The Roundhouse complex was earmarked as an area in need of great and costly improvement. The growing physical isolation of the area as a residential island was noted, 'and on the west the first stage of the Inner Motorway will define its physical limits'. The report admits: 'The total available open space is well below the minimum requirements of this population; this situation, however, is incapable of improvement until nearer the end of the life of the older housing, some twenty years hence.' Even if we accept this *incapability* of the Corporation, its sterility is evident in even minor improvements. For instance, twice in the 1967 report the Planning Department emphasised the need for a pedestrian crossing over the busy main road negotiated by the children of the area to get to and from their school. The school was opened but not for six years did the crossing appear.

Again the Housing Department recently pointed out that

> Trends since the war, in terms of the upkeep and occupancy of the blocks, the general replanning of the City, advances in social and housing legislation and public attitudes to housing, increasingly call into question the walk up flats as places to live at acceptable contemporary standards. The landscaped gardens within the courts have mostly been eroded by over use, vandalism and lack of maintenance, and replaced by expanses of tarmac. Visually many of the blocks are in bad condition and urgently stand in need of extensive structural repairs.[6]

However, financial decisions usually override such considerations and for Roundhouse the solution has been determined by economic priorities. These tenement blocks are, to use one planner's phrase, going to be 'tarted up'. Such a 'modernisation' programme started in earnest in 1973, some four years after it was planned. Roundhouse is here to stay at least for another twenty years, increasingly isolated by plush, extravagant, non-residential buildings, a new church, a purpose-built, multi-storey car park and eventually the new Inner Motorway from which 'noise might be a problem'.

Roundhouse is now a residential island, physically senile amongst new superbuildings belonging to 'them'. It is referred to as 'harsh', 'deprived' and 'obsolete'. It lacks many neighbourhood facilities and suffers in common with most downtown neighbourhoods from high rates of school absenteeism, delousing of children, job instability, unemployment, high crime rates and many other indicators of official social malaise.[7] A sorry picture perhaps; certainly the physical state of the Inner City sums up the fact that 'the interplay of organisation needs and preferences among the multiplicity of Corporation actions overrides the establishment of a human renewal pro-gramme'.[8]

Neighbourhood Identity

The social order inside the bricks and mortar tells a different story however. Objective conditions and subjective sentiments do not always tally. Roundhouse residents do not reflect the physical decay of their housing.

To say Roundhouse is 'one big family', as its most ardent supporters do, is perhaps going too far, but the analogy is not out of keeping with the extensive kinship network of the area. In common with many working-class communities, as des-cribed by Young and Wilmott[9] and Kerr[10] for example, Roundhouse is made up of large families knit together by blood and marriage; thus some of The Boys have as many as 35 relations living in their neighbourhood. The majority of families are long-standing residents who have lived in the Block, as it is known from the inside, for 15 and 20 years. Indeed with the Catholics' desire to marry their own kind and their affinity for living in residential pockets, there is an implicit assumption that the young marry someone from their own area and prob-ably live close by afterwards. Many flats house three genera-tions, grandmother, husband and wife and their offspring all living together; with early, often rushed, marriages it is possible that the great-grandchildren may be around the flat for a while as well. As has been documented frequently elsewhere, family life in lower-working-class neighbourhoods is taken very seriously and the power of the Mum and Grannie is consider-able in domestic and childrearing matters.[11]

The much-quoted outward characteristics of a less-skilled working-class neighbourhood are also to be seen here. The too-early-aged mother pushing an old pram piled high with dirty clothes making her way to the launderette, 'the bagwash', trailing a stream of kids is seen every day, the kids making bon-fires on wasteground; the 'oller', the continuous noise of children playing and shouting; women meeting on the land-

ings; men on the Corner* with The Boys close by; all these
pieces of social action blend into the picture. To celebrate or
romanticise the warmth of the working-class community is no
longer in vogue, nor should Roundhouse's warm umbrella be
allowed to disguise the hardship and 'unacceptable' standards
many of its residents face. Yet the neighbourliness and cheerful-
ness of a community-like neighbourhood is undoubtedly there.
Despite the obsolete buildings with their small rooms, inadequate bathrooms, taps which don't always produce water, poor
sound-proofing and no lifts to help tenants climb the five
storeys, most residents do not want to move. Despite the lack of
facilities, the absence of grass and trees, a garden and even a
backyard there is a waiting list for flats in the neighbourhood.
The smell of poverty is outweighed by the newly weds' desire to
stay close to the family and amongst good friends. 'Everybody
knows everybody in the Block. They all pull together. If anyone's
ill or short of a few bob you can always borrow a bit to get
something in for the kids' tea, like.'

There are numerous difficulties in defining Roundhouse as a
community, not least being its position in a densely populated
conurbation. However, following sociological definitions of
community which emphasise that 'one's life may be lived
wholly within it'[12] and others referring to locality, community sentiments and awareness of sharing a way of life, the
neighbourhood can be seen to tend toward such an arrange-
ment. Strong sentiments are regularly voiced celebrating
staying close, with money-lending, baby-sitting and clothes-
swopping also proliferating to back up these special claims. The
low incidence of children in care with the local Social Services
Department, and the constant demand put on the Housing
Department to keep all flat vacancies for local offspring and
'Catholics only', provide further indications of local solidarity.

These community qualities are not without blemish however.

* 'The Corner' as it is referred to by everybody is not in fact a corner at
all but a central point to the area in front of the main archway into the
Block.

Some of The Boys were themselves shocked to find cases of unnoticed and severe hardship when they were employed by a Government scheme to decorate old-age pensioners' flats.

> Man we did a really bad flat today. She was blind and he was a bit queer, screwy like. The place was a tip, bottles, tins and that and it stank of puke. I couldn't eat me dinner or nothing, it all smelt of sick. (*Des.*)

Roundhouse has several 'really bad' cases of poverty and hardship which its residents know little about. Mainly these 'cases' involve old people who are outside the kinship network. The neighbourhood also has its 'loners' who are seen as 'snobs who think they're better than anyone else'. Some adolescents avoid a local youth club, some parents won't allow their children to attend a nearby play group because it's 'too rough'. Yet the view that Roundhouse is closer, more neighbourly and more interdependent than other down-town neighbourhoods is held by Corporation officials, church officials, and many residents from adjacent areas; the 'togetherness' of Roundhouse is simply not in dispute.

Yet these apparently definitive 'community' criteria cannot be taken on face value or as coming from the wishes of all residents. Many Roundhouse families simply could not afford to 'move up' into better housing. Most of the better housing is on the far away estates well out of the city and divorced from friends, baby-sitters and the general help of the family, and also, particularly for the young family with only one wage-earner, the new 'fair rents' have made such a move a doubtful benefit. 'It's OK for me mam to move to Cantril Farm, she's got our Bobby and Ann bringing in [wages] as well. She's never been better off now we're all earning and she's got the place like a little palace. But we'd never have a penny that's our own if we got a place out there.' (*Dot.*)

Since there is no likelihood of such a move being feasible, the answer for many is to look on the bright side and celebrate what Roundhouse has got that the new estates haven't got—a community atmosphere and neighbourhood solidarity.

The neighbourhood's Catholicism is also a 'common fate' which draws residents together in what the local priest perceives as 'tribal religion', by which he means that rituals rather than theology concern his parish. The Protestant Orange-Day celebrations provoke the annual consolidation of these sentiments, with Roundhouse 'standing like a medieval fortress' defending its tradition with vigour. On this special day the Orangemen, though the women are far more prominent, take their trip out to Southport. The height of the trouble usually occurs when the Orange parade, on its way home, marches up the hill right past Roundhouse. What seems like its complete population is waiting in force. The police are also out in strength—on horses, in uniform, in plain clothes, as they hold back the crowds lining the roadside. As the parade comes nearer the children of Roundhouse start chanting anti-King Billy ditties. The closer the parade comes the louder it plays and the more vigorous its dancing girls become. Songs and chants are shrieked, fingers raised, tongues pulled, fists clenched, bottles thrown. For some ten minutes the three sides strain in the deafening noise, then slowly the parade passes and everyone returns to the Block; the fortress has not been taken, King Billy goes back to 'Everomer', the drawbridge is lowered.

These strong, religious customs show up in Roundhouse's internal celebrations. Very conscious of their identity in these matters the people miss no chance to demonstrate their Catholic solidarity—even though Mass attendance is only about 10 per cent of the parish per week. For the retirement of their local Canon nearly every house was painted outside in bright colours. Hundreds of yards of gay home-made bunting were draped from windows, landings and balconies with great extravagance. 'Everyone' turned out to pay their respects to the Canon, as Roundhouse performed yet another socially cementing ritual and replied to outsiders.

Growing Up with Roundhouse
It is not often that the adolescent who lives down-town thinks of

the Inner City as a homogeneous unit. Perhaps when he's in the Kop and Liverpool are playing Arsenal he feels all the Liverpool Boys are together against the Cockneys; perhaps for a while he shares his identity with his city contemporaries who'll 'never walk alone'. But take away the threat to Merseyside and more often than not you're back to neighbourhood identity, reputation and territory.

It's safe to say the youth of each down-town neighbourhood hold stereotype ideas about the area down the road or across town. For The Boys, 'Granny' is a neighbourhood where the Niggers live, where prostitutes operate, where you're likely to get 'rolled' for your money. 'Everomer' is where the Protestants live, where the kids take and drive away cars, where flats are always getting broken into. 'Granny' and 'Everomer' are neighbourhoods close to but distinct from Roundhouse; the areas' adolescents rarely mix well. The 'boys' of each neighbourhood would almost certainly argue their area was the toughest, their men the hardest and their mates the best. Most would not want to move, or even allow much praise for another part of the city. The Roundhouse Boys are no exception and they cling tightly to the ethos of their neighbourhood. To understand the nature of this ethos a brief look back at the area's stormy past will be useful.

The older men from Roundhouse recall how tough a place it used to be. There was always fighting, outsiders would never dare walk through the Block, policemen would only do so in pairs. Colly's father reminisced at great length as we sat in the Bridewell one morning waiting to bail Colly out.

> There'd always be someone fighting or running away from the police, but once you were in the Block you were laughing, you could hide in anyone's place in those days, just sneak into someone's back kitchen till the coppers had gone . . . and there was a good few murders, I don't mean in The Block itself but around the area. That feller who done the Cameo murders, he only lived in Stockbridge Street, people was coming up just to see where he lived.

The Cameo Cinema Murders in 1949 involved a gang associated with Roundhouse. Two cinema staff were shot and killed during a raid on the cinema's takings. Murders of this nature were unusual at the time and created much public interest. A senior police officer involved in the case claimed in retrospect,

> The Cameo murder had shocked the whole country and certainly never before in the criminal annals of Liverpool and for that matter the whole of Merseyside had a case aroused such intense interest. Throughout the two trials the Crown Court and St George's Hall was crowded each day as it had never been packed before. People queued all night in the hope of being admitted to the public gallery and the queues began immediately at the end of each day's hearing. (*Liverpool Echo*, 1967.)

The leader of the gang lived in the Roundhouse area. Each day of the trial the local paper, and sometimes the nationals, carried his address for all to see. There was much public interest throughout the whole affair and the evolution of Roundhouse's reputation crystallised considerably at this time. According to the judge at the trial the accused came from a 'caste', hence the jury were advised, 'You must not judge this man by the language he uses because the caste to which he probably belongs are accustomed to using such forcible language and swear words.'

Right through the fifties till the mid-sixties the press invariably talked about the Roundhouse reputation and the problems it caused. Reporters commented, for example, that, 'The unfortunate reputation of Roundhouse has in the past caused the people living in the area to keep very much to themselves.' . . . 'The district used to be looked upon as one of Liverpool's toughest areas. Its name has been mentioned during the hearing of murder trials.'[13]

The local Canon agreed the reputation was unfortunate. 'They're no saints, but on the other hand they're no worse than people in any other part of the city. I think it is a great shame that so many people have to suffer from the bad deeds of a very few.'

In 1964 the opening of a youth club was heralded by *The Liverpool Echo* with the headline 'Six Months—And Kids Will Break You'. The new youth leader remarked, however, that the 'reputation of Roundhouse is out of all proportion to reality these days'. He also felt it was 'not as violent as it is said to have been in the past'. Since 1964 press reports have presented a less sinister image of the area though even in 1968 headings like 'Liverpool's Famous Roundhouse' were used, and readers reminded 'the area has had a bad reputation' and has been 'a harsh introverted area full of poverty' where 'anyone with an official label is distrusted'.

This reportage should not however give the impression Roundhouse is always in the news. Indeed over recent years the area has become considerably less newsworthy. Roundhouse today is less introspective and more amenable, it is stable residentially and, as far as many of its elders are concerned, is anxious to lose its old reputation. The Boys and the men on the Corner are not so sure. They view the old image, which still remains in their gossip, in the pubs and clubs and on the downtown grapevine, with considerable pride. Many of The Boys are genuinely convinced Roundhouse is still as tough as anywhere can be when it really comes down to it. Streak's comment or its equivalent is often heard: 'It used to be hard, it's dying down now. But if it came to the crunch and there was a really big fight and it was The Roundhouse youth versus say Granny Garden's youth or something like that, I know who'd come off best. There's some fuckin' good fighters round here boy.'

Believing they come from one of the toughest areas in town holds great advantage for The Boys. They gain dignity and stature and a sense of importance from such an image. Hence some comment made by 'the boys' from another area about not wanting 'no trouble with you lot' is seized upon and repeated continuously till everybody has bathed in the glory. The street-corner milieu expects the Roundhouse torch to be carried on into the future. The Boys feel the obligation to do so and indeed

c

it is only because they believe Roundhouse really does Rule that they can avoid having to go out and prove it.

Although they emphasise the tough aspects of their neighbourhood's identity The Boys also take a pride in the community-like atmosphere and closeness of their neighbourhood. They too are not keen to move out of an area which offers so much.

> If my family have to move with this modernisation* to fuckin' Netherley or somewhere I'll refuse to go. I'll never leave round here. I'll always come back. Like when I was in London, everyone was nice and that but I couldn't settle. You know it wasn't the same . . . You can't explain it good enough with words, it's a sort of feeling inside.

Already several of the older boys have stayed behind when their parents have moved to estates. Jock stayed with his grandmother, 'ninnie', in her flat although 'she's fuckin' bats' rather than move away. Streak agreed: 'You never really left the Block did you, you was always down here.' Jock and Pablo have now got a flat near the area, and Craber, whose parents have also moved, is living with them even though his 'official' new home is nearer his work place.

Other factors are involved in The Boys' desire to stay put, however. The attraction of down-town life is not comparable with the alternative wilderness of the new estates, where 'There's no shops, no clubs, nothing out there and it costs a quid to get a taxi back if you've been down-town.'

Hence both the hard, tough image and the close, 'together' sentiments of their neighbourhood please The Boys, and they tend to believe that nowhere else has quite such qualities. Yet the down-town adolescent does not live in the past, the ethos the neighbourhood transmits to him is only his starting point. The present goings-on offer plenty to talk about and interest is taken not just in peers but juniors and seniors from the neigh-

---

* The flats are shortly to be modernised and it is likely that the Housing Department will 'discover officially' gross overcrowding and prevent its continuation after modernisation.

bourhood. The 'hard man' at the pub bar receives praise for his contribution to the area's potency.

> See that feller over there, Lorney, he's as hard as fuckin' nails. They reckon he took on three niggers one night and murdered them. . . His lot were always fighting in the older days. They were bastards, they used to fuck anybody who walked through the Block, the coppers and everything. (*Acker.*)

The 'boys' of tomorrow are also monitored, hence The Ritz and The Tiddlers, younger adolescent groups in the neighbourhood, are also given praise where it is due. Some of The Ritz played in a local football team which 'got kicked out of the league again, just like we did. They knocked fuck out of St Dominions after the match; Mal was supposed to have given it to some bloke.' (*Des.*)

The Tiddlers' escapades, especially during Year Three, were also much talked about by The Boys. 'Little Des and his lot, they, boy, are fuckin' mad. I mean real madmen. The way they drive dannies [cars] round like that, they'll kill someone that lot, they're going to be real cases in a few years.'

All this said, however, The Boys' view of their neighbourhood's image and how they should embrace it has undergone considerable change as adolescence has progressed. By the end of Year Three many of the network were doubting whether they should simply act out the traditional expectations of the street corner. Emo looked back on his schooldays, for instance, emphasising how being an ambassador of Roundhouse had had its disadvantages. Having been allocated to a separate (grammar) school from his mates, he had had to face competition alone. 'They [other boys in his new school] was always saying our end's harder than yours, and wanting to see you out to prove it. I was always getting into trouble for fighting and I never wanted to, it was just because I was the only feller from Roundhouse.' (T.)

By late Year Three some of the network, setting up their own homes, found that a Roundhouse address was a distinct disadvantage in trying to make hire-purchase arrangements. A few questioned the utility of the old reputation. 'It's bad news when you can't get a telly just coz you live in Roundhouse, you'd think we were all con men or something.' (*Joey*.)

Perhaps the clearest change of stance occurred on the football field. During Year One when The Boys were all about sixteen years old they were happy to boast that their football team had been kicked out of the local league. As Pablo put it, 'The football team's reputation is as bad as ever—every game we played there had to be a fight. Players were supposed to be under 17— we had one 19 and one 20. And fights every time, people getting knocked out. We are really bad for fighting, then we complain we're getting victimised.' (T.) Yet members of the network who played for the local team more recently (Year Three) greatly resented their latest ejection from the league. They felt they had been playing good football, they were winning matches and making deliberate efforts to censure any excessive physical play amongst team mates. Despite this the team became involved in a mass punch-up in which both sides were at fault. However, only Roundhouse received censure, only the other side's story was believed, only Roundhouse were 'kicked out'. The dialogue between their past image and their aspirations for a new one found The Boys in a dilemma for which they usually blame themselves more than they should. 'The trouble with The Boys is they think they've got to be like the older fellers used to be, always acting hard, but they'd get more respect if they played good football and won the league and the Charity cup and that.' (*Streak*.)

Much more will be said later about toughness and fighting. What the football saga illustrates is the effect of past reputation and traditions on The Boys of today. Because their neighbourhood is 'close', and because there is widespread social interaction between age groups, especially on the Corner and in the local pubs, The Boys receive the neighbourhood's traditional 'real man' ethos loud and clear. One local man in his twenties who is friendly with The Boys suggested to them in a pub conversation the transmission processes involved. 'You lot are just like we was. We'd always be fighting coz we knew the older fellers had. Like yourselves, you see us lot playing for Heriots and see fellers go in hard, and say I can be just as hard.'

This 'inevitable' imitation and repetition of traditions is often mentioned by The Boys as important in understanding their own behaviour. It comes close to an explanation of deviancy often associated with the 'culture of poverty' perspective. Such a view emphasises how children growing up in a 'criminal' or 'rough' slum area take on attitudes and imitate and act out the behaviour they see around them.

> Once it comes into existence it tends to perpetuate itself from genera-tion to generation because of its effect on children. By the time slum children are age six or seven, they have usually absorbed the basic values and attitudes of their subculture and are not psychologically geared to take full advantage of changing conditions or increased opportunities which may occur in their lifetime.[14]

This view indirectly attaches 'blame' to parents. Since this criticism of some working-class parents, who are thought to be incompetent and irresponsible over child-rearing methods, is also commonly held by the general public, it is pertinent to consider the relationship between Roundhouse parents and their offspring.

By its very nature this study is concerned with adolescents who spent most of their waking time around the neighbour-hood and the city; comments about the home and child–parent relationships are obviously tentative. The Boys during the fieldwork period knocked around the neighbourhood almost continually. They were rarely at home and therefore com-municated with parents only occasionally. This fact is important in itself: the street-corner adolescent is not greatly influenced by home; those days of parental control have largely passed.

There is a positive correlation in Roundhouse between those youngsters who are always playing out and later hanging around, and their level of delinquency. This is to be expected. The 'street kid' is more exposed to the potential excitements of the environment. The parked cars and lorries, the easy-to-enter empty buildings, warehouses, shops, schools closed for the holiday—all provide escape-hatches from boredom and a lack of excitement. Children who live in a commercial quarter of town, and who play out whenever they can, will most likely get themselves into trouble sooner or later. If this is not in dispute, what is more contentious is the responsibility of parents who allow their children out in the first place. The unending criticisms from the middle-class public nearly always emphasise that 'decent' parents would not let their children play out unsupervised till late at night. How can down-town parents allow their little sons to be exposed to such a world of risks if they really care?

The neighbourhood's views about law-breaking are difficult to pin down and such an analysis is outside the scope of this study; but a large amount of incidental evidence does allow some tentative comment. Roundhouse is not 'sub-cultural' in the sense that parents and children hold a contrary view of society's rules, nor should the neighbourhood be regarded as synonymous with models of theft sub-cultures.[15] There are too many occasions when residents emphasise the correctness of the law, and the validity of the dominant normative order, to make such an analysis valid. It is more pertinent to see Roundhouse as a neighbourhood with a low standard of living which employs certain communal and sometimes illegal devices to try and improve those standards. Whilst Gerald Suttles's description of a slum area's make-up is valid for a wide variety of settings, it is particularly fitting for Roundhouse: 'a social compact in which respectable residents and those not so respectable are both tolerant and protective of one another'.[16]

Within the neighbourhood there is a spectrum of standpoints, ranging from those who will have nothing to do with law-breaking or stolen property right through to those who make their living from theft and 'being smart'. (Within this spectrum is the complication of people saying one thing and doing another.) The tolerance of the 'respectable' residents, whilst it might include disgust at criminal goings-on, would very rarely find grassing to Authority acceptable. The majority of older residents simply accept the presence of theft operations, and will receive stolen property, barter with 'sellers' on the doorstep and sometimes make it known they are in the market for various types of 'knock-off'. This sort of illegality allows certain bargains to be obtained, and indeed represents an important redistribution of wealth which more affluent sectors of society would be reluctant to part with. It is hardly surprising that nearly all residents would assist in protecting law-breakers from apprehension, not asking about what crime has been committed until later. 'In the old days you used to get fellers running into anybody's house to hide from the police. I remember some feller hiding in our back room when I was a kid, I didn't know who he was or nothing, he just waited till the busies (police) had gone then made off.' (*Les.*)

The stability of the neighbourhood and its functional 'social compact' ensures such practices continue to thrive. In a neighbourhood where 'everybody knows everybody' and most people see 'knock-off' as a necessary part of life style, a normal citizen, even one resentful of such practices, has to turn a blind eye. This is the sort of protection to which the much-heard comment 'once you're in the Block you're laughing' refers. Once in the Block, the adolescent with stolen property under his coat will not be reported to the police; of that he can be sure. Once 'in the 'ouse', he may be 'murdered' or 'busted out of the four walls' or 'belted round the back kitchen', that is merely a domestic affair.

There are some delinquent practices, however, which the neighbourhood unambiguously condemns. Theft *within* the neighbourhood involving Roundhouse residents is not tolerated. Vandalism of neighbourhood property, except perhaps when a flat is empty, is also tabooed, censured by a whole range of residents who would usually 'say nothing'. This condemnation is, of course, tied up with community sentiments—a conclusion reinforced when Roundhouse is compared with some other down-town neighbourhoods, where, since kinship networks, residential stability and neighbourliness are less widely established, house break-ins, purse-snatching and vandalism are committed by local youngsters against their own neighbours.[17]

Focusing inwards on to the individual family situations and parent–child–adolescent relationships involves the same difficulties of generalisation already discussed, even more acutely. How far the youngster accepts neighbourhood traditions is open to the effects of older adolescents, his peer group, and the identity and reputations perpetrated in the conversation culture of the pub, the Corner etc, is obviously related to how much freedom of association parents allow their children. Again there appears, just with The Boys' family experiences, a whole spectrum of parental stances. The nature of parental control can only be tentatively identified.

Firstly, there are a series of pressures on the practising Mum, pushing the children out of her direct supervision. The mother of a typically large Roundhouse family, tied to the baby of the moment, simply could not cope, in her small, often grossly overcrowded, badly sound-proofed flat, if she kept all the kids indoors. There is no garden, no organised and supervised play space, not even a back yard. The flat is above ground level, and once outside the door the children are on a narrow landing which is a thoroughfare to passageways, corners, stairs and freedom. Kids will demand to play out, mother has no option and the saga begins. Over the months and years it becomes standard practice for little Tommy to disappear 'out' for most of his free time. As the last infant gets to school age, mother returns to work—if she ever gave it up: she is likely to be a waitress, day or night, or perhaps a sales assistant or an office cleaner. She will be unable to look after the kids during the holidays, she will be tired when she is at home. Since working is necessary if ends are to meet, nearly all mums undertake it, accepting it as normal. The kids consequently have very free, unrestricted and exploratory childhoods. They learn to accept independence and decision-making from a much earlier age than their garden-bound, supervised, middle-class contemporaries.

The consequences of the mother's response to the pressures of poor wages and inadequate housing facilities affect her children. They are 'out of sight, out of mind', and as long as no adverse feedback about their behaviour reaches her she assumes they're 'not doing no harm'. She tends not to look too deep and so to avoid any added worries, a process noted elsewhere.[18] Hence parents aware of what 'the proper' way of bringing up children is, what school preaches, what the media suggest, suffer varying degrees of role conflict. Mothers, in public at least, sometimes have to rationalise that it's never their kid that sets fire to a stolen car or breaks into a local warehouse, and if the evidence to the contrary is overwhelming, then someone must have led him astray. This self-delusion infuriates the more informed, but rather unsympathetic, older brothers and sisters of the accused ringleader who is supposed to have led everyone else's 'good' kids astray; they complain typically, 'She thinks her kids are little angels, that Mrs O'Mally does, and they're the biggest robbers of the lot. She comes out saying, "Don't you be saying things about our Tony, it's your Jimmy that should be seen to, he's the ringleader." '

The Mrs O'Mallys are probably representative of all those mums whose attitudes are midway between that of the occasional mother who is indifferent to her child's behaviour to the extent of deliberately not noticing he's picked up things in the supermarket till he's home, and the mother who puts her name on the housing-transfer list because she simply can't accept the area as suitable for bringing up children. Neither example is common; most parents simply carry on 'doing what they think is right'. Father leaves the bulk of child-rearing to Mother, except when he's called on to act as deterrent, and Mum places child supervision where she can in a whole list of time-consuming priorities. Parents are not unaware of what is thought 'proper' in supervising and socialising their children, but the awareness does not help in doing it as directly as they would like.

They will support the local primary-school staff whenever
their support is asked for, because they genuinely believe school
will help their children. The headmaster, for instance, decided
to encourage school uniform, not for authoritarian reasons, but
with the idea that it could act as a 'moral emblem', encouraging
his children to continue the 'proper' standards after 4 pm. In
his terms, given the amount of trouble his older pupils were
getting into, this was reasonable. Not in favour of a traditional
expensive uniform, he suggested a grey smock-top with a crest.
The parents' committee rejected this idea and recommended an
expensive traditional uniform comparable with those worn by
children attending the city's 'better' selective schools. The staff
explained this parental behaviour as 'defensive' and 'their way
of combating a sense of inferiority they feel about their area and
the way their children are, in comparison to those from better
areas'. Perhaps this is so, or perhaps the decision was a positive
desire rather than a defence mechanism, but certainly such an
example is not untypical of mothers who do care and do want
their children to 'get on properly'.

Parents are also concerned about the neighbourhood's image.
When a documentary film about unemployment was made
around the area, a group of mothers crowded around the producer, telling him, 'Don't you show nothing that will give this
area a bad name.' This same topic often crops up at residents'
meetings. Dig a little deeper into community pride, and sometimes there is some dismay that the neighbourhood already has
a bad name. Again, what parents and residents would *like* for
themselves and their children is not often what is possible or
realistic. Hopes must be mediated by grinding realities; the
neighbourhood might have a bad name, that's life, but we must
make sure it gets no worse. Scapegoats are sometimes found.
Hence a petition to prevent a notorious family from moving
into the Block was got together amidst talk about 'their
daughters are on the game' (prostitution), and 'we don't need
any more robbers around here'. The petition was successful,
mainly because the family was outside the kinship networks of

the neighbourhood; it seems to have been a gesture of concerned residents trying to emphasise their interpretation of 'respectable' values.

Yet despite most people's desire for the area to 'get better', for 'proper' behaviour to come to the front, in their more pensive moments most conclude that it won't. The kids still have to play out, you still haven't time to be chasing after them, they'll still get themselves into trouble whatever you tell them. And when they get a bit older they won't listen to you anyway. In the end the kids will have to learn for themselves what it's all about. As Bone's father concluded: 'I've tried to sort him out but he takes no notice. I've told him where he'll end up if he keeps getting caught. But he's old enough to take the rap now, it's probably the only way he'll learn.'

In summary, despite the physical decay of Roundhouse and its low standard of living, local morale is high. Roundhouse residents share a closeness and solidarity which leads to a high degree of tolerance in interpersonal behaviour. The eccentric old men, the senile women, the alcoholic neighbour, the ever-fighting husband and wife, even if gossiped about, still find acceptance. This neighbourhood tolerance is also extended to a certain amount of adolescent deviancy, especially in relation to receiving stolen property.

Parents and children are caught up in this condonation. The pressures of the large family, the lack of facilities and obsolete architecture, all push the energetic child out of parental control. Once out and about, parental words are often not a strong enough deterrent for the street-corner boy. As we shall increasingly see, he is subjected to other versions of what is right and wrong behaviour. Parental views are only one standpoint; the youngster mixes also with the peer group and the men on the Corner. He learns to adapt his beliefs and behaviour to his company. Mum knows only the half of it.

Before considering The Boys' adolescent behaviour, we must look at the general course of growing up for some of the more delinquent youngsters from Roundhouse who are younger than

The Boys. Growing up in Roundhouse throws up a whole series of hurdles worthy of consideration. As they move about their social habitat, Roundhouse youngsters cannot fail to be influenced by traditional solutions, prejudices, stereotypes and various 'focal concerns'. This social complexity acts as a springboard from which The Boys and so many other youngsters take off.

Notes to this chapter are on pp 225–6

2 Delinquency on the Move

When you're a kid you go down-town and rob yourself a dinky. When you get a bit older you rob clothes to sell to somebody like. When we was older we used to go over to Birkenhead. It was dead easy over there to take trannies [radios] . . . Then we went on the cars . . . we didn't get catseyes then, we'd take gear from inside, but they're wise to that now, they don't leave radios loose. (Jimbo.)

It would be a mistake to meet The Boys at the age of sixteen (Year One) without knowing anything about their childhood and earlier life experiences in Roundhouse. This short chapter involves a brief analysis of the delinquent activities of two other younger social groups from the neighbourhood—The Tiddlers and The Ritz. Whilst unrealistically divorcing delinquency from these groups' total life style, this chapter hopefully furthers several themes.

Firstly, the delinquent careers at present being followed by these adolescent groups gives some indication of The Boys' recent past, identifying the sorts of processes and concerns of their early adolescence also. Secondly, the innovatory and adaptive nature of delinquent action is brought out. Such processes are usually missed, because research into delinquency has of late paid little attention to longitudinal and detailed ethnographic study. Over the months the down-town adolescent hangs out all his linen. Looking at his behaviour from ground level and getting tangled up in the action allows an identification of processes withheld from the outsider, sociologist or otherwise. Thirdly, in conjunction with the next chapter, the analysis to follow emphasises the importance of the *context* of delinquency: the significance of the neighbourhood and the social organisation of its adolescents is monumental, a fact which general theories of delinquency have tended to obscure.

The picture then is of different-aged peer groups being involved in delinquent action simultaneously. On occasions these groups interact, but more generally their delinquent style is distinctive and independent because of their different expectations through time. Figure 1 illustrates this simultaneous delinquency and its changing nature. This diagram is a crude representation of the phases of delinquent activities of the three adolescent groups studied—The Boys themselves, The Tiddlers and The Ritz. Movement is traced over a three-year period, the second and third years based on direct participant observation, the first on formal and incidental conversations carried out fairly early in the research. The diagram has several limitations. Firstly, the three groups are not samples as such, but actual social entities or networks, and thus age distributions are not 'even'; there is no smooth numerical increase as we move from left to right and downwards. Secondly, the headings used in the diagram are illustrated only implicitly on the pages to come, since in reality transition and change do not occur evenly and exactly on a particular date. Overlap of, backtracking and withdrawal from, delinquent styles are continuous. Thirdly, these delinquent 'careers' are relevant only to the members of the networks analysed during the specific fieldwork period. 'Careers' are labelled such only because clear patterns have emerged retrospectively for these particular adolescents.[1] As we shall see, small changes in the contingency mixture might have sent individual solutions in quite different directions, either more or less proscribed.

The Tiddlers
The staff from the local primary school, which takes 90 per cent
of the children from the area, see most of their intakes as leading
a Jekyll and Hyde existence. The staff argue that there is a set
of standards which demands conformity, producing consistency
and thus security within the school; the kids enjoy this security
and know where they stand. This, they say, contrasts with the
ambiguity of standards outside, where the children are not sure
how their parents, brothers and sisters and peers will act and
react. The staff argue that, 'In school a kid will hand in a penny
or fifty pence but he'll go shoplifting as soon as school's over.'

	Year One	Year Two	Year Three
The Tiddlers	Naughty 8–10 yr	Small beginnings and petty theft 9–11 yr	Joyriders 10–12 yr
The Ritz	Petty theft 13–14 yr	Further instrumental delinquency 14–15 yr	Catseye Kids 15–16 yr
The Boys	Instrumental delinquency 15–17 yr	Catseye Kings 16–18 yr	Partial withdrawal 17–19 yr

Figure 1. Delinquency on the move

There is some truth in this. Compared with their highly
structured day in primary school, the inner core of The Tiddlers
—Frankie, Bobby, Chalkie and Tiddler himself—find the rest
of their day and all their holidays without much discipline; as
long as they appear at meal times and a stipulated bedtime
there will be little adult complaint. Street life and life around
the Block is full of potential excitement. One favourite activity
is 'bonnies in the 'oller', making bonfires on waste ground with
anything combustible. Smoking cigarettes is also an important

pastime; the easiest way to get them is to 'scrounge' them from the older lads: 'Give us a ciggy' is a phrase repeated incessantly by The Tiddlers, though they are usually rewarded only by a dog-end. Another method is to buy cigarettes—from pocket money or empty-bottle money or again by scrounging: 'Lend us two pence.'

A great deal of naughtiness involves seeing what one can get away with, knocking on doors and running away, letting car tyres down, smashing bottles and, a favourite, 'giving cheek' to adults. The adults come in all shapes and sizes, with baths-attendants, store detectives and old men being preferred. The Tiddlers will also try their luck with older boys.

> Chalkie   Give us a ciggy.
> Fatch   Fuck off, get your own.
> Chalkie   O' fuck off yourself, you tight bastard.
> Fatch   Go on, beat it, before you get kicked.
> Chalkie   Come on then.

Fatch grabs hold of Chalkie who immediately submits. 'OK, Fatch, I was only messin'.'

Seeing what one can get away with soon involves stealing. That things are stolen is revealed to The Tiddlers from an early age, and at this stage the 'subcultural' effect of growing up in an atmosphere that encourages theft is quite important. Kids soon learn from each other how easy it is to shoplift. Frankie can often be seen in a local department store 'up to no good'. He is only as high as the counter and can remove goods with great ease; a little hand appears, grabs the spoils and simply disappears in the crowd. Razor blades, toothpaste, soap, cosmetics, generally make good sales around the Block. There are plenty of people who will buy something cheap without asking questions. 'Some of the women says, "If you get any more, lad, you bring them to me" ' (Chalkie). 'This one, she says, "Now I'm not saying go and rob none, but if you get another tin I'll take it off you" ' (Frankie). Tiddler, who seems to have no sense of fear at all, will simply stand outside shops offering stolen goods to passers-by.

As these kids get older they start to come into contact with Authority. Departmental-store detectives and staff are usually the first to apprehend The Tiddlers, but, given the age of the children, they can take little further action. The store staff usually end up operating a ban on those they consider 'known trouble-makers'. The kids talk of this as being 'barred out': for The Tiddlers it simply adds to the fun. Just going into a store becomes a game in itself, a further experiment in what one can get away with.

A favourite target for the little ones is the parked lorry. Confectionery vans, 'sweet lorries', are the most obvious temptations. Large numbers of goods vehicles are parked in the area with padlocks that fall off and skylights that small children can get through. Occasionally the whole neighbourhood is full of children eating mints: they have mints in their mouths, in their hands and stuffed in their pockets. The word had got round and youngsters queued up to take their share, as much as they could carry, from the van. Local warehouses are another favourite with The Tiddlers. One evening the doors of a furniture removal and storage firm's warehouse were opened, no one could remember how in the excitement. Several locals helping on a holiday play scheme at the time felt a certain responsibility for the kids involved and tried to gather them up so they wouldn't bump into the police whilst carrying stolen property. Their efforts were just seen as extra excitement—the kids simply evaded their grasp and piled into the warehouse dragging out anything and everything. Records, knives, lampshades, cartons of books, festooned the area. This activity continued till the police arrived. No one was apprehended, everyone simply vanished at the critical moment.

This particular escapade was simply expressive and experimental—though such affairs also act as apprenticeships for later more serious and dangerous operations. The occasional break-ins the youth club suffers should be seen in this light, where the kids involved know their mischief, even if discovered, would not be taken to the police. They also know the club has little to

D

offer them in the way of valuable spoils: what the escapade does offer them is excitement and practice. Similarly The Tiddlers would appear with things of no obvious value to them which happened to be available for removal: a ladder, a bucket, a tin of paint, will always provide amusement. They can be broken up, set fire to or thrown down the tenement stairs. An umbrella doesn't have to be used to keep the rain off.

Holiday playschemes, usually run on a shoe-string, provide some stimulation and acceptable supervision for the youngsters. Even so it's usually the same old trips—not Chester Zoo again —which soon bore them. So they will chase chickens, push prams in ponds, trespass on private property, give cheek to the bus conductor, get thrown out of the swimming baths and sum up a thoroughly boring trip to the airport with the final comment, 'That was fuckin' last, the best thing about that was the robbing.'

As they get to secondary-school age, The Tiddlers take an increasing interest in adulthood. They become 'little men' before their time. Care is taken over hair style and dress in an attempt to look like their older heroes. The Tiddlers will smoke, swear, 'act hard', they will show you their home-made 'prison' tattoos and their razor-sharp knives. They are afraid of nobody, they claim, and to prove it will tell their seniors to 'fuckin' watch it' as long as they are out of kicking distance. The Tiddlers are allowed fairly free association with The Boys mainly for their amusement value. The Boys take considerable interest in The Tiddlers' escapades.

> *Joey* They're fuckin' mad, Frankie and his lot. See Frankie, he's got his hand bandaged up, he did that climbing through a barbed-wire fence on the top of Bishop's wall. I says that'll stop you robbing for a bit lad. He says fuck off, I've got this hand, haven't I?
> *Fosser* Did you see them in that old van last week, about ten of them all piled in with Tiddler driving like a madman. They're fuckin' mad those kids . . .

'Fuckin' mad' is a role type used regularly by older boys in the area to describe The Tiddlers' behaviour. In this context it means daringly dangerous without adequate concern for the consequences. More often than not the 'nutter' who's 'fuckin' mad' will suffer for his lack of strategy and consideration of the long-term consequences of his action. Hence The Tiddlers are seen as 'bound to get stuck down in a few years' and 'odds on for borstal'. At present The Tiddlers are indifferent to the outcome of their small beginnings into crime. They will tell everyone how they got caught shop-lifting in a way designed to imply they are fearless, even in the hands of the law.

> *Bobby*   They take you up to the office till the copper comes. Then he gives you a warning like and then they let you go, there's nothing to it.
> *Chalkie*   They don't always let you go, 'coz this jack [policeman] took me home and told me old girl, and she fuckin' murdered me.

Whilst a lot of ten-to-twelve-year olds who live in Roundhouse fall into the 'little men' category and get involved in escapades which are strictly illegal, The Tiddlers stand out as the most reckless and acknowledged 'wild' group. Their behaviour was, by the end of Year Two, no longer simply mischief, naughtiness and 'cheek'; it was behaviour the police were, and are, concerned about. The Tiddlers are now Junior Delinquents. Early in Year Three the group got hold of a couple of large bunches of car keys. Initially they would wander around the nearby streets trying to open car doors and take what they could from inside. Stealing from cars is the stock solution for obtaining extra money used by many of the area's youth and The Tiddlers had grown up with this particular pattern, as had The Ritz and The Boys.

Yet The Tiddlers' need for money was less than that of their elders, who were interested in clothes, drinking and big spending generally. They found the simplicity and pettiness of shop-lifting, once it became routine, rather boring. The desire to be adult, brave, hard, to be excited and captivated by a situation, led them elsewhere. For one thing the kids from Everomer were taking cars and riding around in them. There was even a programme on TV about how the Everomer kids were having races around their blocks in stolen cars. What Everomer could do The Tiddlers could do better. Tiddler himself was the first to learn to drive, that is to learn how to connect up the ignition and drive a car in one gear. He sat in a few cars with Bobby to begin with, by way of practice. One night I remember standing with a few of The Boys by 'The Cockle'; Tiddler and Bobby had just forced open the door of a car and were trying various keys in the ignition. The next minute the engine was revving, then it was cut out, then started again, before the two little men got out and walked coolly away, much to The Boys' amusement.

From these tentative beginnings joyriding has become a common practice amongst The Tiddlers' age group. The Roundhouse joyriding team, though not as active or sophisticated as Everomer's,[2] has built up to about a dozen early adolescents displaying varying degrees of motoring expertise. The Tiddlers have shown considerable initiative and ability in learning car-key codes, makes of cars, types of gear change and various methods of starting cars such as making a circuit with a pair of scissors. Chalkie and Tiddler are now in fact fairly safe drivers, with gear changing and improved cornering part of their repertoire. Further, it is no longer enough to take any old car; the status of the car has become relevant, with Cortinas and Marinas (which the police also drive) being highly favoured. In lots of ways these youngsters are showing a desire for the straightforward respectable status of being a car owner. They talk at length about the merits and drawbacks to various cars, the only big difference from the talk of the ordinary car owner being their addition of status concerns important to their image amongst the conversation culture. Hence talk is often centred on how fast you've been, have you had a chase off a police car, have you had a crash, a lucky escape and so on.

The new joyriders have further influenced patterns of delinquent behaviour by leaving 'stolen' vehicles inside the tenement-block courtyards. Since the police cannot officially move these vehicles until they are reported missing, Roundhouse residents' notification to the authorities of an abandoned vehicle often appears ignored. Because the car is left abandoned for several hours and since it is regarded locally as 'lost property' which belongs to no one in particular, the little kids of the area will adopt it as a sort of mobile fortress. If left long enough the vehicle will, after its play value has been exhausted, be broken up and set on fire. This practice of one age group inadvertently handing over the car to another is common to other city neighbourhoods and increases the likelihood of the very young graduating to more daring escapades over time.[3]

Taking and driving away is not a new offence in Liverpool, although during Year Three reported offences increased rapidly until about 200 vehicles per week were being reported missing from the city area. Although the Roundhouse area, as a grid reference, shows a high incidence for this offence, this figure is due mainly to the high concentration of parked cars in the area. Nor do the adolescent joyriders account for the bulk of offences; most taking and driving away is committed by older journey-men simply wanting to get from the city centre to outlying estates. Nevertheless, joyriding became during Year Three something of a craze for The Tiddlers. Its significance in this study is that it illustrates the innovatory nature of much delin-quent action. Delinquency changes in character. The Tiddlers, whilst they have been involved in shoplifting and petty larceny, in keeping with certain delinquent traditions in Roundhouse, have also broken new ground. The Boys regard such joyriding escapades with a certain amazement. They regard The Tiddlers as 'nutters' and 'madmen' because 'They're doing things now we never dared do when we were kids, they're much worse than we ever were.' (*Mal.*)

A further innovation of a more serious and potentially very dangerous nature involved a petrol bomb. This incident occurred one Sunday afternoon when a police sergeant was bending over a stolen car outside the Block. As he bent down a petrol bomb came over the wall and exploded close to his feet, not injuring him. The whole incident was watched by several of The Boys as they stood on the Corner. One of The Tiddlers who'd made the attack was able to make a simple getaway completely undetected.

There was much unconvincing talk during the next few days about a plan to stone and petrol bomb the police station, but no actual incidents took place, nor are likely to. The petrol bomb seems to have been an isolated incident. It should be seen as part of The Tiddlers' attempts to be 'gangsters' or adult as they see it. By showing hatred of the police these early adolescents were reacting to their own feelings about Authority in conjunction with the hatred that they know The Boys, those they are striving to copy, feel for the police. The Tiddlers' conception of risk and fear of Authority is relatively undeveloped; they are still spontaneous in their adventures, and would be described as 'mad' or 'got no sense' simply because they lack an adequate conception of risk as regards the consequences of getting caught, which their elders know only too well.

To a large extent, parents are unaware their children are involved in such delinquent escapades. While they know of the various goings-on they tend to feel the kids involved are not theirs. Parents will usually only take disciplinary action if proof of their child's misdemeanour stares them in the face. Thus Tiddler's mother promised his teacher after he had been caught shop lifting, 'He won't cause no more bother, I take his shoes and trousers off him when he gets in so he has to stay in and watch telly.' Chalkie has not been caught yet: 'Me mam has a good idea what I'm up to but when she asks where I've been I just say I've been in the Block or playing footy, whatever I think of.'

The Boys and The Ritz recall this same sort of parental treatment. They remember vividly their attempts to hide their 'evils' from parents and their denials when accused. Fosser recalled how 'They used to lock me in my room and take my shoes. But I'd never stay locked in boy, I'd wear any old pair of fuckin' shoes. I'd never stay locked in, I used to hate it.' (T.)

The Tiddlers, then, are growing up in much the same way as The Boys before them. Forced from an early age into the Block's social milieu with its strong expressive influences, The Tiddlers looked for things to do, things to play with, excitement and a chance to show off, like all kids. The joyriding escalation has been the solution that has come most meaningfully to them. Though they are regarded by their elders as 'madder' than they ever were, this is probably merely an impression created by the novelty of such escapades to the neighbourhood. Whilst the actual delinquent styles differentiate The Tiddlers' from The Boys' early adolescence the likelihood that they will become The Boys of tomorrow is of greater significance. The Tiddlers are known to the police with two of them already on supervision orders.

The Ritz

At their age level The Ritz are again the most easily identifiable social network of friends who live in Roundhouse. Although there are individuals of the same age living in the area who are regularly involved in delinquent activities, as a group The Ritz are unique. A survey of names and addresses of fourteen to sixteen year olds who attended Juvenile Court in Year Two reveals that for the Roundhouse area only seven adolescents outside the network were apprehended. Observation suggests that whilst other adolescents from the area are delinquent they usually turn to shop-lifting, truancy and petty theft, most of which remains undetected. The Ritz are delinquent more often and in more serious ways, so they have tended to become known to the police; most have been convicted at least once, and by the end of Year Three up to four and five times.

Although referred to locally as a 'little gang', The Ritz are merely a peer group of friends who have grown up together and spend much of their free time together. Figure 2 represents an interpretation of the size and closer friendships of the core of the network during Year Two.

	Mal		
Sammy	Jaw	Bone	Fin
Rob	Quinsey	Toggle	Mack
	Boon	Mickey	
	Woodsey		

Figure 2. 'The Ritz'

With the exception of Toggle and Mickey, who passed the
11+ exam and were placed in 'grammar' streams at schools
outside the area, all The Ritz went to the local primary and
secondary schools. With the exception of Bone and Mickey they
have all grown up in the area. They all recall the same naughtiness, adventures and freedom in early childhood that The
Tiddlers enjoyed. Fin recalled how 'we used to pinch things
from the barrows [street traders] and round the market. Meat
and fruit and that, and go to this old empty house and make a
fire and sit round guzzling'. (T.) Rob and Toggle claimed they
had never been involved in childhood theft. Toggle felt this was
because 'My old man would have murdered me if I'd got
caught then. I wasn't even supposed to go in shops at all unless
I was going on a message. I never robbed at all till a couple of
years ago when I started going round with this lot.'

For most of The Ritz, however, early adolescence was a time
for petty shop-lifting and other opportunistic theft, not always
for the intrinsic value of the goods.

> *Jaw* Me and Quinsey done a car in for a packet of fags one night. It
> was only for a laugh. He said, 'I bet you wouldn't screw that car for
> those ciggies,' so I did.
> *Quinsey* We'd do cars for last week's *Echo* in those days, we weren't on
> to catseyes or anything then, it was just for something to do in those
> days.

By the end of Year Two, theft was being taken more seriously,
and shirts and pairs of trousers would be taken, as would articles
to sell round the Block. Jaw came on to the Corner one afternoon and rather than discuss how fortunate he was not to be
'grassed on' for selling stolen goods complained, 'We've just

been all round the Block trying to flog some blouses and we only got ten bob each for them in the end.'

At this time Fin and Mal, who were physically bigger and more mature than the others, were interested in becoming more adult and getting away from 'kid's stuff'. As Figure 1 suggests, The Boys were well into 'catseyes' at this time (Chapter 3 has a full discussion of car-radio theft), and Mal and Fin were attracted by this, especially because of its financial returns. These two 'worked' with some of The Boys and soon learnt techniques enabling them to 'screw' cars for themselves. Mal and Fin had an 'older' style than the other Ritz boys. Their language and image suggested their desire to be 'hard' like one of The Boys.

> *Fin* Me and Mal are just going down-town to spend some cash, we're loaded. We did two cars this morning. The first one, I had it down me kecks and we stopped and got icecreams. We was just walking along eating these icecreams, dead cool like, when this cop car goes past with the jacks looking at us. We just carried on walking like we didn't care.

Mal and Fin tended to break away from the rest of the group and get caught up in the increased policing activities with regard to 'car attacks'. During a six-month period they made a great deal of money but were twice caught red-handed. Not sufficiently deterred by police warnings they continued till eventually they were both sent to Borstal (mid Year Three).

The core of The Ritz were not drawn into stealing 'catseyes' for several months. Year Two saw them involved in more spasmodic delinquencies. Decisions about law breaking became more personalised. Sammy and Rob for instance would not entertain the idea of 'screwing' cars, whether for loose objects or catseyes. Their reasons were mainly related to the higher chances of getting caught and the greater severity of consequent court decisions. Rob also had an idea that there was a limit to when stealing was OK and breaking car windows and ripping out radios was beyond that limit. They remained involved in little more than shop-lifting, playing truant, 'borrowing' scooters and mopeds from nearby carparks and trying to get

into the cinema with stolen tickets. For the rest it was oppor-
tunism as usual. Jaw had a particularly successful haul.

> I walked into this shop where there were loads of watches and clocks.
> I took a couple of watches off a stand. The woman didn't notice. Then
> she went off to get some change or something for this old feller. She left
> the till open so when this old bloke wasn't looking I helped myself and
> walked out with £19.

This was no idle boast and Jaw had a pocket full of money
and the watches to prove it. Being much smaller and younger
looking than the others, he always tried to seek their attention
and would soon spend the money somewhat over-generously to
aid his acceptance.

Bone and Quinsey found themselves in trouble with the law
for the second time.

> *Bone*   The word got round that Fleets (warehouse) had been done in,
> so we went down to see what was going on. It was only mouldy old
> sweets and toys, but we went in and sorted out our gear [what they
> wanted to take]. I came out and went and stood round a fire on the
> 'oller while Quinsey took the gear back to his place. After about
> five minutes two plainclothes came and said, 'We saw you handing
> out sweets.' They'd got Quinsey as well. We both got done for that,
> Quinsey got probation and I got scrubs.

For the most part Year Two's illegal action was made up of
these spasmodic, occasional opportunistic thefts. The Ritz were
not on the prowl for 'trouble' at every spare moment. They
merely wanted things to do to break up boring periods: perhaps
a game of football or a visit to the youth club, or if the situation
arose at the right moment perhaps a car break-in. For instance,
a few of them had burgled a house outside the area when they
spotted the key left in the door and found quite a lot of cash.
Woodsey had taken a casette recorder from under the seat of a
car.

This pattern only changed when The Ritz got caught up in
the catseye craze. Year Three saw 'delinquency' becoming a
more important theme. 'At first we thought it was dead easy.

We thought we'd never get caught. The older boys had stacks of cash so we thought we'd get some as well.'

For about three months, the summer when most of The Ritz left school, both they and The Boys were 'screwing' cars regularly. Mickey and Toggle's involvement was only temporary however. As we have said they were more academically inclined than the others, and both were awaiting CSE results and had apprenticeships fixed for the autumn. Caught in a carpark taking a radio, they were persuaded by the consequent police procedures that given their prospects they would be wise to stop 'robbing'. This they have done and are both still working. For the rest however, with poor job prospects, less money and more time, screwing cars continued. The core of The Ritz of Year Three—Mal, Jaw, Quinsey, Woodsey and Boon—have become the new 'Catseye Kids', and despite several arrests are still not completely deterred, though more cautious. Their delinquent careers are following closely those of The Boys before them and will almost certainly continue to do so. A stocktaking of visits to Juvenile Court by the end of Year Three shows these five will shortly have to face decisions affecting their continued freedom. Their chances of continuing car-radio theft and enjoying the financial gains it affords will have to be weighed carefully with the possibility of a period of incarceration if they are caught again. Their convictions to date are as follows (names are not used, to ensure anonymity).

A   Discharged for loitering with intent; supervision order under a social worker for attempted theft; Attendance Centre for theft from a vehicle.

B   Police caution for shoplifting; fine for shoplifting; supervision order under a probation officer for burglary; Attendance Centre for theft from a vehicle.

C   Police caution and visit from a Juvenile Liaison Officer for shoplifting; police caution for taking and driving away a scooter; supervision order under a social worker for attempted theft; heavy fine for theft from a vehicle.

D   Police caution for burglary; conditional discharge for

burglary; fine for shoplifting; supervision order under a
probation officer for theft from a vehicle.

E   Supervision order under a probation officer for theft
from a vehicle and resisting arrest; heavy fine for
attempted theft; loitering-with-intent charge pending.

Such brief discussions about The Tiddlers and The Ritz do
not do justice to their situations. More will be said about The
Ritz and their relationship with The Boys and the catseye
business in the next chapter. The changing nature of delinquent
action through time and the variations of those involved should
now be clear however. Both these groups of youngsters have
'grown up' on the Corner in the sense that much of their spare
time is spent knocking around the neighbourhood and becoming involved in the ideas and actions that effervesce there.

Parents, it has been emphasised, are not always in a position
to offer their children an alternative to playing unsupervised.
Mum, especially, tries to keep her children out of trouble, but
because of a whole series of structural constraints and family
contingencies is unable to offer a real alternative to young sons
who pester to be allowed to play out. This is not to deny that
family mismanagement and family stress occur, and affect the
children, but it is the appearance of the youngsters in the
neighbourhood, for whatever reason, which is of the greatest
significance. The family and the home must take their place in
the etiology (the search for causal explanation) of delinquency.
Some parents do keep their children out of trouble, but usually
by literally not allowing them out. Given that youngsters must
have some freedom, and given that most family situations
simply do not make such confinement feasible, however, the
family in this study is relevant mainly as an agency which has
only limited control over adolescent deviancy rather than as an
instigator of delinquent motivation.

It is to the street-corner world in which many Roundhouse
youngsters become immersed that we must look to understand
the creation of delinquent action. Here views are less conservative, traditions and mythologies of great significance, and delin-

quency accepted as a possible means of achieving goals. The street-corner milieu, although it is an extension of parental values, also feels the need to conceal its more deviant activities from conventional residents *because* it comprehends their values as dominant.[4] This chapter has stressed that the street-corner world both transmits delinquent traditions and provides an atmosphere for innovation and creation. The street-corner adolescent thinks out and applies himself a great deal more than he is often given credit for.

Understanding that The Boys' earlier adolescence involved the same sorts of interests, behaviour and pressures as these younger boys now feel, we move on. The Boys' story also begins on the Corner, for it was from there they became involved in theft behaviour to the extent that they became the Catseye Kings.

Notes to this chapter are on p 226

3 Catseye Kings for a While

It was a dead cert, just sitting there waiting to be whizzed.

To Authority in particular and outsiders in general, The Boys don't exist. The members of the network are merely downtown adolescents who look much alike, who live in a 'high delinquency area' and if the facts be known are 'persistent offenders'. By the end of Year Three, taking twenty-five members of the network, only one had no form of criminal record. The average number of indictable offences was just over three, with several of The Boys scoring six and seven convictions. Many had run the gauntlet of 'warnings'—probation, fines, attendance centres, more fines, approved schools, detention centres, borstals. The Boys, taking any official measure one likes, are viewed as severely delinquent, and consequently fit to receive the connotative definitions and degrading labels saved for their type.

During a six-month period starting at the end of Year Two, The Boys as a group almost certainly reached the peak, in terms of intensity of misdemeanour, of their delinquent 'careers'. For a while they became the Catseye Kings. Amongst other things this chapter deals with their rise and fall. Depending on where you are standing this is a story with many morals. As far as The Boys are concerned there are only two sides, theirs or Authority's. The sociologist involved in this contest must take sides, whether he likes it or not: every time he records an incident and leaves another buried, every time he quotes an actor and ignores another, he is taking sides. He is the 'third man',[1] he not only reconstructs the action but then further interprets, by 'writing up' his own version of his original perceptions. By writing a lengthy chapter on The Boys' 'delinquency' there is a tendency to imply to the reader that illegal behaviour is a serious preoccupation of The Boys. Having spent two years of fairly close observation in this group who as individuals at least are regarded as highly delinquent and 'persistent offenders', I know The Boys in fact are not persistent in their rule-breaking at all. Indeed, put in the context of a wider society full of deviancy at all social levels and in all social classes, The Boys' 'delinquency' is mundane, trivial, petty, occasional and very little of a threat to anyone except themselves. Yet this is not seen as relevant to their disposal; instead they are 'dealt with' as if they were different from everybody else.

> When society defines certain people as outsiders, it needs to emphasise the ways in which these people are different from the insiders, those who are normal. Thus criminals are not just people who have broken the law but are also generally dangerous and not to be trusted.[2]

Hence The Boys are regarded by some, most of whom wield power, as malicious, thoughtless, devious, wild, vandalistic, with a chip on their shoulder and coming from 'a jungle'. The Boys' life-style, if all its aspects were known to our typecasters, our 'highly respected' citizens, would be stigmatised as depraved and damaging to the well-being of society. With minimal appreciation of their situation, The Boys would be earmarked. They are heavy drinkers, spending a great deal more time and money in pubs and clubs than they should. They take short cuts wherever possible, showing no self-control and ability to defer gratification. They are drug users and even pushers, they get involved in fights in which people get so badly beaten that they have to go to hospital. They damage other people's property to the value of hundreds of pounds. They steal from cars, shops and warehouses, and when apprehended show contempt for Authority. They are ill-mannered, lazy and unwilling to take jobs they are offered, and even when they do work show no loyalty for their employer.

Starting at this inaccurate, prejudiced—almost racist—stereotyped, but everyday interpretation of The Boys' style, this chapter will move towards a deeper comprehension.

The Boys' Network

There must be hundreds of neighbourhoods in Britain that talk about their own 'The Boys'. This title usually refers to a recognisable peer group, a network of lads who've grown up together and are seen around together in various combinations. For our purposes The Boys represent the largest and most recognisable adolescents' network of this kind in the area. The Boys are not a gang, they do not possess such rigid defining criteria; they are a network, a loose-knit social group. A gang is often identifiable to outsiders as such, a network is not. Thus probation officers and policemen would probably not be able to grasp the extensiveness or nature of The Boys, but would only identify one small part of their network.

In operational terms membership is defined by the use of the passport 'he's one of The Boys'. Such a passport is not made out at some special moment of initiation but has evolved over the years. Being one of The Boys involves having grown up with, gone to school with, played out with and hung around with, played football with and gone on holiday with all the others who have done the same and minimally enjoyed each others' company. The membership list is not completely static; thus Figure 3 indicates some change over a twelve-month period, involving for example the departure of Craber and Joey from the core almost to the edges of the network, and the movement inwards of Jimbo.

The core membership is made up of the largest unit of close

MID YEAR TWO

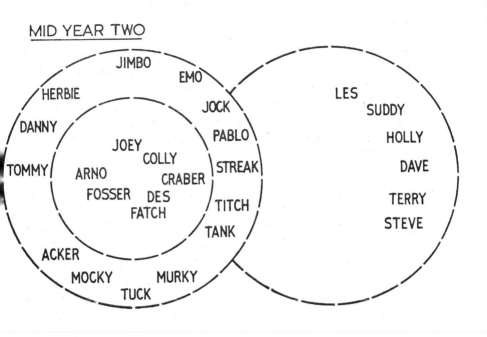

MID YEAR THREE

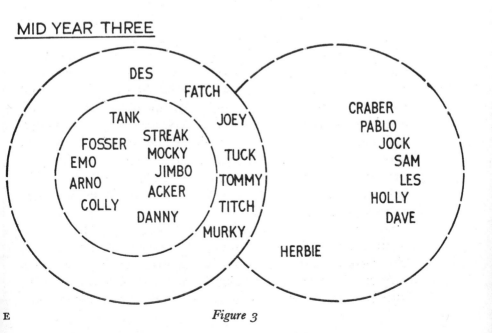

Figure 3

companionship illustrated in terms of time spent together and efforts to collect itself together socially. The pattern of the network socially is not synonymous with delinquent companionship, however. Companionship related to delinquent activities is regarded by the network as less important and more fluid than wider friendship. Thus at the end of Year Three, Arno and Streak 'robbed' together but did not 'go round' together except when with a larger gathering of the network.

At the edges of the network are probably about six marginal members, each recognised by some but not others as being 'one of The Boys'. Here simple friendship and personality preferences may be important. The core membership is not a special magic circle however, it has no special privileges or power. If one has a passport one can move inwards at any time; there is freedom of choice. Thus Murky, who works long hours and rarely gets involved in delinquent activities, is no less welcome when he does appear. As long as he acts within the basic edicts of the group and doesn't go absent for extensive periods, he will always be welcome to join in. Credentials are only 'checked out' over long periods; once you're 'one of The Boys' you will remain so until contrary evidence is presented.

The Boys are identifiable to other locals and regular faces also. The adolescents of both sexes in the area would be able to make a roll-call of the network, as would the bar staff and regular 'boozers' in the local pubs. Any member of the network could go into 'The Turk', ask 'Have you seen any of The Boys?' and receive a sensible answer such as 'Colly and Jimbo were in a bit ago.' These insiders over the months have seen varying combinations of the network so often that the total membership has crystallised almost incidentally in their mind's eye and they know who The Boys are.

Most of The Boys left school as soon as they could. They left because they were bored and tired of being told what to do. They saw various occupational alternatives. If they tried hard they could get an apprenticeship, otherwise they could get an unskilled manual job, hopefully well paid, or again they could just hang around and not do very much at all. In general they opted for the straightforward weekly wage packet of the un-skilled manual job.

Not all The Boys left school at the end of the fourth form. Danny and Streak stayed on at the local secondary school to do CSEs when their mates left. These two were not the bright boys of a dull bunch however. Almost half of The Boys had passed their 11 + exam and attended grammar school. Fosser had lasted nine months, Fatch and Danny the year, Pablo and Colly stayed nearly two years, Herbie and Streak stayed till the end of the third form. All these boys went back to the local school. Emo and Murky stayed on at grammar school till the fifth form; Emo missed his exams because of a traffic accident, and Murky acquired seven CSEs. Of the boys that stayed on at school all but Murky, who went straight into an apprenticeship, joined The Boys on the Corner the following year (Year Two).

Although The Boys had a couple of months 'off' after leaving school, to absorb their newfound freedom, they were soon all looking for and trying out manual jobs. They felt the role of adult was not far away; once they had a job and plenty of money to spend they could assume the conspicuous consumption habits that would put the seal on their adulthood. At this time their delinquency was still opportunistic; several had been to court on shop-lifting offences but delinquency was still related to fun, excitement and adventure, the 'spoils' were not all-important. Five of them had been caught together breaking into a sweets and tobacco shop.

> We were all on the Corner when Arno says he knew where there was a place we could do dead easy for ciggies and that. We broke into this empty shop next door through the roof and we were knocking a hole in the wall to the next door to climb into the shop. We'd just made a hole and Tank was going to climb through, when a torch goes on at the shop door and someone starts banging. It was the busies, someone must have seen us go in. We all tried to get out of a skylight. It was fuckin' funny. We all had on women's overalls out of the shop and that. Anyway they got us all in the end and dragged us out. I was a bit scared when they got hold of me like but I was made up [pleased] because there was a fire engine and big spotlights and everything. (T.)

The Boys all got a £20 fine for this escapade (Year One). At this time they still saw 'robbing' more as a leisure activity or something you did when it was easy. A shirt, a pair of socks, a pair of bootlaces would be 'whizzed' if no one was looking. A goods lorry, a 'bondy' warehouse, would be broken into or a shop window broken and 'gear' grabbed quickly. The hundreds of parked cars around the area provided another form of opportunist theft, doors to be forced for a camera, a brief case, even a packet of cigarettes if there was nothing better to do.

When The Boys first left school the job market was still fairly buoyant. Jobs were 'easy come, easy go' with no one being very concerned about getting the sack—there was always another. Pablo, who had turned down another year at school mainly for the more immediate returns of the wage packet, had a fairly typical first year and a half out of school.

It was a dead-end job, plumbing. They start you off at fifteen and they kick you out at seventeen. I worked there about six months and got sacked. We was waiting for wages on Thursday afternoon; I was a gas-fitter's mate. There's a feller who comes round with the money, he was trying to be funny like and says get in there and dust the shed out with a brush. I just refused like, a few swear words and the sack. Really make you small like, just saying go and brush the shed out . . . I refused. (T.)

I was out of work about two weeks then got a job at Purax. I was a van lad driving round the country delivering furniture. I was only getting about £10 for a fifty-hour week. I did five months and got the sack from there. We was bringing all the felt in from another firm and we was messing about and I pulled one of these polythene bags of felt. I pulled it and it ripped. And just by chance one of the fellers who owned it, one of the sons, had seen me and he brought me to the foreman.

After about two months I got a job on the Isle of Man boats. I was only on there the day like when I got the sack. I started off on the Friday morning and the boat wasn't leaving Liverpool till midnight the same night. I got no sleep right through the day. We did three trips. From Liverpool to Douglas and back again and back to Douglas. So that was right through the next day I had no sleep. I fell asleep on the second trip. The steward came down and sacked me. I had to stay in the Isle of Man about five days I think it was. He asked me then did I want to stay in the job. I said no, walking round collecting cups, no chance, I refused that so I came home. I was out of work for about six weeks then and got a job in Leeces. I stuck that for about three months. I was a depositor for the dough, putting it in the pans for the bloke to put in the oven. That got boring, they were getting on at me about my hair. They wanted me to get a hair net or get it cut. They kept on at me to get it cut. Then I was on me holidays and took a week off as well, like. Then I went in and got told to get down to the manager. He told me to get it cut or wear a hair net. I refused and he sacked me. (T.)

Herbie was lucky: his father got him an apprenticeship in the firm he worked for himself.

I was there eighteen months as an apprentice, signed my indentures and everything, then I spewed it [left], it was getting on my nerves. The foreman was a divvy. I started out with the Army.

I was going to do an apprenticeship with the Army but everything they tell you like £24 a week, it's a load of rubbish. You get nothing like that. They never told me nothing about you've got to be seventeen and a half years old before you come on the full money, and out of that your lodgings, your bedding, this, that, the other. I was picking up £5 and £6 a week. And that was no good for sending me mam home a few bob like, not enough for buttons. I was under seventeen and a half years old and you get seven months to make your mind up. So I left after two months and came back to the Block and signed on the dole. (T.)

They got me a job in Topsons. It was bad news, in work at eight o'clock in the morning, soon as you're in you start doing this all day, putting your foot on this and doing that. It was fuckin' terrible. And for £7 a week at seventeen. I spewed it and got my money stopped by the dole for six weeks, I only got just on £2.

Then just before Christmas me old man got me a job in Kirkby. He said get up there, they want a dumper driver there, I think they want them with a licence though and I'd only got a provisional licence. He said try and kid your way in and tell them you've got one. So I said OK and went up. I couldn't find the place at first so I came back down and he gave me instructions again for going back up. This is after Christmas I went up, they said OK, join the union and all that, and come and start on Monday. He [foreman] said, have you got a licence? I said yes, he hadn't said what kind of a licence. He said, well you'll have to bring it in tomorrow but you can stay today and we'll pay you for it. And when I was going home he said don't forget your licence. Next morning he says where's your licence, I said, Oh I think it's down me grandma's. So next day I had to show it him and he says it's a provisional isn't it, well I said you only asked for a licence, that's all you do need to drive a dumper. But a feller got hurt there and only had a provisional, and the insurance wouldn't pay him. So he says oh you'll have to spew it. So I was only there two or three days and they was going to stop my dole till I explained like and I was all right then. (T.)

At least twenty of The Boys who left school that year had the same record of short stay, poor attendance, poor pay, boring jobs. They were coming round to the idea that it wasn't worth putting up with dead-end jobs unless the pay was good. One of the men in the Block found Colly, Fosser, Joey, Fatch and Des a job at the place where he was working.

> *Fosser*   It was only for a bit like, they had a special lagging job that needed doing. That was the best job I ever had, boy, we was bringing home £20 a week then but it only lasted a couple of months.
>
> *Colly*   It was a good laugh as well, all the boys together like. We'd all go straight to the ale house and have a few bevvies and a pie before we came home and we all bought a load of clobber [clothes].

The Boys, although mostly only sixteen years old, were now readily accepted in the local pubs where the philosophy is that if they're old enough to work and earn money, they're old enough to drink. The pub was fast becoming the centre of The Boys' leisure time, and which pubs were good, which weren't, how much one had had to drink, were important topics of conversation.

By the end of their first year 'at work' (Year One), The Boys had discovered the pleasures and satisfactions of work—the pay packet. They had not become committed to the work ethic; they had realised their dispensability, the boredom of unskilled work and the tyranny of the boss. They had never approached a job 'committed'; they simply continued the attitudes acceptable at school—isn't it boring, do as little as you can and give as much cheek as possible without causing trouble for yourself. When you're 'treated like dirt', 'always getting told what to do', 'get sacked for fuck all' and have to work long hours for poor pay, then indifference, defiance and non-commitment are vital defences to avoid a greater exploitation, an exploitation of dignity. Here again most of The Boys learnt from experience that the attitudes and approaches held by older brothers and other adults were correct. 'Work *is* bad news.' The Boys did not simply imitate their elders and accept the lazy tradition.

The Boys felt and will continue to feel that work is dead-end, boring and exploitative. They have shared their work experiences in discussion, the picture is quite plain. They come to a set of rational decisions about the value of work. A good job is judged mainly on two counts: 'is it a cushy number?' and 'does it make your wallet fat?' If there are no well-paid, easygoing jobs then work must be regarded as a doubtful way of spending one's time. This was their philosophy at the start of Year Two.

Corner Boys and Cash
It was about this time I started hanging around with The Boys. My appearance came directly after their summer holidays, some of which they'd spent at Sandhills so I was a familiar face to them and the younger kids of the area, and was spoken of as 'Howard from Sandhills' to those I didn't know. Having taken August off most of The Boys had given up their jobs. They were in no hurry to find new ones. By this time the Press was full of talk about unemployment which soon exonerated The Boys from the effort of looking. Well paid jobs were increasingly difficult to get. The city's unemployment figures for fifteen to eighteen year olds were around the 2,000 mark. 'What's the point of going down [Youth Employment], they've only got a load of crap, the well-paid jobs go to the married fellers with families and that.' Indeed The Boys agreed amongst themselves that the sorts of jobs they'd had last year were 'not worth a wank' and basically experience had damped down any enthusiasm for work. Elliot Liebow noted that Tally's men held a similar stance. 'At any given moment, a job may occupy a relatively low position on the street-corner scale of values.'[3]

The Boys, reinforced by their fifth-form leaver mates, started to hang around. The autumn involved little more than sitting in the youth club, playing table tennis, wandering around town, going for a cup of tea at Flems, a local department store, or finding a pub with a dart board. At first I stayed around the youth club, but as I became more accepted in my new 'lazy' role I would perhaps get asked to join the procession like anyone else who was hanging around. After a short embarrassing period I was able to slot into this routine. I too was hanging around, and there was no immediate reason why I should not be taken along, since my general form had already been scrutinised at Sandhills.

Hanging around apparently just doing nothing is a disturbing phenomenon for many outsiders. To the middle classes and affluent workers, with their structured day based on the work ethic, 'leisure' is something you earn, not something you take for granted. The Boys' experience of school and work had convinced them, however, that all in all hanging around was less boring. Certainly there were times when everyone was still bored and fed up, but at least 'there are no fuckin' bosses on your back all day'. These days were not without structure. As with their nights-out-down-town, of the following year, these 'bumming days' had definite form. An average day's repertoire included standing or sitting on the Corner, hanging around the youth club, playing table-tennis there, visiting local pubs for a few drinks and a game of darts, going to Flems, wandering around town, going to the 'chippy' and playing football in the Block. The Boys could decide the order of these events, the sequence of 'tasks', *they* structured their day. Superimposed on this repertoire were certain 'compulsory' events: Thursday was dole day, Friday lunchtime 'everybody goes to the pub', Saturday is football day. This repertoire evolved slowly and was adapted with changing circumstances. The functions of such a structured day are several. Undoubtedly having certain things to do added meaning and interest to life. Also the set structure allowed someone who got up especially late, or had to 'go on a message' or stay in the flat to do something, to trace The Boys quickly and easily. 'Are you waiting for Colly, he's got to go to the UAB?' 'No, he can catch us up, let's get off.' By Christmas I was part of the scenery and could likewise 'catch them up'. If I only had a couple of hours I could find The

Boys in a few minutes and, like several others, join the procession.

The onus put on conspicuous consumption during Year One
only added to The Boys' desire, and hence need, for money.
Their weekly dole, after some had gone to 'the old girl', left
them with little more than £1.50. Some money could usually be
got from older and more affluent members of the family but not
on a dependable basis; some weeks everybody was 'skint'. The
shoplifting and occasional profit on a 'middleman' transaction
brought in a further supplement. Sometimes for instance one of
The Tiddlers would appear with a 'knock off' which one of The
Boys would take and promise a certain amount for the day
after. 'No, I'll buy [beer]; I've just made a duce [two pounds]
on a suit Chalky gave me; I got seven for it and gave him a
fiver.' (*Acker.*)

Most of The Boys had been to Court for the sort of minor
offences mentioned before, such as stealing a shirt, a pair of
trousers, cameras and transistor radios from cars, and cakes
from a lorry, to mention a few. Tuck, in the meantime, had
been going out 'on the rob' almost nightly after the pubs shut
and had been caught so often he had ended up in borstal. This
surprised nobody. Role-typed a 'fuckin' nutter' or 'idiot', Tuck
had 'no fuckin' sense, he didn't know when to stop'. The fear
of incarceration was in general not a serious consideration at
this time; if anything Tuck's ill fortune was held up as a consequence of his own greed; he was an example of an inept
robber, not of the unwisdom of stealing itself.

With the winter setting in, the Corner was a less inviting
place, and The Boys would get up later and meet in 'The
Turk' at about midday. At closing time they would walk back
up to the Corner trying to kill the rest of the afternoon. On the
Corner:

Fosser I'm fuckin' bored, bored, bored (beating a stick on the kerb in
unison).
Colly Give us a blower Joey.
Joey It's about time you bought some ciggies, isn't it?

Colly I'm skint, Joey (bangs his pockets), haven't got a bean. Fatch is the one with all the poke [money].

Fatch Fuck off, I've got ten bob to last me till Thursday.

(Later.)

Joey Hang on, there's me old girl, I'll see if she's got a few bob. (Shouts over to the group): Come 'ed boys, let's go down to Flem's for a cup.

We all set off down to Flems, six strong taking up the pavement, not too worried about bumping into passers-by, blue denims, long hair, 'real Liverpool'. Once in the store, goods are picked up and examined and the group make their usual boisterous, apparently 'offensive' conversation. 'There's the floor walker [store detective]. All right, luv, got your wig on today.' Fatch is explaining the store's inter-com system to me: 'Soon as they see you they call 44, which means everybody on that bit [section] should keep an eye on you. See that old git there [uniformed security officer]—he'll be up here in a minute walking next to us.'

During the cup of tea and munching of a large supply of sugar lumps, the salt was mixed with the pepper and the colour of the waitress's knickers identified. 'Hey pink drawers, do yer want a feller?' 'No thanks luv, I've got one at home.' 'Well what about another?' She smiles and walks away. She comprehends the down-town style and is not offended by the patter which upsets the suburban visitors. By the time we got back to the Corner, Jock and Pablo were there. It was tea time and we all wandered over to the chip shop, vaulting the safety barrier yet again. Once stocked up everyone walked back to the Corner and sat on the pavement with their backs resting on the wall. Little kids attracted by the smell were fended off without the chips they were attempting to scrounge. There was always plenty of action at this time of the day with people passing almost continuously. The police panda creeping past would always provoke the usual abuse, a nice-looking girl the usual commentary. If it was one of 'The Girls', a local girl, an exchange of friendly abuse might start up.

Joey Hey Brenda, where've you been?
Brenda Where you should be—at work.
Joey Work, get yer drawers off and I'll make you work.
Brenda Would you now, dirty ticket.

This quick snappy dialogue is an intellectual game in its own right and did much to keep The Boys amused in what was becoming an increasingly boring period.

Christmas was coming round again. Christmas, for The Boys as for most other people, is an extra excuse to indulge in extravagant consumption for an extended period; only this year who had all the money, because it wasn't The Boys? The annual new suit and shoes, the 'fat wallet' to buy everyone a double and then another, seemed unlikely to materialise. A few pounds were being made on the occasional 'job'; a record shop and electrical wholesalers had been 'done' and some 'leathers' had been whizzed from a shop window. Keeping an eye on the parked cars had provided the occasional bonus, but as far as The Boys were concerned all in all they were skint. They made a fairly conscious effort to plan a couple of 'robberies' which never materialised. There was no question of worrying about the morality of planning property thefts, which seemed like crimes without real victims. The Boys' main concern was how much could they sell the gear for, and how likely they were to get caught.

Joey, Fatch and Colly were the first of The Boys to steal catseyes. These fixed radios seemed almost standard equipment in the newer and more luxurious cars continuously being parked around the neighbourhood. Some of the 'older fellers' in the area had been taking radios and selling them to a 'dealer' or middleman for up to £7 a time. The word was around that this middleman was ready to increase business. At the time few people had been caught for this offence and a sensible way of making money seemed available. 'Catseyes talk' was started and carried on amongst The Boys, their older associates and eventually with The Ritz, for over a year. Joey and Fatch, under the supervision of Joey's older brother, took several catseyes from cars in the area. One dinner-time they came onto the Corner rather pleased with themselves because the night before they had broken into two Rover cars and removed radios. The others already knew this. Joey announced: 'We've just got paid, fellers, lots of lovely poke. Come on you cunts, you don't deserve it but we'll get a few bevvies in.' About six of us went down to 'The Turk', where for the next couple of hours the lager flowed freely. Everyone was happy and full of friendly jibbing.

During the next couple of weeks there was much talk about Rovers and catseyes. Rover 2000+ models were the main target for the ensuing 'attacks', because the plastic casing housing the speaker could be removed with one hefty boot up on to the dashboard. The holding brackets were then easily accessible and the radio could be taken quickly. That these cars were the most expensive and luxurious around town was a coincidence, though not without consequence as we shall see.

It was about 9.30 pm when we walked down the hill towards the centre. Colly had just seen 'a real beaut' in a Rover parked on waste ground in William Street. Although I was regarded as a friendly spectator I was briefed to keep look out, 'dixy', at the top end of the line of cars. A two-tone whistle, not unlike a police siren, was always used as a warning of possible trouble. Colly had a 'punch' with him, a spring-loaded centre punch used in the leather industry. Several of The Boys used these to break car quarter-light windows. Tonight the window shattered at the second attempt, and the door was opened quickly. Joey, who had on the correct footwear, put the boot in accurately. Colly did the rest, unscrewing the brackets and yanking the radio away, so snapping the connecting wires. The door was shut and Joey went off down the hill with the radio under his jacket. Colly joined me, concealed his punch and we walked back up the hill. I admitted to a certain amount of elation and a great deal of relief. Joey would make his way back to the

Block and then meet us in the pub. 'We take it in turns to carry the radio, coz if you get caught with it on you you've had it. There's no point in everyone getting done for it, so the one who's got the radio goes off on his own.'

Colly remarked on how smoothly things had gone this night compared with the evening before. 'I really shit myself last night. I was in this Rover when these fuckin' headlights went on. I thought it was the busies. Joey pushed the door shut with me inside and just stood outside leaning on the car with me ducking down. He said "It's only someone going off".'

The catseyes capers spread. By the end of January at least twenty of the network were screwing cars, some regularly, others occasionally. A dialogue built up amongst The Boys and other regular faces who were interested in the knock-off business. Who was screwing cars, on the catseyes, or simply on the cars were important topics for the conversation culture. During the daytime wandering around the area, 'pipe-ing', looking over a car, became a regular practice, even if merely to pass the time: did it have a radio, was it the right kind to bring a high price at the fence, was the car door locked, was there an alarm, was it in a safe place to screw? Pipe-ing eventually had to become very subtle; the outsider, particularly the lurking plainclothes policeman, should not to be able to realise a couple of boys were pipe-ing a car at all as they walked past it. Talk during February centred around the techniques of removing radios from the dashboard without detection or damage to it, the problematic part of the exercise; expertise was scarce initially. At this time some radios were having to be sold at a reduced rate owing to damaged buttons. Walking down to the dole one morning with Titch and Fosser an innovation was born. We stopped to look at an open sports car which was somewhat novel at that time of the year. Titch recognised its radio as being of the same make as one he had damaged in taking it out of a car the week before. He yanked off the control buttons hastily and we were walking down the hill again in seconds. 'They'll fit great. That'll be a few quid for tonight. I'll fix that other radio in ours and take it in when we get back up.'

Titch told the others about his cure for damaged radios, and within a few weeks a regular exchange of spare parts was occurring, with spares for future use being taken off radios difficult to actually remove. Also, the large group expeditions for taking a car radio, which had been common initially, soon disappeared on the pre-planned thefts. For one thing such a large group was too obviously 'up to no good', and secondly the subsequent share-out was too small in relation to the risks taken.

The larger network spent much time discussing its new business during the leisure hours on the Corner and in the pubs. Here information about technique and policing activities was disseminated, as was news of each duo's or trio's actual efficiency and 'cool' during screwing operations. The trio was the most popular combination for going on the cars at this time.[4] Number one would keep dixy, whilst 'two' forced open either the quarter-light or the door and perhaps booted the dashboard casing. 'Three' would then remove the radio, usually by unscrewing brackets and snapping connecting wires, whilst 'two' also kept dixy. 'One', who had so far taken the least risk, would then put the radio down his trousers or in his coat and make off on his own for the safety of the Block. In this way risk was fairly evenly distributed. Who did what also varied according to the various combinations of talents available, with 'nerve' and technical expertise being important variables and 'divvies' not being trusted to do the booting.

For some three months The Boys were the undisputed Catseye Kings—they stole catseyes and they lived like kings. The regulars were earning as much as £35 per week on the cars and spending the cash as quickly. Single thefts were now hardly worth talking about; newsworthy comment had to be more daring.

Colly   Ay ay, here comes greedy arse. You can get the bevvies in today lad, four catseyes last night.
Fatch   Three, man, three. All on me own as well, no trouble.

Colly You're just greedy, lad, you want to save a few for everyone else.

Emo I couldn't screw a car on my own, I'd fuckin' shit meself.

Fatch Easy, lad, easy . . . Anyway who's talking, Colly, you've whizzed more than me this week.

Colly Who, me? I don't screw cars, I'm a good boy.

Such a skit on innocence by Colly was the nearest The Boys got to considering the morality of their behaviour at this time. Things were too good today to worry about tomorrow. Till the end of the spring they bathed in the extravagance of getting up late, spending a few hours in the pub, drinking, smoking and playing cards, having a good meal, playing football and going back to the pub again for the evening ritual. Even over a year later these days were recalled vividly. 'They were the best days of my life. They were fuckin' great. We were loaded the whole time. I'd spend 30 quid a week just like that. I'd buy a pair of shoes for 6 quid just like that, peel them (pound notes) off. If you were skint in those days you'd just go on the cars for a couple of hours.' (*Fosser.*)

The Boys didn't always have to go pipe-ing, quite often other youngsters or adolescents in the area would pass on a useful message which would trigger off a spontaneous joint operation involving whoever was around at the time.

Jaw Have you seen that Rover in Bleak Street, there's a catseye-5 in it?

Colly Shall we go and clock it boys?

(We walk down the road.)

Joey It's too near the main road.

Colly Oh, come on, you can do it from that side by the wall and make off through the 'oller. I'll go and get me punch, I'll see you on the Corner.

The Boys' car-radio offences were not going unnoticed however, and as the summer arrived their delinquency became blocked by heavy policing. The police were now recording over a hundred thefts from cars within the Roundhouse area per month (see Figure 4, p 184). Although outsiders were certainly coming into this high-density-parked car area, it was The Boys who were affecting the statistics most dramatically. Increased policing was inevitable and both uniformed and plainclothes Task Force officers patrolled the area.

Initially the increased number of confrontations with the police, whether through routine stops or encounters on car parks, did not affect the network's enthusiasm for taking car radios. Such encounters were seen as occupational hazards to be overcome. Over the months, however, the police presence became too intense to be ignored and The Boys' behaviour adapted in two ways. Firstly, catseye talk changed, with leisure-time conversations becoming increasingly dominated by discussions about the police. Secondly, The Boys made contingency plans and modified their behaviour in response to their contest with Authority.

Before discussing these changes however something should be said about The Boys' view of social morality, and the way they saw their behaviour in relation to the wider society. One aspect of catseye talk during the summer (early Year Three) was concerned with the question of why people stole. Such questions had become pertinent because of the increased risks involved in going on the cars now the police purge had begun in earnest. Certainly The Boys accepted that they didn't all rob for the same reasons. Boys like Danny and Murky were not 'real' robbers according to the others but were involved mainly through their membership in the network. Because the majority of the network were reluctant to miss opportunistic theft chances, a night officially designated for 'going on the ale' was sometimes interrupted to get a 'dead-cert' radio. Hence relatively law-abiding boys would find themselves keeping 'dixy' simply because a catseye chance had been spotted, and for being involved in a theft would sometimes receive a 'dropsy' of about a pound. This tended to tempt them into more deliberate 'car attacks', especially when they'd 'had a few bevvies' or were skint. It was somewhat ironical that Murky was one of the first of the network to get charged with attempted theft from a car although he was simply keeping dixy for someone else and was regarded by his mates as 'straight'.

Arno also had to be explained, since he was working on a building site and bringing home a good wage. One day that spring a few of The Boys got involved in one of the increasingly popular discussions about why people went on the cars. Most agreed the catseyes were a means to an end—money. This was consistent with their admissions about fear during theft operations.

Fatch   I shit me-self doing it like, I always do, it's worst when you're in the car and you're coming away with it. A cop car can come round the corner and that's it, you've no chance to get rid of it or nothing.

Jimbo   There's too many on the cars now, they all think they can just go on for ever without getting caught.

Streak   I'm not going to be a robber the rest of my life. If I could get a decent job, say twenty quid a week, I wouldn't rob. But when you see your mates with their pockets full and buying gear and that, you feel you've got to get some as well. You're not going to stay in while they go out every night.

Joey   Oh, we've heard that before, that's why everyone says they rob, but you and me aren't doing so bad.

Streak   But that's what I mean, that's what makes you steal.

Jimbo   But look at the likes of Arno, what's he bringing home [from work], 25 quid a week. What does he rob for? Greed. That's why he robs, just fuckin' greed.

Joey   I can't see where his 25 quid goes. If I had twenty-five and even put five away I wouldn't be skint by Thursday like he says he is.

Fatch   Arno does it to be one of the boys like the young kids do, he does it to be big.

Streak   Oh no! Look, say I'd got a job and I was earning say £30 a week and I was walking across the 'oller' and I saw a Rover with catseyes, and it was a cert, I'd fuckin' get it.

Jimbo   But you said you *wouldn't* rob if you had a good job.

Streak   Oh yer I did . . . what I mean is if I had a good job, plenty of money, I wouldn't go looking for cars no more, I'd only do one if it was right by the Block or something. I suppose I'm just a fuckin' natural robber.

The Boys then *emphasise* different reasons for going on the cars, yet all, in explicit terms at least, come down to the most

F

commonly expressed reason, money, money which is to be spent. Then as now their basic view of delinquency was that it should be instrumental, that is theft-orientated and in terms of concrete gains. The excitement element in some delinquent action is not denied as relevant, and likewise The Boys will mention boredom and a lack of action as providing the immediate push; but as Emo pointed out to Bone and I, 'If there's nothing on telly and nobody's going down-town or nothing you might decide to walk around and pipe a car. But you wouldn't do it just 'cos you were bored, you wouldn't do it if you weren't going to get the poke [money] for doing it.'

Bone   But you can't tell me the little kids all screw cars for money, they do it 'coz they think it's big.
Self   Would you screw a car just for the hell of it?
Bone   No not me, not now anyway. I used to when I was a kid like.

The Boys regard delinquency which is merely for 'fun', just expressive and without concrete gains, as kids' stuff. Such days have passed for them, they no longer take risks which involve a possible court appearance just for the hell of it. The switch away from expressive delinquency towards instrumental delinquency as adolescence progresses is universal in Roundhouse.[5] As the next chapter emphasises, the real excitement for The Boys involved spending the money gained from the catseye business. It was the spending of money on clothes, and the long, excessive nights down-town that really appealed to The Boys and their views about an ideal manhood. Without understanding the significance of the good times The Boys' delinquent behaviour cannot be fully grasped. Indeed the excitement of going on the cars had, by the end of the summer, because of the risks now involved, reached such a high voltage that screwing cars was no longer even regarded as 'good news'. It was simply something which had to be done if the good times it paid for were to be continued.

The Boys were perfectly aware that their catseye escapades were illegal. They knew their parents mostly disapproved of such behaviour. They, for their part, also tabooed certain types of action. They held up certain concrete examples which acted as stereotypes, or role types, to exemplify incorrect behaviour. Thus simply in terms of 'stupid' behaviour Tuck took the prize. He, still in borstal at this time, was held up as the all-time 'nutter' who illustrated how not to approach law-breaking and how not to come to terms with Authority.

> He was fuckin' stupid, he didn't know when to stop. Everyone told him he'd get stuck down but he just wouldn't be told. (*Des.*)
> Once he'd got a few bevvies in him he'd do anything. One night we'd climbed into Flories' [a local butchers] back yard, and he just punched in a window, like that, with his bare hand. He was a mad bastard, Tuck. (*Colly.*)
> No one goes robbing when they're on bail, not unless *they want* to go down. (*Jimbo.*)

The Boys had other stereotypes of this sort to delineate the limits of reasonable behaviour. Another figure, Clepto, although a local boy, gradually became seen as an outsider, someone unwelcome. Had he been a middle-class youngster Clepto would have been under psychiatric care long ago and classified as an 'affectionless' or psychopathic personality. He was without moral standards even in relationships with 'insiders'. 'He'd stab his own grandmother in the back for two bob,' Joey declared. Even Danny, who tried not to be unkind to anyone, agreed. 'He'd no right to take those records from Eilene's flat. Fancy stealing from one of your friends. You can't get any lower than that.' 'He robbed my hat from Sandhills as well. He swore blind he'd bought it but I know it was mine.' (*Joey.*)

Clepto represented the antithesis of how anyone should behave toward their friends and neighbours. Some things were not allowed, were simply taboo. Every one of The Boys has commitments to certain people and places, for some acts there is *no* justification, *no* excuse. Clepto was ostracised for breaking these commitments; he was treated as an object, he had to leave. Nearly any of the older Roundhouse youth could come out with Tommy's comment. 'Stealing from someone in the Block, that's different. I couldn't do that. I don't know why, I just couldn't. I could never ever steal from a mate like that Clepto did. He's the world's number one cunt.'

The Boys can become attached to and identify with local people and their possessions. Their list of commitments might be smaller than that of the middle-class adolescents but it is still highly potent. Acker's view of local citizenship rests on such a protective fraternal commitment. It was almost with disbelief he complained, as Streak and other men have done similarly, of one imposter in particular. 'There's a sneak on our landing somewhere. Someone told the busies about me having stolen gear in the house. You wouldn't believe it, would you, a grass on your own fuckin' landing.'

Fosser learnt these aspects of community commitment when he was only a youngster.

> I robbed a purse from the flat next door. Someone said they'd seen me. I knew it was bad like, but when they found out it was me I shit meself. I got called all sorts at home—snake, sneak, slimey bleeder, no one would talk to me or nothing. I swore black and blue I never robbed it at first but I had to own up in the end. Boy, I really learned my lesson there.

Nearly all the late adolescents I know from the area would hold the same perspective Fosser now holds—some things are *wrong*. The commitment to social rules, to 'significant others', is implanted in The Boys. They have internalised rules and formulated values which are consistent with the larger complex of values held by the wider society. Consistent with, but not as abstract or generalised, not as translatable into the wider public expectations of 'correct' behaviour. It should be said Roundhouse is not typical of the City's down-town neighbourhoods in this respect. Its kinship and community sentiments impose a stricter moral order than is found in many less tight-knit areas. Everomer youth for instance are less subject to even locally generalised commitment about other people's property and feelings.

Thoughtful researchers of the past like Cyril Burt have also asked how we can expect people without property to respect property rules. If you ask The Boys the answer is they don't, they can't. Respect is related to some form of meaningful commitment, at the very least the expediency of having too much to lose of one's own. Once we move into the realm of catseyes, warehouses, chain stores, commitment is replaced by encounters with outsiders' coercion. The Boys of course will not necessarily deny the validity of authority or society. Streak, who gives more thought to such matters than most, would thus 'admit' or say: 'Screwing cars is wrong. Someone could have worked hard to get it like. Say someone's worked his way up and he's got a new shining Rover, it's bad news having it done in.' Bone would disagree or he would 'rationalise' in some people's eyes. 'I wouldn't like to rob from someone really poor but these posh twats, I take a real delight in robbing from. Sometimes you go by the church and you see all these fuckin' big twats with big cars, big flash camera and all the gear and you think, I'll go and pipe that car, and it's got a cassette so you screw it.'

Yet Murky, basically a hard-working non-robber, would not condemn his mates. 'It's not wrong, well I'm against it like, but they must be soft to leave the cars so things can be stole. And the lads have to go out of a weekend and need clothes and that. I'm not saying that's the best way of going about it but they can't get a job, how else do they get poke?' (T.)

And Joey, who Murky exonerates, admits: 'Screwing cars is wrong if they can't afford it. But a big per cent of the cars we do, the people have a good few bob. If they've got money to pay for Rovers they're all right. But you can't say we only rob from the rich, can you, we'd screw any car if we thought we could get away with it.'

In short, the network's commitment to the wider social morality is spurious, limited and close to a position of expediency where outsiders' property is concerned. Their commitment to moral restraint tends to be neighbourhood-bound, extending beyond only in relation to 'significant others' and people or situations which are similar enough to their own kind's predicament to allow an empathy and thus restrict their expedient behaviour. This discussion of social morality will be returned to at the end of the chapter. We now turn to the contest between The Boys and Authority over the continuation of their theft behaviour. Contest is a fitting term, because as we have just discovered it is getting caught rather than the morality of their behaviour which concerns The Boys.

Contingency Plans

As their list of encounters with the police built up, The Boys became fully aware Authority was homing in on them. A period of 'lucky escapes' dominated the catseye talk. Through the pooling of their experiences The Boys soon pieced together the police situation. I was standing on the Corner with Streak and Des when a passing police jeep reminded them of an incident I had missed the day before.

> I hate fuckin' cops, the last two days they've pulled us, well stopped us, not pulled us. This jack came up the street and started talking to us. Me and Fosser, it was, were standing here where we are now. He says mind if I ask you your name. I didn't say what for, or what you going to do—arrest me, nothing clever like. I told him me name and where I lived, so did Fosser. Anyway, yesterday he came round the corner and said, 'It's Mr Green, isn't it?' And I went yeh. Then he said, 'Where's Mr Mulholland?' That just shows you, he must have looked up that case me and Jock was in when we was about fourteen [three years ago]. He must have looked that up. Anyway, I said he's at work and he went: 'Haven't you got no time for him now. Keeping out of trouble, are you?' I said nothing. Then he said, 'Where's Foster?' And I said in bed. You know I wanted him to fuck off 'coz he wasn't half annoying me.

Talk about confrontation with and intimidation by the police was plentiful during this period. Although I discuss these 'interactions' later, they must be mentioned here to help explain the changing behaviour of The Boys. Colly and Jimbo had become best friends. They appeared on the Corner where several of us were already standing.

> Me and Jimbo have just had a fuckin' lucky escape. We were just going to do this Rover and a big red Cortina pulled up. Two plainclothes

dived out. This cunt with a sheepskin on says, 'Against the wall you two.' Colly had a punch down the back of his kecks, but this feller must have thought it was his backbone or something 'coz he missed it. He couldn't do us for nothing, so he says, 'If I see yous around here again I'll run you off your fuckin' feet, now beat it.' We walked away dead lucky.

Jimbo That's twice this week I've been lucky. I was going to do one in the other day and this jeep came screeching up. All I did was just bend down and pushed the punch into the ground [mud] but they never stopped me.

Mocky They pulled our Tony in last night you know. They caught him red-handed, me old man had to go over and get him out. He got fuckin' murdered when he got home.

The Boys suffered more than lucky escapes however. As their life style became less straightforward, talk became increasingly centred on the meaning of Court and convictions. Talk about 'being up' at Court was not new; someone in or close to the network was always 'up' for something. The more regular or unlucky 'delinquents' of the network already had records for petty theft and nearly all had been to Court or been cautioned by the police. The catseye campaign had led to heavy casualties by mid Year Three.

Tuck was due out of borstal, Tank due out of approved school. Colly had walked round a corner straight into the arms of a police sergeant who, remarking on the young man's fatness, had pulled a car radio from under his jacket and taken him in. Murky had been convicted of attempted theft. Jimbo, who had already notched up a long series of convictions, was on suspended sentence for screwing a wine merchant's. Fatch and Emo were both convicted of loitering with intent and received £25 fines and severe warnings. Arno, convicted yet again for theft from a car, received a £50 fine. Apart from actual convictions other 'warnings' were handed out in the form of police attempts to secure conviction with insufficient evidence. One police perjury failed, with Joey (charged with loitering with intent) being acquitted. The message that they were under the spotlight registered just the same. The widespread talk amongst locals about these convictions and Court appearances also furthered the feeling that going on the cars was an increasingly hazardous business. Talk centred on the devious methods by which the police were obtaining arrests and report of policemen's binoculars on high buildings and the use of plainclothes women detectives increased both fear and resentment.

There are several aspects of this 'terreur' by Authority to be considered, the first being the immediate effects of these increased pressures and convictions on the Catseye Kings. In reality each of The Boys had, as he always has, his own unique solution to such contingencies. At any time each of The Boys has his own process and it fans out, like every other slightly differently to the Others. A few processes can be looked at in these terms and some general points made as to their typicality in illustrating the view from The Boys.

As far as Authority was concerned, Tank and Fosser had abused lenient warnings and just about run out of chances. Tank, as said above, had been in approved school, and Fosser's list of convictions, although very petty, sounded—especially when read out loud in Court—like a railway timetable. At the height of the catseyes craze, Fosser received his final warning. He was caught, on his own, taking a radio from a car and had been rather unexpectedly remanded in custody at the initial hearing. Fosser explained this piece of bad news in terms of his relationship with the police officer who arrested him. 'I'd made a cunt out of him on that case dismissed with Joey, remember, he wanted to get his own back, he was telling the sergeant all sorts to make sure I got sent to Risley.'

Fosser was sent to Risley remand centre for ten days. 'Grisly Risley' has a reputation for harsh treatment of adolescents, whether convicted or not. Fosser eventually got fined £50 along with a stern warning that next time he appeared in the dock he must expect to be sent to borstal.

The Risley shock disturbed him considerably. He talked later of having to put a blanket up against the window to keep out the rain and cold. He had no towel, no toothbrush and few visitors. 'I was only in there ten days and I was nearly cracking up. And they treated you really rough, one time I was thrown down the stairs.'

Before his conviction Fosser had a month to consider his fate. After the ten days in custody he was remanded on bail till his case could be heard. That month was a traumatic one for Fosser. He decided to get a job in an abattoir which he felt would help his case. This meant he was not with The Boys in the day. But he also chose not to be with them during the evening. He was quiet and sulky during this period and hung around the youth club with The Girls. He was, he later realised, preparing himself for borstal. The only time he really spoke to me during that month was when he came into the youth club very drunk. Fosser was trying to come to terms with things. He was coming to understand the forcefulness of Authority. 'He [the solicitor] said, look at it from the worst six months to two years [borstal], though there's a chance it could be a heavy fine. I deserve borstal. If I don't go down I'll call the judge a soft cunt, I'll say to myself you soft cunt when I'm standing there.' 'I just want to work with the community work-shop [one was just starting up near the area] for years and years as it goes on.'

Suddenly work and going straight seemed like a good alter-native, suddenly 'robbing just isn't worth it'. The Boys were very worried about Fosser who was usually right in the centre of their network. Danny realised, 'Fosser's just trying to keep out of trouble till his case is finished. He's just keeping to him-self so he doesn't get into any bother.'

When Fosser 'got off' with a fine he didn't remember to call the judge anything, he seemed quite happy with the verdict. He was going to pay the fine off 'in no time' and 'not rob any more'. Fosser was as good as his word till the autumn, getting involved in no serious stealing escapades. Although he worked with the community workshop at £11 a week he did not pay his fine off. He was involved in minor shoplifting during the summer, but as this was in a Welsh village he didn't regard it in the same light as at home.

Tank, on the other hand, never made any attempt to 'keep out of trouble'. He had come out of approved school in the spring having been screwing cars every weekend he had been allowed leave. He was back on the cars quite regularly within two weeks of his final release, seemingly untouched by the whole ethos of the institution. He too started a job with the local workshop. The workshop however was short of contracts at the time and the 'workers' often had time off in the day. Influenced by Tank's persuasions Fosser drifted out of the grip of Authority's 'terreur', back into the short-term logic of going on the cars. He had spent four months keeping out of trouble, he was bored, skint and ready to try his hand. The duo were caught and charged with attempted theft. Both were remanded on bail with ten days to speculate on their fates. Fosser returned to his unhappy shell and was simply, in his words, 'waiting for the crunch', kicking himself for not knowing better since he 'should have learnt from last time'.

Tank took the whole affair differently, or rather indifferently. He spent his two weeks of freedom telling everyone he was sure to go down. His older sister was perhaps aware of his reasoning. 'It depends how hard you've had it as a kid. It's OK for some kids, they've had things harder—they don't mind borstal. Our Tank he's used to it, he's always got battered, he just takes it.' Tank's hard coating was needed to give him some protection from a poor family life. Most of The Boys realised this and sometimes argued in the way a social worker might, pointing to the missing father, weak mother and vicious older brother. Pablo, his cousin, remembered how Tank had to 'rob basies [boots] and jeans so he could go to school without looking a show'.

Tank's attitude to the institution was different from that of his mates; they had not 'been down', they still had the fear of the unknown. Tank would always say 'it's like a holiday camp', which made little sense to the rest. Others in the network tended to see things like Fosser, who whilst regarded as simply 'dead unlucky' and 'jinxed', also acted as an example of what could happen to anyone on the cars.

Joey, Colly and Jimbo presented a different set of solutions to the challenge against their theft behaviour. They took stock one weekend when we went off camping. The Ritz were now becoming involved in the catseye capers and their 'progress' was watched with interest.

Joey There's so many on the cars now that someone's getting caught every day.
Colly It's not The Boys though as much as Ritz's lot, they're out every night now like we were.
Jimbo Yes but they don't even wait till it's dark and they're not doing it properly, that's why they're getting caught. If you see them with a radio you can tell straight away by just looking at them, and they're walking dead fast and that. They'll all get caught, that lot.[6]
Colly That's it, if you're careless like you will get caught, but if you rob properly you've got a good chance of getting away with it.

Throughout the summer Joey, Tommy and Jimbo, along with Fatch, Emo, Arno and Streak in particular, tended to agree with Colly's analysis of the situation. These were the calculated risk takers of the network. They all had convictions behind them, all knew their possible fates if apprehended, yet they all kept on screwing cars. Their delinquency did change however. It became more covert and necessarily devious. Risks had to be minimised. One solution was to work outside the area. For a short period the neighbourhood's middlemen who fenced the radios would take two or three of The Boys in their cars to plunder the suburbs and neighbouring towns. This unintended consequence of extra policing had further ramifications when Colly and Joey, now in much closer liaison with the criminal network of the Inner City, did their first big job as 'skivvies' for outside 'brains'. The details must be spared but suffice it to say nobody was caught, a couple of thousand pounds of merchandise was involved and the two boys made £75 each. This 'job' was a fairly isolated case at the time; there was no question of Joey and Colly suddenly going 'big time', but their experience and contact may well have consequences for the future.

A second unintended consequence of increased policing involved the catseyes business. The Boys stopped carrying

'punches': police discovery of such a tool would almost certainly lead to a charge of equiped for theft, attempted theft,
loitering with intent or even carrying an offensive weapon,
depending on other circumstances. For the unhappy car-
owner this meant it was no longer his small quarter-light that
was broken: now The Boys simply put the boot into the main
front-door window causing extensive and expensive damage.
Various other minor amplifications also ensued from the contest with authority. Cars nearer the Block became prime
targets, as the carrier had more cover and the 'attackers' more
confidence. Cars were increasingly screwed late at night under
cover of darkness.

Titch, Mocky, Murky, Danny and Des, although caught up
in the opportunistic delinquency of late childhood and early
adolescence and the catseyes craze of Year Two, were never the
'full-time miscreants' that many of their mates were. Although
like all the network these four had little compunction about the
immorality of theft behaviour from outsiders, they had tended
to become involved more through their mates than their own
propulsion. Like most down-town adolescents they had 'done
their share'[7] of robbing but usually when the risk was low and
the escapade 'a dead cert'. Mocky admitted he simply didn't
like robbing since he'd been to Court: 'Me nerves go and I
really shit meself.' Murky for his part had got a well-paid
apprenticeship with regular overtime, which left him firstly
with little time and secondly with little need to go 'on the
mooch' for illegal earnings. Danny and Titch were still
susceptible to the 'dead cert', especially when they were skint,
but they were regarded by the network as 'not really robbers,
not really'. These lads had started to move away from the pre-
meditated excursions and by the end of the summer had re-
sponded to Authority's purge. Obviously as far as Authority
was concerned these adolescents if apprehended were 'just as
bad as the rest', but not for those who know them.

> *Emo* You missed a good night last night, we all got rotten, we did the
> winey, the lot.

Colly You can tell how rotten he was 'coz Danny came on the cars with me.
Self Danny.
Emo Yeh, he was really bevvied, he didn't know what he was doing. He'd never go robbing if he wasn't bevvied, you know that.

So far changes in delinquent behaviour have been seen as brought by outsiders' obstacles in the form of Authority's coercion. There were other factors involved for some of the network however. Several of The Boys were going steady with girlfriends by Year Three and felt a certain commitment to their partners' wishes. Des, during Year Two, had been considerably involved in delinquent acts, firstly with his brother Tuck and then with Fatch. By Year Three, Des was 'courting steady', and with his girlfriend Jean becoming an increasingly important influence on him he decided, at the height of The Boys' catseyes success, to opt out. At first as a catseye regular and very much one of The Boys he found this nearly impossible. 'What do you do when you're with The Boys and they call you a shit-house 'coz you won't do a car with them. The last time I got caught I didn't want nothing to do with it anyway, but I wasn't being called a shit-house so I did the window.'

Des was suffering considerably during this period; he was balancing 'the near certainty of immediate loss of status in the group against the remote possibility of punishment by the larger society if the most serious outcome eventuates'.[8]

It was only when the purge by Authority came and The Boys started reconsidering the catseyes as a way of life that Des was able to opt out. With his attachment to Jean putting an increasing commitment on him to be good, and with his best mate Fosser's temporary 'going straight' example, and the fact that his brother was in borstal, Des now had the necessary compunction to tell everyone quite bluntly he was keeping out of trouble; he 'didn't rob no more'. He got engaged, spent more and more time with Jean, and correspondingly less with The Boys. Such a break did not come easily especially when courting involves 'sitting in me tart's house every night looking at her old man's gob down on the floor [glum]. It's fuckin' terrible and they know I'm a robber, I reckon he hates me.'

> *Self* Don't they know Squid [their son] robs?
> *Des* Oh, they think their kids are fuckin' angels. They don't know anything about what Squid does.

Shortly after he got engaged, Des told me, 'I reckon I'm getting out. It's no good here with people calling you a shit-house and saying you're under your tart's thumb.' Des was right to sense The Boys' annoyance, for they felt snubbed by his disappearing act and held him up as a warning:

> That's what happens when your tart gets the upper hand. You stay in every fuckin' night and never have a good night out. (*Emo.*)
> If there's one feller round here that's gone down a hundred, no two hundred per cent, it's Des, he's real fucking suck'ole. (*Arno.*)

Intensity of feeling later died down when more of The Boys had partly 'opted out', but at the time the mutual antagonism was intense. Des made the break because he wanted to, willingly giving his loyalty and love in return for Jean's.

Joey's dilemma was more tragic. As long as I've known Joey he has lived for the unity of The Boys. He has always been a great inducer of social cohesion, emphasising the importance and pleasures of equality and comradeship and being 'one of The Boys'. If we were going for a night out down-town, Joey would suggest we went for so and so, or would call up to the landings to someone else that we were ready to go. If ever there was serious disagreement, Joey would always try and smooth it over, though not always successfully or without occasional melodrama. He could sometimes be quite subtle in his approach and perhaps not even deliberate. In 'The Turk' one evening:

> *Joey* You couldn't have a worse set of mates than this lot. Do you know what they did today—skived off at lunchtime and left me and Colly decorating. Didn't say a dicky bird, just fucked off to the boozer. (By autumn several of The Boys were doing part-time decorating with a local workshop.)

Fatch Well we tried to find you but we didn't know what number [flat] you were in.

Joey (pretending not to hear) You couldn't get a worse set of mates anywhere.

Emo Oh fuck off Joey, you couldn't get better mates than you've got round here.

Joey You reckon. Christ, look what happens now, of a Saturday, everyone fucks off to their tarts about 9 o'clock. Their fuckin' birds come before The Boys nowadays.

So the conversation went on, with Joey suggesting that the girlfriends should be kept in their place and not allowed to interfere with The Boys who if they were *real* mates would see to it. At this time Joey practised what he preached. He had been 'going with his tart' for six months and although he obviously liked her he would not allow this affection to change his relationship with The Boys. Joey has a typically traditional attitude to women still particularly common in working-class culture.

Joey I give her a good fuckin' smack when she starts arguing. She knows when to shut it. She used to go with coons. I remember walking down-town with her when we passed some nigger she'd been with. She looked back at him like she was interested. I pushed her up against the wall and really smacked her. I said go on then after him then. She fuckin' shut up after that.

Self I reckon it's bad news smacking birds, Joey.

Joey They expect it round here except when you really poke them. Once I smacked her and she fell over and hit her head. I was down there holding her saying I didn't mean it, was real sorry and everything and not to tell her mam or dad.

Joey's bird did put up with him, did wait till he was ready to see her, did get used to being smacked about, did get used to him meeting her at closing time. Joey's bird did get pregnant.

Joey's loyalties were torn. He realised the pressures were on him to get married. Mary's parents, his parents, her friends and his mates all expected Joey to do the right thing. There was no scandal or moral outrage when 'courting' girls got pregnant, indeed the 'pregnant marriage' was quite normal. It was quietly taken for granted Joey and Mary would get married in a few weeks. Joey was aware of the pressure, and indeed accepted the marriage in principle, as it appealed to his sense of loyalty. His dilemma was that at seventeen years and as a central figure in The Boys' network, marriage seemed an unfair trap, forcing him to withdraw from everything he valued and enjoyed. Marriage, fatherhood, responsibilities living with the in-laws, and having to get a job versus The Boys' company, nights out, other women. Joey took a week off work to sort himself out and presumably get the wedding organised. I spent a good deal of time with him that week and became involved in his moods and oscillations. His perspective seemed to change daily and not slightly but from one extreme to the other. On one day he was going to get married, find a place of his own, he wanted to be a father. The next evening down-town, 'What's the time? (9 pm.) I was meant to meet my bird at 7 to take her to the pictures. But she can fuckin' wait till I'm good and ready, when I'm rotten drunk.'

Despite Joey's vacillations his mother had set the wedding day. This came and went but Joey was still not settled and there would be no marriage until he was. He still spent his time with The Boys who avoided the topic. He still treated Mary with a certain indifference, much to the disgust of her friends: 'He thinks he's God's gift to women, she's better off without him, she's too good for him.' (*Vera.*)

Joey sensed the change in The Girls' attitude, the despair in Mary's face. 'It's not that I don't love her, but once she gets her claws in and starts whining as soon as you leave her . . . she's trying to make an old man of me.'

Quite suddenly Joey announced that he and Mary were going to live with his brother, who had a flat in the Block. A month later they got married and took a flat in The Skies, a nearby block of flats to which several young couples were moving because no flats were available in the Block. It took Joey four months of almost constant drama and melodrama to come to this resting point. Whether his 'solution' is permanent or temporary is hard to say. What is clear to Joey is that what he has thought and fought out is a reasonable *compromise* (which might surprise the social worker who classified him as 'maladjusted' and 'unable to compromise' at the age of twelve). He has left The Boys as a social group, seeing them only after work and perhaps one night a week, and on Saturdays to play football. Instead he goes out with Mary and another couple. Joey is not likely to go on the cars or 'break-in' jobs in the near future. His law breaking, because of his commitments and his belief that he is now adult and responsible, is liable to be less dangerous and more covert, reverting to such activities as the receiving of stolen goods to furnish the new flat, and the occasional middleman deal for a smaller kid.

Streak at nineteen years has also *had* to get married, but he is very happy with his lot and has found few problems. Before he'd met Moira, Streak said much the same about girls as Joey, 'Just keep them in their place. Once you let a tart start getting on top of you you'd better go home. The only answer to it is a fuckin' good smack. It is, honest to God [I'd smiled]. You know when they start domineering and that the only answer's a fuckin' good back-hander.' Yet six months later you'd see Streak and Moira out every night. 'She's great, I can talk to her just like a mate, have a really good laugh. We can go down town and have a great night out, just like with The Boys.'

Streak decided he should 'settle down'. He managed to find himself a well-paid job with a joiner's firm, but was laid off within two months. He made a concerted effort to find an equivalent job but could only uncover badly paid 'boring' butt-end jobs which he refused to take on the principle that his dole, now he is nineteen years old and married, is better than 'slogging your guts out' for the 'extra few bob'. He never completely stopped 'robbing' and has now returned to screwing cars with Arno. Despite having had their final, final warnings, these two still accept the risks because, 'We're better robbers than the other fellers, we don't shit ourselves and we're dead careful.' Streak, because of his genuine commitment to his new

G

responsibilities, would almost certainly go straight if the legitimate employment market would encourage him to.

Colly, Arno and Jimbo, it should be said, would not settle so easily. They have all been in and out of jobs during Year Three, but have consistently supplemented their income by any theft opportunities that have presented themselves. All three are big spenders, can drink away their wage packets in two nights and be skint by Monday. But unlike their reformed or less delinquent mates, they will not accept their moneyless situation. They are committed to having a good time and have only themselves to look after; they don't see why they should compromise.

Although socially active members of the network until mid Year Three, Jock, Pablo, Dave, Les and Craber had never really got involved in the catseyes capers. By Year Three they had become a recognisable group within the network and eventually were no longer really 'one of the boys' in the remainders' terms. Early in Year Three Jock started selling marijuana on a small scale. He preferred this smaller illegal income to any other, as he argued in 'The Turk' one night.

> *Jock* It's a good thing to do the cars if you can get away with it. But you can do fifty catseyes and on the fifty-first you'll get caught. You're going to get caught doing cars, know what I mean, you'll definitely get caught. Selling dope, if you do it good, you're not going to get caught and I've got a fireproof way of doing it, so I'm not going to get caught.
>
> *Streak* But you can get caught selling dope and if you do you'll get the fuckin' rap.
>
> *Jock* That's the chance you take.
>
> *Streak* Yeh but that's what I'm saying, no matter what illegality you do you can get caught.
>
> *Pablo* Jock's right. I used to do a few cars, but not as many as the fellers do now. I wouldn't take the chance now.
>
> *Streak* You two are pot-heads though. The Boys like to go out downtown so they need more cash than yous (sic).

The increasingly important 'nights-out-down-town' as we shall see in the next chapter shed much light on the 'focal concerns' of The Boys. Their life style is ideally an expensive one. The Jock group has slightly different ideas and their development is worth brief consideration. In the first place it illustrates another form of 'deviant' solution, but also it is a further indication of the break-up of The Boys' network and a fanning out of solutions to the bad times.

Both Jock and Pablo had been involved in the early 'general' theft behaviour of The Boys as they had run the gauntlet of uninspiring jobs (Year One). Jock's record of being sacked was probably the most telling: he claims eight sackings in one year. They had both obtained a few convictions during early adolescence. Pablo had been convicted with Acker for breaking into a jeweller's shop, for which he was fined £20. He also had shoplifting and drunk and disorderly convictions. Jock's record was very similar. During the summer at the end of the first postschool year, Jock and Pablo went off hitching around Europe. Probably due to their 'hippie' experiences, when they returned home they took up with Holly, a well-known character in the area who was a seasoned drug-user. Both started using marijuana, and with Voggy, a friend who has now left the city, they quickly moved through the whole gamut of drugs available in Liverpool for social and illegal use.

Jock remembered, in a taped conversation here abridged.

> I'd been on pot for a while when Holly said there's better stuff than pot like—but we said we didn't want to take any pills or nothing like that. But after a bit we were trying everything. We done the downers, mandrex and speed [barbituates and amphetamines]. I remember the first time me and Voggy took speed. I was asleep but I was walking, we were in Wilkies [a big departmental store]. Now the day before I'd robbed a shirt out of there. How I robbed it, I went to try on a pair of cords in the changing place and there's a gap into this other room where they keep the shirts. So I put my hand through, robbed a shirt, put it on and walked out. But when I told Voggy, this time you know when we were speeding, we started trying to jump over the wall into this room like. There was thousands of people looking at us and Voggy was shouting let's get them shirts. I was fuckin' bad, really bad . . . I went unconscious. Next thing I was in this room with the nurse out of the shop, Voggy was shouting and asking for mandrex. He just wanted more gear [drugs] he was a really weird guy . . . I took speed whenever

it came in, then I stopped taking speed and started taking acid, but I gave that up after a while, it wasn't no good for me.

Me and Voggy had a flat in Faux Avenue for a bit, we got to know all the students and that lot and started selling dope. Right through the day there was people ringing the bell. But I didn't like what I was doing, what it could do to the people like, so I stopped selling speed and just sold draw. (Draw, pot and bush are the local names for marijuana.)

Jock now sells marijuana only. He does this in a small way, not as a 'pusher' but simply as a go-between for people who wish to place orders.

Pablo's drug career is similar, though less dramatic. He too has been involved in more serious drug experimentation, but like Jock considers himself law-abiding: neither of them has been involved in stealing and consequent Court cases for over a year.

The Jock group had attracted Craber to its ranks by mid Year Three. Craber has a steady job and comes from a 'salt of the earth' family, where stealing is regarded as wrong under any circumstances. Although Craber has been involved through The Boys in minor delinquencies, he generally disregards robbing as a solution to anything. The quieter pot-smoking group thus appeals to him. 'I couldn't get up and go to work at 7.30 if I was going down-town getting rotten every night. I'd rather be with Pablo and that lot, you have as much fun and you don't have to spend half as much poke.'

The Jock group has a membership of about six and is now a recognisable entity. It represents a less total alternative for The Boys who either work, want to stay out of trouble or simply don't enjoy the network's core style any more. Although aware their drug use is illegal this group have not come into much contact with the police, are otherwise fairly law-abiding and have avoided the 'amplification' processes undergone by drug groups elsewhere.[9]

So much more could be said about the 'becoming' of each of The Boys. What the above descriptions emphasise is the reality of the fanning out of solutions by the network in response to, initially, the bad times and later, to Authority's purge of the catseye business. Many factors have influenced decisions as they stand at the end of Year Three. The responsibilities of steady courtship, early marriage and perhaps the new baby are real pressures to settle down and get a job, however butt-end it is. The saga does not end here, by definition of course, and whilst we cannot predict The Boys' future with any accuracy it is likely that some will return to criminal careers sooner or later.

Although The Boys' story is far from complete it is fitting here to try and summarise their position as a social network. They themselves seem uncertain of their future as a peer group and watch the signs of dissolution with interest as the predictability of their mates' behaviour lessens. Some are married, some are locked up, some are carrying on in the old style, others breaking new ground, evolving alternative leisure styles. With this metamorphosis has come a reduction in the network's power to enforce conformity and this has multiplied the disintegration. The Boys are becoming a leisure group—a night out, go to the match, see you in the alehouse, group. They are still close, but as a total network not so close. They themselves wonder if they will get back to the old days when The Boys ruled.

> Joey'll be back round the Block when he's got settled.
> Tommy'll be out of borstal soon.
> I'm going to get a flat in the Skies near Joey and Acker, but I'll always come down to go out with The Boys.
> I go round with Woodsey now. I'm working the same sites as him.
> I'll still play football for The Boys like and go to the discos.

Chapter 5 will return directly to the significance of the catseye business and its effects on the personal identity of the members of the network. The impact of the catseye business will be with The Boys for many years. At least half the network are now semi-permanently on the threshold of the institution. For them any future law-breaking is likely to lead to incarceration. The law is immediately repressive. They also understand more clearly the meaning of being caught and put through the prosecution process. In the long run, however, will such a threat continue to act as a deterrent? For once the line is crossed, as Tank pointed out during his stay in Detention Centre, 'They can't lock you up for ever, not unless you do a robbery or a murder or something. It wouldn't be so bad coming back here, it's bad like, but once you've been down and know the screws and that . . . I wouldn't shit meself again if I got sent down.'

When the prosecution and the penal system become the only way a society can shepherd its citizens it is clear that rights and responsibilities on both sides are obsolete. Extensive use of coercion and the routinisation of the contest between law-enforcers and breakers endangers the 'accommodated' acceptance down-towners have for society. Such an on-going contest is likely to lead some of The Boys into a rejection rather than an indifference to the message of the wider society as the years roll by. Roundhouse does contain its little group of 'villains' whose whole code of behaviour is actually committed to non-work and theft as a career. A few of the network could well enter this subcultural world.

Formal Overview

The Boys' delinquency has been presented in its full. Their deviancy has not been glossed over. In the same way the next chapter will consider what appears to some as bizarre leisure activity. If such behaviour, by viewing it in context, can be explained as rational and well chosen we will not need to resort to stereotyped answers and psychological explanations emphasising personality disorder. A larger perspective is now needed in which to place The Boys' behaviour. How does the network's life style slot into the wider society? Sociologists have developed sophisticated models and theories to explain delinquent behaviour, and a discussion of some of these perspectives and their relevance for this case study will be found in the last section of this chapter. For the present, however, and with the non-academic in mind, this section will attempt a formal analysis of what The Boys' delinquency means.

To some extent commonsense explanations we give about deviant behaviour depend both on the sorts of questions we ask and the preconceptions we have about those we are discussing —in this case city adolescents. I had started working with and forming views about Roundhouse and other Inner City 'street kids' during my time at Sandhills. Having spent long enough in business to forget my undergraduate sociology, my standpoint was fairly neutral. Indeed my actual research was over a year old before I opened any books on the subject in earnest. Since my ideas had come from confrontations with kids rather than with sociologists, the encounter with academic delinquency theory was a depressing affair. 'Fresh' from long hard months at Sandhills trying to persuade Roundhouse youngsters that communal life really worked if only they'd do their share, that 'skivving' helped nobody, that work could be fun, that group decision-making was important, I could hardly have avoided making my own generalisations about behavioural motivations. Sandhills had soon had me asking if The Boys in particular had a social commitment to anything or anybody other than themselves; then later, as the barriers came down and we had made friends, I was asking why should they be any different? Where did I stand when they saw a day trip to a seaside resort as an unrestricted shoplifting exercise, a fight as the reasonable way of settling a dispute with the natives as to who 'ruled'? Eventually I decided that the question I should be asking was 'Why not delinquent?'. Why should The Boys behave in a disciplined 'Christian' way, why should they be committed to society's rules, who had encouraged them? When had The Boys received that 'conscious, rational, deliberate and demanding'[10] socialisation that middle-class children like myself had received, and how could it make sense to their situation?

Sandhills, however, because of its reciprocal communal demands on residents, seemed to present The Boys with a real comprehension of what a generalised commitment, a voluntary restriction of impulse and short cuts, was all about. And most of the time The Boys showed that, because they cared about coming to Sandhills, they would and could exert self-control for their own and the common good. Yet once back in the downtown world with The Boys, I witnessed the return of their 'fuck you mack, out of my way' stance, contrasting starkly with their Sandhills behaviour. Such comparisons only emphasised that it was The Boys' urban struggle rather than their malfunctioning personalities that precipitated their deviant behaviour and lack of concern for outsiders. The assumption often made by 'highly respected' and influential members of our society, who are often magistrates as well, is that a lack of social commitment is potentially dangerous and in need of correction. If only, they argue, everyone would obey the rules and do as they're told by those who know best, all society would benefit and everybody would be better off. Those deviants who refuse to accept the good sense of this argument cannot be allowed to practise their refusal; they are a potentially dangerous minority who must be taught the errors of their ways.

The question 'Why not delinquent?', the proposition that The Boys should break the rules if they only hinder and never help them, is not the usual opening query. It will however be the theme of this section. First let us ask why people do keep society's rules and do conform to the 'correct' social morality at all. Analytically, positive commitment can vary from a deep moral conviction to particular values and rules through a long dimension to the other extreme, a sophisticated technique of expedient, impression management which is a matter of knowing how to appear 'respectable' or how to 'keep your nose clean'. The latter involves knowing which rules it is most useful to keep and be seen to keep, and which rules one can break without repercussions. Society's educational, socialising and control agencies obviously aim at the 'moral conviction' goal as an ideal type. The ideal citizen thus limits his freedom of action himself; it is his own decision, he 'internalises' the common purpose of the wider social environment and accepts his roles or function within set rules, in common with others so that social interactions work smoothly. Sartre would call the taking on of this commitment 'intero-conditioning'. The church, the school, youth clubs, character-training courses, all seek this moral conviction in adolescents.[11]

If we see man as less morally committed and less socialised in the sense of not being totally programmed, we also see the populace as nearer the other end of the dimension.[12] Here social order is possible more in terms of extero-conditioning, one strand of which Sartre would call the 'fascinating of the seriality' or mass of the population into keeping to the rules of those in Authority. The fact that so many rules in society, which are not always logical or fair, are kept sufficiently to allow a complex, industrialised, densely populated, yet socially and economically unequal society to function without rebellion or revolution is evidence of some sort of restraint. As already indicated this social compliance may be related to expediency more often than to deep conviction. Howard Becker agrees.

> The normal development of people in our society . . . can be seen as a series of progressively increasing commitments to conventional norms and institutions. The 'normal' person when he discovers a deviant impulse in himself is able to check that impulse by thinking of manifold consequences acting on it would produce for him. He has staked too much on continuing to be normal to allow himself to be swayed by unconventional impulses.[13]

The businessman, the professional, even the affluent manual worker, all have things to lose by being caught. So their deviancy is subtle, their techniques of managing public identity sophisticated.[14] Deviancy here is based on activities considered safe from the pointing finger.[15] But let us not pretend we don't break the rules or contemplate infractions that, if enacted, would see us behind bars. Take away our possessions, our reputation, our social status—part of our identity—and ask who's righteous now? Some of course will still claim righteousness, some will still stick limpet-like to the correct social rules. But many of us would find that, thus stripped, we would no longer be 'fascinated' by the prevailing social order, no longer seduced by having things to lose.

Where does Roundhouse and where do The Boys fit into this scheme of things? Because of its low standard of living, relative powerlessness and exclusion from legitimate ways of achieving affluence, Roundhouse accommodates or stretches the dominant view of social morality. Roundhouse to some extent condones certain forms of law-breaking. The Roundhouse social compact protects itself from social-control agencies that try to enforce the rules too strictly, and indulges in officially frowned-upon but functional practices, such as handling and receiving 'knock off'. Parents often pay only lip service to the 'correct' middle-class way of bringing up children—they have neither time, training nor resources to do otherwise. This does not imply indifference or lack of care. It does not suggest that parents encourage delinquency. Most Roundhouse parents do not dismiss or contradict the dominant normative order—'how it should be'; they merely succumb to the pressures which prevent them behaving 'correctly' because they have little choice.

Psychologists and educationalists make much of the need for a 'thorough' primary socialisation for all children so that they understand and feel the expectations of society. This process is typified by the well-thought-out deliberate, consistent child-rearing techniques of the middle classes. Such indoctrination produces 'impulse control',[16] self-discipline and the 'low threshold of guilt',[17] so often identified as fundamental to the socially conforming behaviour expected by 'respectable' middle-class society.[18] The desirability of this potent form of social control which many middle-class families have the motivation, time, facility and capital to impose on their children is of course rarely challenged. Instead the lack of such control is the black mark awarded to 'delinquent', 'unruly' children and their parents.

Yet to provide Roundhouse children with such an indoctrination, unless their family is upwardly socially mobile, could possibly be doing them a disservice. Good as gold Gary could hardly be kept in the consistent care of his 'significant others' by playing with his toys in his playroom. Roundhouse kids have few toys, no playroom, a shared bedroom and often a shared bed. Gary couldn't play in the garden, the park, the playground, the back yard, since there are no such enclosures where his behaviour could be supervised. Give Gary all the 'proper socialisation' trimmings so he's polite, doesn't swear by the minute, turns the other cheek, keeps his clothes clean, stays out of trouble, and then send him out to play in the Block, and you would be making his childhood an isolated, boring and perhaps even miserable affair. For such trimmings are not functional in the street, where excitement has to be made, not queued up for.

Nor is the 'fascination' of having plenty of the good life ever-present to convince the down-town adolescent he should be happy with the status quo. The Boys only tasted the 'fascination' of having plenty of wealth, and thus power, in the consumer society, perhaps 'sedulously fostered by commercial "teenage" culture',[19] when they were the Catseye Kings and 'living like lords'. For them 'fascination' is not something given *per se*, and so worth protecting through backing up the rules and values which perpetuate the status quo, but something to be achieved through trying to take from others who appear to have more, which involves deviating from the rules of the dominant ideology. The argument that these 'deviants' sometimes 'steal from their own kind' and from those with less does not invalidate this attempted redistribution process, but is merely a minor spin-off of other constraints, such as a poor neighbourhood's isolation from more salubrious areas and its struggle with those in the same boat for what little the Inner City offers.

In short The Boys have nothing to lose from deviating, and whilst they are uncommitted to new 'significant others' such as the wife and the baby they will make their protest openly and expressively. The evidence is before their eyes—they are dispensable, there are no decent jobs and no prospects of a secure future. They see affluence about them but cannot reach it.[20] Putting up with the 'bad deal' is not the response of the thinking and doing man. The Boys aren't and don't want to be heroes, for starters they just want their share. The boot that shatters the window is a product of many years and many experiences.

The street-corner man, whatever the outsider's popular image, thinks and talks a great deal about economic realities and the distribution of society's wealth. But because the street-corner population is mainly adolescent and with nothing to lose by direct action it is less compromised and less concerned with what outsiders think. I have argued elsewhere that the street-corner milieu represents a further accommodation or extension of the already accommodated view of official morality held by more conservative members of the neighbourhood.[21] The Boys' commitment to the dominant ideologies of correct behaviour is consequently spurious and limited. In general however it cannot be regarded as contrary. The street-corner man in Roundhouse goes one clandestine step further from, rather than walking out on, the conservative version of the local value system. Some local cultural milieux may be 'subcultural', but the Roundhouse ideologies do not move to this extreme. Only at the height of the delinquent behaviour could The Boys' network be regarded as approaching a subculture of delinquency.

Dealing with this period when The Boys were the Catseye Kings, and given that their action was not affected by considerations about the morality of their theft behaviour, their involvement can be understood in rational, problem-solving terms. Whether these down-town adolescents deviated or not depended on the choices open to them for obtaining a share of the good times. With legitimate channels in the form of well-paid jobs or careers closed, The Boys' delinquent action was largely determined by the availability of illegitimate opportunities of which they might *choose* to take advantage. As we have shown, several factors encouraged their choice in becoming car-radio thieves. The radios were available in large supply, a middlemen service was on hand to exchange stolen property for money and the neighbourhood tended to turn a blind eye to such infractions.[22] What's more, the street-corner milieu actually encouraged such action and provided a continuous flow of helpful information.

It is when we consider this *context* of delinquent action that the same qualities emphasised in conventional occupations stand out. Throughout Years Two and Three The Boys showed that at all times they were considering and rethinking the utility of going on the cars. They chose to be delinquent and they chose their response to the prosecutions that followed. For them, at that time and in terms of their position in society and the possibilities it offered, the *rationality* of being the Catseye Kings should not be doubted.

*Theoretical Discussion**

It is not the task of this book to test out various hypotheses thrown up by the delinquency theory polemic. This chapter however, because it documents the micro-sociology of delinquent action and the commonsense meanings the actors give for their behaviour, does act as a test case for at least some aspects of various sociological explanations of delinquency which are discussed below.

Merton assumed all sections of American society to have internalised the middle-class-powered normative order. He thus asked 'Why delinquent?' and answered in terms of the importance of the differential' access to legitimate opportunity structures. The relatively deprived, status-frustrated lower-class minority were exonerated from keeping to the rules and deviancy was pushed on them by the social structure. Albert Cohen, taking up this Mertonian perspective, assumes lower-class adolescents have also to a large extent internalised middle-class standards of success and status. Again it is their relative failure to find opportunities to satisfy these goals which leads to the eventual development of a delinquent subculture, which is the antithesis of the middle-class culture since, by a reaction formation, the normative order is stood on its head.[23]

---

* This short section assumes some knowledge of sociological theory. It can be ignored, without detriment to the 'story' by the non-sociologist.

Cloward and Ohlin also start with the Mertonian explanation of delinquent motivation. One question they ask is 'Under
what conditions will persons experience strains and tensions
that lead to delinquent solutions?'[24] For these two crimino-
logists it is only when there are tensions and strains, when
circumstances are abnormal, that the adolescent will move
against the moral and normative guideline of society. The
Mertonian school has thus worked from the premiss that
exonerating circumstances in the form of alienating or frustrat-
ing tensions are needed to lead adolescents and others into
breaking out of their commitment to the normative order laid
down by society.

The cultural-diversity perspective represents the main
alternative sociological explanation of 'Why delinquent?' to the
Mertonian approach, and has found considerable credence in
the British scene. This perspective does not involve the deviant
population's internalisation of the dominant value system. Instead it contends that certain elements of the working class in
particular are socialised into a lower-class culture or sub-culture
which in many respects differs from the conventional order.
This perspective has become generally accepted as descriptive
of the English situation, particularly since Downes's thesis
which went to great lengths to show that American research is
culture-bound. Downes argued that the working class in
Britain has its own cultural and historical heritage which
encourages the less skilled adolescent in particular to dissociate
from middle-class aspirations and life styles and reaffirm his
working-class status.[25]

From the mid 1950s, work by Mays, Morris, Sprott and
others developed this subcultural or cultural diversity perspective considerably. Certain sectors of the working class, especially
the unskilled or 'rough' working-class families, who often lived
in deprived down-town neighbourhoods, were seen to have a
particularly distinctive set of cultural and normative standards.
This sector of the population was seen as most likely to contain
the deviant elements of society, as crime statistics always sug-

gested. Hence for a down-town area of Liverpool in the 1950s Mays claimed:

> Delinquency [in underprivileged areas] has become almost a social tradition and it is only a very few youngsters who are able to grow up in these areas without at some time or other committing illegal acts . . . Delinquency is not so much a symptom of maladjustment as of adjustment to a subculture in conflict with the culture of the city as a whole.[26]

Thus residents in these areas 'share a number of attitudes and ways of behaving in common which predispose them to illegal behaviour'. These subcultural areas are held together by 'an abiding community of ideas, values and attitudes which have developed over years into a social tradition and which are handed on, more or less intact, to the rising generation of newcomers'.[27]

The most obvious difficulty here is that this analysis does not really explain the non-delinquent within a delinquent and criminal area, since it *predisposes* youngsters to delinquency. A related problem is that cultural-diversity theory does not explain adequately why delinquents give up much of their criminal behaviour in their late teens or early twenties if they have grown up in a subcultural milieu.[28]

Walter Miller's construction of the 'focal concerns' of the lower class represents another version of the cultural-diversity perspective.[29] These 'focal concerns', a term preferred to values, are present in local traditions in which lower-class youngsters grow up. Because of the emphasis of these 'concerns' in their cultural milieu, adolescents are almost certain, in the course of acting them out, to become delinquent.

Miller's work is discussed in more detail in the next chapter. Suffice it to say here that condensing a cultural milieu down to six themes, then claiming these themes to be quite distinctive and immensely potent in predisposing adolescents to deviate, is going too far. Miller has also been criticised severely for failing to comprehend the applicability of his 'focal concerns' to other socio-cultural milieux—of, say, the middle class.[30] For the moment the most significant aspect of Miller's work is related to the socialisation aspects of his etiology. He seems to fall into the over-socialisation trap also, especially if we try and apply his analysis to the British situation. His adolescents in fact have so deeply internalised the lower-class culture as to be completely unmoved by middle-class institutions and control agencies.

All the perspectives so far identified have asked the question 'Why delinquent?' All have resolved the issue of this delinquent motivation by referring to a sophisticated socialisation and internalisation process of a dominant set of social standards. The Mertonian school, including Cohen, emphasised the necessity of strains and frustrations brought about by the internalisation of unachievable middle-class standards. The argument stands or falls on the internalisation of values.[31] The British subcultural perspective rests similarly on internalisation, this time of contrary values which 'predispose' down-town adolescents and others to deviate. Miller's thesis also rests on the exclusive internalisation of the lower-class culture, given that one accepts his definition of it as feasible.

The work of David Matza in attacking the subcultural theorists ventured away, in part at least, from the 'over-socialised', predisposing view of the delinquent. Although still regarded as at times 'brilliant', Matza's work has recently come under heavy criticism.[32, 33] For Matza, the delinquent, however, still held some commitment to conventional moral order; indeed he rests uneasily within the conventional order until driven into drift, 'a kind of moral holiday', through necessary 'techniques of neutralisation'.[34] Whilst this tenuous commitment to the normative order is highly feasible, the actual mechanics of Matza's argument are strained. His view of delinquent motivation still structures a 'willingness' and choice out of the adolescent. Matza's delinquent is a 'fatalistic drifter' who lacks choice in the face of conflict and contingencies.

Although there is much to glean from all the perspectives mentioned, especially the subcultural theories, these wide-ranging and obviously here over-simplified perspectives do not lead, in my opinion, as directly to The Boys' situation as they should. My critique is related to this specific case study and is not attempting any major theoretical discussion.

Roundhouse, as we have said, is not subject to a homogeneous and linear socio-cultural milieu. It neither completely accepts the meaning of the dominant normative order, nor lives by a completely distinctive subcultural blueprint. Instead we find a spectrum of viewpoints ranging from the 'respectable' law-abiders to the street-corner delinquents. There is a considerable tolerance between these moral standpoints, and significant overlap in certain matters. Such complexity leads us to challenge the sociologist's obsession with socialisation and the internalisation of distinctive norms for explaining delinquency in black and white fashion.

As Denis Wrong's enlightening article stresses, this over-socialised view is summed up in the sociologist's phrase 'the internalisation of social norms'.[35] When a norm is 'internalised', it is now frequently implied that the individual is thus conditioned to conform to its message; in other words, the norm becomes part of the super-ego, the conscience of the individual. The earlier work of American sociologists, like Merton, Cohen, Cloward and Ohlin, rested on this sort of process, and the connected idea of man as essentially motivated by the desire to achieve a positive self-image by conforming and competing for acceptance and status within the edicts of these internalised norms. Wrong concludes that so long as we view reality as if 'most individuals are "socialised", that is, internalise the norms and conform to them in conduct, the Hobbesian problem is not even perceived as a latent reality'.[36] Thus deviant behaviour will be explained in terms of special circumstances, ambiguous norms, alienation, role conflict, or greater cultural stress on valued goals without approved means of attaining them. The subcultural perspectives and much gang-delinquency theory are based on these assumptions.

Obviously there is much vitality in all these sociological perspectives. Further it may well be that in some situations these

H

explanations hold true, and that there is room for Mays's 'predisposed' delinquent, Matza's 'drifting' delinquent, Hirschi's 'anomic' delinquent and Patrick's 'psychopathic' delinquent. Such explanations are not by definition incompatible. A framework should be available to encompass differential motives within the context of their situation. In short it is wise to assume that 'delinquent motivations run the whole gamut from total acceptance of social morality through to those cases where deviants are in total opposition to conventional morality, and in large part motivated by their desire either to alter or destroy it'.[37]

The Boys in this particular study tend to lack a solid commitment to the dominant social morality, but are not totally opposed to it. Their position is one of expedience as far as infractions against outsiders are concerned. For this reason society finds it necessary to suppress their behaviour with coercion. Such a perspective leads us towards the position adopted by control theory. As Hindelang suggests in criticism of Matza, 'It is not necessary to postulate the mechanism of "drift" or the "techniques of neutralisation" if in fact delinquents do not have moral inhibitions which normally restrain them from delinquent involvement. If moral commitment does not exist, then there is nothing to drift out of, and there is nothing to neutralise.'[38] Hirschi goes even further: 'Delinquency is not caused by beliefs that require delinquency but rather is made possible by the absence of (effective) beliefs that forbid delinquency.'[39]

This control theorist's stance of 'anomie' does at its extreme lead us to view delinquency as behaviour resulting simply from an absence of control. Such a perspective does not belong to The Boys; Linden and Hackler's view is relevant however as a summary of The Boys' position. 'It is not necessary to view the adolescent as being pushed into delinquency by a group of peers, but merely that, for an adolescent who does not have strong ties to the conventional order ties to delinquent peers may facilitate involvement in delinquency.'[40]

This situation has only been arrived at through considering

the complex counterbalance of the neighbourhood's accommodated ideology, the network's movement in the street-
corner milieu and their experiences with the wider society.
Such a moral stance allowed The Boys to act and react to the
contingencies of the catseye business in 'optimum-balancing'
terms. Their contest with Authority was at a phenomenological
level; as Cohen has suggested, 'human action . . . that typically
develops and groups in a tentative, groping, back-tracking and
sounding out process'.[41] 'The history of a deviant act is a history
of an interaction process. The antecedents of the act are an
unfolding sequence of acts contributed by a set of actors. A
makes a move possibly in a deviant direction; B responds; A
responds to B's response, etc.'[42]

This fluidity and on-going realignment of positions was
illustrated in the changing nature of catseye talk and the fanning out of The Boys' solutions in response to persecution by
Authority. Such problem-solving took place also in the slower-
changing and more stable opportunity structures provided by
the neighbourhood in terms of condonation, a middlemen
system, and an abundant supply of car radios. If such opportunities were different The Boys' delinquent style would also be
different.[43]

The context of delinquent action, then, is a crucial ingredient,
for it is in this melting-pot that actors create meaning and the
propulsion to act. As a micro-sociology of delinquent action
this chapter has emphasised the significance of locality and
confrontation on 'the ground'. This micro-context is of course
only where we find the immediate origins of deviant motivation.
Wider structural factors as part of the political economy are
basic to a full etiology. Thus the ideologies of schooling, the
effects of economic growth, changing attitudes and policies
about crime all belong to a full social theory of deviance. This
study can only discuss such macro-factors as they impinge and
push into the context in which The Boys operate.[44]

It has been suggested throughout this chapter that the street-
corner milieu had a significant impact on The Boys' style. As

yet we have not fully uncovered the substance of this milieu—
its themes and concerns. It is now time we turned to look at
those things the down-town adolescent values and strives for.
Until we can grasp the significance of the good times and the
meanings of leisure time we cannot put The Boys' delinquency
into perspective. For as Matza reminds us: 'A delinquent is a
youngster who in relative terms more warrants that legal
appellation than one who is less delinquent or not so at all. He
is a delinquent by and large because the shoe fits, but even so
one must never imagine he wears it very much of the time.'[45]
We must look at the other shoes The Boys wear and enjoy
wearing.

Notes to this chapter are on pp 226–8

4 A Question of Style

We've had some good times you and me la'.

In trying to explain The Boys' life style and the ethos of their neighbourhood, two main sorts of problems arise for solution. Firstly, are the subjects of study observably different in their attitudes, behavioural patterns and relationships, and in whose terms? Secondly, assuming there are *some* differences, what explanations can be offered for these diversities, what structures and motivators are at their root? These latter problems tend to lead us past observation into constructs and inference in our search for solutions.

A whole variety of quantitative explanations are offered by physical circumstances. Roundhouse as a predominantly un-skilled manual working neighbourhood is solidly stuck in the mud of the Registrar General's occupational classes IV and V, the groups which also receive least of the economic cake. In terms of a social-malaise survey of official agency definitions of 'core problems', Roundhouse also comes out as 'different' by being at 'the bottom end'. So in terms of facility, employment, housing, health and hygiene, Roundhouse is seen, along with other down-town areas, as decidedly different, that is 'de-prived' of certain life chances and living standards.

Explaining behavioural differences regarded as deviant is a

more controversial matter. Dispute arises when behavioural styles other than those overtly and obviously related to local living conditions are looked at. Members of the unskilled working class who live in down-town areas, according to the statistics, are the most delinquent and criminal. They, it appears, are the not-so-lame ducks who rather than 'get up off their arses' take short cuts to things other people have to work for. Down-town Roundhouse also appears to produce more than its share of 'naughty' boys; indeed it breeds a host of those stereotyped delinquents, described at the beginning of the last chapter, according to some 'learned' and 'respected' men of city and societal influence. Once people accept these sorts of prejudices and stereotypes, then questions and answers become blurred and those people with less become those who deserve less. The deprived become the depraved. The down-towners become for the Corporation official with 'an open mind' and 'liberal' views, 'a ghetto of the less able' and for the so-called sympathetic documentary-film producer *The Dead End Lads*.

This chapter looks more closely at the male adolescent milieu and its 'conversation culture'—the themes it articulates and concentrates on. The Roundhouse adolescent talks about more than 'robbing' and does a lot more than screw cars. Indeed, seen in the context of what he does with his day, his week and his year, the down-town adolescent's delinquency, and all that it is *meant* to imply according to 'respectable' society, is only one of several major concerns. For every delinquent act one of The Boys has committed, depending at what stage of his adolescence we are referring to, days, weeks or months can pass before the next. The last chapter concentrated on that period of The Boys' lives when they were (and as boys probably ever will be) at their most law-breaking, uncompromised and 'reckless'. Arguments which can explain this behaviour without descending to 'depraved' stereotypes and socialised robot models stand on relatively firm ground.

For exactly the same reasons this chapter will again come to terms with The Boys at their worst in 'typecaster' terms. Can the down-town adolescent's 'other' controversial activities (eg, heavy drinking, fighting) be shown in terms of necessary style, a style which in fact deserves no 'attentions' and pointing fingers at all? If we remember The Boys spend most of their time as 'straight guys', sleeping, eating, playing and watching football, working, drinking in the local, listening to music, talking politics, etc, and then analyse the few times when they *break out*, we have a 'natural' test situation. If the break-outs prove to be explicable in terms that are normal, normative, rational, understandable, etc, then it is a matter of 'case proved'. Put less dramatically, do The Boys, their depressed situation apart, behave in the same way as other non-stigmatised adolescents, from the middle classes for instance? Is it a question of style related to their situation, or of a malicious, thoughtless, hedonistic 'depraved' ideology their kind live by?

There has been extensive sociological theorisation about this area of 'working-class culture' and life style. Subcultural and 'culture-of-poverty' type explanations have rested heavily on the transmission of tradition,[1] whereas a radical critique of this perspective suggests the whole cultural milieu of least well-off working-class life is no more than an on-going structural adaptation by a population that finds itself at the bottom of a highly stratified society.[2] The question of tradition cannot be ignored—it is always a thorn in the sociologist's flesh. If tradition is defined as the transmission of knowledge or belief from one generation to another, it is no small problem to untangle what is tradition and what is functional adaptation and innovation in a stable neighbourhood. Yet tradition is one of the main ways the Roundhouse male explains much of his style: why he drinks so much and in the same old pubs, why he spends so much money in the same old way, why he fights and has 'always been a robber'. Tradition is epitomised in the everyday answers to the question why: 'That's why'; ' 'Coz I did'; 'I'm one of The Boys, aren't I?'; 'It's always been like that round here'; 'They just copy other kids'; 'There's always been fighting round here'.

His other explanation is that he is forced to be the person he is because he has to react as best he can to the pressures around him. 'You've got to rob'; 'You need a few bob in your pocket'; 'I'd go nuts if I didn't go down-town for a night out'; 'You can't let somebody make a cunt out of you, you've got to fight sometimes'; 'I'd rather be on the dole than working in that place'. Although The Boys rarely put both explanations together, the implications that the two should be combined are there if their actions are compared with their beliefs. This personal diagnosis of their situation implicit in many dozens of conversations is one of the clearest messages that has come from the fieldwork. It is an explanation which we shall return to later when ready to evaluate its validity.

In his Roxbury studies of the 1950s, Walter Miller pulled out of extensive fieldwork notes six prominent themes related to 'lower-class' and especially lower-class adolescent behaviour. These 'focal concerns', Miller argued, were values or dominant emphases in lower-class culture, the acting out of which 'automatically' involved breaking legal norms and being seen as 'deviant' by those outside the cultural system. Such 'lower-class' behaviour is not however explained as oppositional, or as a get-back at the frustrations and alienation precipitated by the wider society; it is a vindication of lower-class adolescents amongst themselves. Consistent with this idea Miller sees the lower-class culture as 'a long-established distinctively patterned tradition with an integrity of its own'.[3] These 'focal concerns' are trouble, toughness, smartness, excitement, fate and autonomy, the meanings of which will become obvious later in the chapter. Since at least four of these concerns can be readily and convincingly identified in The Boys' behaviour, and because both British delinquency theory[4] and The Boys themselves all emphasise the traditional dissociation from outsiders, and the importance of local themes, 'testing' such a framework will be useful and add depth to more formal conclusions.

At one level then this chapter acts as a test of the applicability of theoretical perspectives such as Miller's for explaining some of the unconventional and stigmatised behaviour The Boys get involved in. On another level it is concerned with the meaning of the *good times*, the acting out of which sometimes leads to the deviant behaviour we are trying to explain. Such meaning is tied up in the dialectical relationship between The Boys' basic life situation and the solutions they seek in breaking out of its grasp through indulging in the good times. As Blumensteil has put it, 'dialectically speaking, the social problems pathos is the thesis, the sociology of good times an antithesis'.[5] Such an inter-relationship can be discussed in stages. Firstly, the good times sought by The Boys, although they have changed through time, centre round pleasure-seeking, being in control, and a mood of optimism. Secondly, the significance of the good times is tied up with The Boys' basic and predominant life style and their struggle with the not-so-good times and the bad times.

Hanging around on the Corner apparently doing nothing must be understood in terms of its relationship in this dialectic. Hanging around 'bumming' is not by definition soul-destroying or even boring. The significance of extensive periods of standing on the Corner can be understood only in relation to the mood and amount of choice open to the down-town adolescent at any particular time. The bumming period at the end of Year One for instance came out of a rejection of the badly paid and boring jobs of that year, the only positive pay-off of which was the wage packet and its potential purchasing power in terms of the better times of the pub, the match and free spending. For a while hanging around was a better alternative than those butt-end jobs, but only for a while. The Boys were soon demoralised by the dilemma between being skint and being forced to return to a diminishing casual-labour market. The choices were equally oppressive—they didn't seem choices at all. Standing on the Corner was, because of the lack of alternatives, an enforced choice and it slowly created resentment.

The catseye business changed all this: it offered good times every day of the week. The catseye capers became more than the down-town adolescent's attempt to get enough of the good life—decent clothes, good food and a little for chosen luxuries. It transcended the norm. The Boys discovered the potential of the good times 'down-town' style. They visibly changed gear and for a while moved into a whole new mood of optimism when every day was 'crusty', 'a real cracker', 'a fuckin' great night out', 'a really good laugh' and as Streak always says, 'brilliant, absolutely fuckin' brilliant'. Even the network themselves, it will be recalled, pondered on whether their theft behaviour was not somewhat greedy, especially in relation to the low standards of living that predominated in their neighbourhood. Some of the network looking back on the catseyes days kick themselves for pandering to the good times and not saving their proceeds for more durable enterprises than drinking and big-time spending. But these men are not fair to themselves, they forget the bad times and the routine they were breaking out of. The significance and meaning of the good times lies in the depth and extensiveness of the bad times.

In keeping with this argument, the hanging-around hours during the uncontested catseyes days were quite different in nature from those periods at the end of Years One and Three. To stand on the Corner 'half bevvied' for a few hours, with a pocket full of money and the prospects of a good night out to come, was good news. It was a freely chosen pursuit, a pleasant form of relaxation as the rest of the world hurried by. (Obviously not everyone who stands on the Corner is there for the same reasons and in the same mood.) In contrast, this chapter considers the significance of the good times during the latter half of Year Three. By this time Authority's purge had splintered the Catseye Kings. Some of the network were responding to the reopening of the job market due to local economic expansion, some were still earning a living off the cars, some were bumming on the dole and a few were oscillating between alternatives. Daytime fieldwork was then difficult, and I chose to spend my time with those boys who had started work with a local workshop involved in electrical re-wiring jobs and redecorating flats. The old symptoms were rife in all of us. In terms of the

low wage the job was simply renewed 'bad news'. The Boys'
minds were just not on the tasks set, as their moods and standard
of workmanship showed. It was to the next 'smoke', 'break',
'dinner' and 'early finish' that they turned their attention, with
conversations nearly always focusing on what happened in the
pub or the club over the weekend, interesting local news or
perhaps the idiosyncrasies of the customer. Care about the job
itself was minimal. The whole week stumbled towards Friday
night when, with the pay packet ripped open, the 'old girl's
bit' handed over, the real world could be retrieved.

Colly and Emo, paint brushes in hand, came to terms with
the alternatives open to them at this time.

> *Colly*   I reckon I'll spew this job at the end of the week, it's a load of
> crap.
> *Emo*   It could be worse man, least there's no one on your back.
> *Colly*   Oh fuck that, I'll go on UAB [social security] or the panel [sick
> leave] or something for a bit. Anyway Danny's old man reckons
> there's a demolition job coming up in a couple of weeks and that
> they're looking for a gang at a fiver a day.
> *Emo*   Oh ay, we've heard that one before, there'll be dozens of fellers
> after that job, dropping backhanders and everything to get their
> hands on the loot, you'll have no chance.
> *Colly*   OK so I don't get it, I'm still packin' this lark in. I'd rather be
> skint than turn into a fuckin' paint brush.

Since several others, including Arno, Des, Tuck and Titch,
were not working at the time, Colly was sure of daytime company, and did pack in his job, though he got another a few
weeks later. The 'in and out of work' syndrome affected most of
The Boys during this period, since there was little to choose
between the two poor alternatives.

The early-evening meetings on the Corner to sort out who
was going for a night down-town thus became the one time
when all the remaining network got together. The sources for
the good times during this period varied between catseyes,
wages and a careful saving of the dole for one big show of
financial strength. We can now tune into these periods when
The Boys break out with vigour by drinking, using pot, big

spending, sexual adventures and large doses of energy and humour. To step off the Corner after a day's work or a day of hanging around and go off with The Boys down-town contrasts starkly with the immediate past. It involves moving into a world of potential action. It is at these times that outsiders may be shocked and down-town adolescents appear to be different from and indifferent to the dominant, respectable way.

Wine, Women and Pot

Living down-town as The Roundhouse Boys do is to be involved, even if they are not always articulate and conscious of it, in the struggle for space and the struggle for enough of the 'good life'. Although the Inner City and its city centre is officially 'public territory', part of it is Roundhouse, which for The Boys is 'home territory'.[6] The down-town pubs, clubs and restaurants are, within surmountable limits such as membership subscription and age, mainly 'interactional territories' in that any adult can frequent them. Yet in practice these down-town establishments are still perceived as 'home territories'. The Boys are very much at home in some pubs and clubs, yet feel out of place in establishments frequented by 'them', who in turn avoid what they regard as the 'rough' hangouts.

The space The Boys utilise in their everyday lives, starting at the Block and moving outwards, is so well defined that if they all wore soles which left red footprints their living space would soon become defined on a map as red blocks with concise pathways between and few deviations from the main circuit. On the one hand such a circuit suggests inflexibility, parochial consciousness, limited horizons and a lack of initiative and innovatory energy. On the other it suggests The Boys know what they want, how much they can get without receiving undue persecution and where they are most likely to get it. Of an almost infinite number of permutations of geographical, ecological and social circuits in which they could theoretically live, they actually operate in a fairly stable and slow-changing area of social space. The reasons for and meaning of this choice, if choice it is, will concern us for the rest of the book, and will include discussing what The Boys enthuse over, who they want to be and how they attempt to achieve such goals, the obstacles in their way and the outcome of their search.

Although The Boys were only about sixteen years old when I first got to know them through Sandhills, they were already becoming involved with alcohol and its pleasant effects. At that time they tended to 'import' drink to parties, rather than frequent pubs. As time went on, leisure and pleasure became increasingly associated with pubs and later licensed clubs as well. Pub visits started with the public houses fairly close to home, where youngsters could be sure of getting served, and where they could demonstrate to significant others they were now 'adult' and doing normal adult things like being 'on the ale' all evening.

Nearly everyone accepted under-age drinking; the police only made infrequent checks on local pubs and then only as a 'brief presence'. One evening (early Year Two) a large police sergeant walked into 'The Turk' and turfed Fosser out. Fosser went straight up to 'Wally's', only to be sent out of there by the same policeman a few minutes later. Thinking this was the end of the matter Fosser returned to 'The Turk', and continued his drink, which had been kept for him. No sooner had he picked up his glass than in came the sergeant. 'Hey sonny, I'm not playing bloody games with you. Now out, landlady, this lad's under age, make sure you don't serve him again. Now out sonny, before I run you in.' The policeman left, having gone through the formalities. Fosser returned and everyone carried on drinking, having booed down the landlady's 'bitching'. In short, no-one really saw under-age drinking as wrong in itself. If you were old enough to work, you were old enough to drink and spend your earnings as you wished.

For The Girls of the same age, 'drinking' was not quite so easy. For some of them, 'the old girl', 'me mam', had to be avoided, as she was not keen on her sixteen-year-old daughter being seen in the local pubs. For this reason 'The Cockle', a pub full of young people, was used by The Girls for their little group meetings over lager and lime. 'The Cockle' was just far enough away from home to be out of convenient reach of the Roundhouse elders and was quite safe for the girls worried that 'Me mam would batter me if she caught me in the boozer.'

By late Year Two, most of The Boys were making a handsome living from the catseyes. They were now fully accepted in any pubs they wished to frequent and were becoming increasingly interested in 'going down-town'. Although Roundhouse is 'down-town' to the outsider it has more specific meaning for The Boys. 'Are you going down-town?' means two things, depending mainly on the time of day. If said on a Saturday morning it means are you going for a wander around the departmental stores and record shops, etc; said in the evening it means are you going drinking in the down-town pubs and wine lodges. Drinking down-town is something special, it is pleasure *par excellence*, the ultimate in conspicuous consumption, excitement and sometimes trouble.[7]

From time to time something exceptional happens while The Boys are down-town. A fight, a near-fight, a rub up with the police, a broken shop window, someone carried home—over the months the examples mount up. The latter half of Year Three provided such a catalogue, with major outings of up to a dozen of the network doing the town possibly on a Thursday but most probably a Friday, Saturday and Sunday. Thursday nights out would finish about 11 pm, Friday and Saturday would involve going on to a club till 2 am, and Sunday going to the local disco till about midnight.

How many nights a week The Boys went down-town was determined almost exclusively by how much money they had. They would rarely 'do' the down-town pubs if they had less than a 'duce' (£2), but instead would spend the evening in the local pubs. The changing circumstances of Year Three meant The Boys had progressively less cash; nights out for many of them were reduced from four to two a week. Several of the network were skint for half the week, whether because of commitments such as flat rent, wife and baby, or because the dole and the lowly paid jobs they had returned to were no substitute for the proceeds of the catseyes business. Although some boys continued to subsidise their income by 'going on the cars every now and again', the network as a whole simply had less and most of that was gained legitimately.

It was about 7 pm one Sunday night (mid Year Three) when I got on to the Corner. Colly and Joey, as usual, were already there having a discussion as to the merits of Johnny Cash versus Bob Dylan: basically Bob Dylan couldn't sing, as opposed to Cash who never had anything sensible to sing about. Fosser and Emo soon arrived. Danny shouted down from his landing that he would 'follow yous down' when his shirt had been ironed. Jimbo smoothed over in his new leather coat, amidst 'get a load of you smoothy arse'. (The tendency to get dressed up for evenings out had increased over the months.) We walked down to 'The Turk' and after a quick glass of lager and the addition of Danny made our way to the louder, brighter, more interesting city centre. Always The Boys go the back way to places, across waste ground, down alleys, then suddenly you're there in the action.

Tonight talk is about football, about Liverpool's win the day before, about what a good side they are and how they're going to win the league. First stop was the Long Bar. Joey ordered the drinks, out came the cigarettes and the night started in earnest. It was rare an evening passed without the police and Courts being discussed. If it wasn't one of the 'older fellers' or one of The Boys, it was one of The Ritz or even The Tiddlers who had been 'pulled in' or 'been up'. The week past had seen Boon arrested. Along with Mal he had been removing a radio from a Hillman car when a police jeep 'screamed up'. There was a chase with Boon heading for the Block.

Fosser He came running into the Block right past us with this copper legging it after him. He turned dead sharp, you know he had rubber soles on, anyway he stopped dead sharp and this copper who was just about to get him fell flat on his arse. Boon fucked off up the landings and this copper just gave up. We was in bulk laughing.

Danny   They must have put out a description 'coz they stopped me and Emo yesterday.

Emo   That's 'coz my hair's like Boon's and I've got purple cords. This copper asked me name and that. I knew what he was after. I just said I work, you've got the wrong bloke.

Fosser   They must have got Boon's name in the end 'coz they came into the club and asked for him and just pulled him in. Mocky [Boon's brother] was there, he went over to tell their old man.

Colly   They'll really fuck him for making a cunt out of that copper. He'll get fuckin' murdered.

Joey   Come 'ed Boys, let's get off.

The next stop was a wine lodge. The 'Winey' was always a fascinating place full of faces of character. No one really enjoyed the task of drinking the large 'docs' of wine which were poured from enormous barrels behind the bar. Fosser's simple philosophy, 'Wine, lovely wine, you'll never get drunk if you don't drink wine,' probably summed up the reasoning for stopping at wine lodges. The Boys rarely stayed more than ten minutes, just long enough to 'have a few wines'. Our next stop was 'Calottees', another wine lodge from where, the same ritual performed, we moved on to 'Queers' Street' and its trio of pubs. 'Ma Black's' saw everyone sitting in the usual corner and back on lager. By now everyone was unwinding and feeling happy. The pace of drinking was allowed to slow and joints of marijuana were built. This operation was now quite 'incidental', with no one concentrating or watching as they had done a few months before when smoking pot was a novelty. Now it was 'institutionalised', it was part of a normal evening out. Fosser put on the 'record of the moment' at the juke box, and the joint was passed around. There was less talk now as everyone concentrated on the music and the pot. Everyone agreed it was 'good draw' and within a few minutes we were up and on the move again. We went into 'Queers' Bar' which was always enjoyed for its free entertainment thrown in by the two 'fairies' behind the bar. The Boys would always try and get these two barmen 'talking like queers' but the bait, as tonight, was not always taken. The next two calls were 'tarts' pubs'—bars always visited by a lot of young girls. The Boys tended not to take girls very seriously so early in the evening, 'chatting up' being left for the licensed clubs much later. However, discussions about sex and chatty dialogue with girls was always probable. Since we were propping 'The Pendant's' bar up, the two girls who were trying to get served had to push past. Colly and Joey, the experts in the quick repartee game, went into action, soon tying up the girls in their own suggestions much to the amusement of the rest of The Boys.

Colly I'll have a whisky, luv.
Girl Will you now!
Joey Make mine a double, one for each hand. (Shapes his hand close to the girl's behind.)
Colly Do you want a feller Mary?
Joey Do you want a hand Mary, where do you want it Mary?
Colly Oh don't go Mary, I've got something to show you.

The newly christened Mary and her friend went to find their mates, a little embarrassed but not offended, knowing Liverpool boys and their humour.

By now everyone was merry, a bit intoxicated; with some enthusiasm we continued on the route, with temporary stops to wet the walls in back alleys. At 'The Bassett' we came across some other 'boys' from Roundhouse who called for a brief chat before the last down-town call, at 'The Beer Cellar' for another lager. Then it was two taxis back up to 'The Turk'. Almost everyone who mattered socially to The Boys would be in 'The Turk', 'Wally's' or 'The Cockle' up the road by this time of night. Jimbo wanted to roll another joint so we went up to 'Wally's' to see if there was a corner we could sit in. Pablo, Jock, Craber and friends were there and were greeted as 'the potheads' to which they retorted something about plonkies (wine drinkers). With Arno leading off, everybody was soon singing. The old favourite 'You'll never walk alone' was followed by The Boys' own home-made song.

Give me the lager, gi'me the wine to-ni-i-ght,
Give me the lager, gi'me the wine to-ni-i-ght,

I

Lager in the morning, lager in the ev'ning, lager all through
the ni-i-ght,
Wine in the morning, wine in the ev'ning, wine all through
the ni-i-ght,
(Change to slower pace.)
Roundhouse, Roundhouse, top o' the league,
Roundhouse, Roundhouse, top o' the league.

It had become somewhat of a tradition at this time to sing these chants as loudly as possible, stamping on the floor in unison until the landlady, 'an old ratbag', came in and threatened to call the police. In true style she made her threat, returned to make another and say she'd call the police, then again to say they were on their way. Nobody took much notice of her and carried on singing till it was suggested everyone go up to 'The Cockle' for a final drink. We marched up the road, some more obviously drunk than others, and all generally 'disorderly'. The smoke-room of 'The Cockle' was packed out with 'the children of Roundhouse' as Fosser called them while he lurched in the doorway blessing them with the sign of the cross. Everyone was 'getting ready for the disco' and The Girls in particular were dressed up. Most of The Ritz were there as well since they were still a bit young for down-town pubs.

Jimbo, although 'well stoned', built another joint. He had been rather quiet all evening and now explained a little that he had wife problems (it should be remembered that he is older than the other boys). He had been trying to decide whether they could afford a flat instead of having to live with his in-laws. He asked me about housing applications and what I thought about marriage, and after a short chat we let the matter drop. (I was expected to know about housing, legal matters, politics and so on—Colly would ask me the weather forecast!) Jimbo made a conscious effort to enjoy himself to the extent of over-laughter, Fosser was chatting up Irene Mull-honey, Emo and Danny were sharing a joke, everybody was engrossed in dialogue. Colly and Joey decided The Boys should be 'getting off' and, about twelve strong, we made our noisy unsteady way to the Disco.

To the outsider a noisy, sweaty, smoky dance in a dark old house has little appeal. But to the children of Roundhouse it is a warm, friendly, exciting atmosphere where one can be oneself without feeling self-conscious. There are a few social rules about who dances with whom and how many times, and an intensely active grapevine works overtime if need be. For most of The Boys the evening finishes with a spot of courting before they wander up to bed, usually well pleased with the night out.

Such a night out was, and still is, typical. Most Roundhouse males indulge in these evenings as often as they are able. The things that matter, give pleasure, are mainly good company, a good atmosphere and getting drunk, often to the extent of 'spewing up' to start again. Nights out down-town provide all these aspects and often more besides.

The Boys are really part of the first generation to add social drug use to this inventory of pleasures. As already mentioned, the 'illegal opportunity structure' makes pot readily available to down-town adolescents. The Jock-Pablo group have used other more potent drugs, but The Boys have remained within the safety of marijuana. Jimbo recalled:

> About a year ago, all the fellers like Colly and Streak and those who are smoking it now, you'd offer them a drag and they'd say 'piss off you mad bastard', they reckoned it was bad stuff. But now they're all on it. I think it sparks Streak off, he's dead happy when he's had a draw, and he'd never have had it a year ago.

The Boys' use of pot contrasts with that of more 'serious' users like the Jock-Pablo group whose language and life style are considerably influenced by the drug scene. The Boys' initial reluctance to use pot was typical of the non-user's attitude in whatever social class. Once they had watched others and realised its relative mildness they sought its excitement. This is again not unique to the working class, and in fact is generally seen as a middle-class deviancy.

Drug use is only discussed here in relation to nights out down-town. Some of the network simply do not use drugs socially and would not smoke pot, mainly because they are non-smokers anyway. Several however smoke it simply because it is there and handed to them. Bone, Danny, Fatch, Arno, Tommy, Herbie, Emo, for instance, simply see a few drags on a joint and its possible mildly euphoric effects as comparable with a couple of pints. For them the main criterion of the evening is having a good time, and whether they get drunk or 'stoned' is not relevant as long as the effects are positive. Others, Jimbo, Colly, Fosser, Joey and Mocky, take pot more seriously. They use it more often and are more discriminating between good and bad 'draws'. Even these Boys on a night out however settle for a general euphoria, summed up by Colly as being 'pissed out of me head and stoned out of me mind'. Emo suggested during a conversation about drugs that part of the drug scene was involved in 'trying to be big'. 'Like if someone was offering "acid" to some of the lads in "The Basset" or somewhere they'd take it, buy it that is, but they wouldn't trip or nothing, they wouldn't use it. They'd say they had, like, afterwards but I bet they wouldn't take it.'

This is probably true. The Boys are wary of drug use, being aware of the position the media adopt. However, they do not have media mentality. They feel that the media and Authority try to persuade them that deviance is not fun—that you get caught and punished and that you don't get pleasure anyway. Thus pot leads to other things, other things lead to addiction, then you jump off the tops of buildings or die an agonising death. This is of course a statistical possibility and certainly even soft-drug use is dysfunctional for a few users. The Boys for instance were aware Voggy had become fairly ill while using large doses and combinations of drugs; but they were also aware, in Jock's terms, that 'he was a weird guy anyway, he didn't live in this world half the time whether he was stoned or not'. Voggy was role-typed as an example of someone fairly unstable.[8] Realising he was an exception, but aware of the possible dangers of drug use, and aware also that Holly, Jimbo, Jock, Pablo had all been 'seriously involved' in drug use and had through experience decided to return to pot smoking, The Boys had a fairly total picture: the evidence before them basically meant—stick to pot smoking. This maxim was re-inforced one fateful night.

It was a normal pre-disco trip down-town, the significant difference being that Mocky had a bottle of capsules he had bought from a regular face in one of the clubs the night before. Seven of us were sitting down at our third pub of call when Mocky took two tablets and offered them round. After a long discussion, Fosser, Emo, Mocky and Titch took two pills each, with the rest of us saying we weren't interested and didn't think they should be either. We moved on into Queers' Street and sat down again with another round of drinks. Fosser asked for and received another couple of pills because the first two were 'doing fuck all for me'. We moved on to our next call, every-body getting into the spirit of things. Fosser, however, started to become unsteady. He knocked a table over on his way to the toilet and we had to get him out quickly, as there was a bit of a commotion, a near fight and threats of calling the police. Things got worse; Emo became unsteady and once outside he went running off down the street. Joey was blaming Mocky in no uncertain terms as he and I tried to urge Fosser along. Titch and Mocky seemed unaffected, which was fortunate because Fosser's next antic involved sprinting bursts along the pave-ment without consideration for life or limb. It was decided he should be taken home. Joey and I took an arm each, which as Fosser became more and more docile, eventually meant we were carrying him since the taxis would not stop for such prob-lematic passengers. Joey insisted Mocky dump his bottle of capsules: 'If we get stopped by the busies now and they find that lot, we'll all get pulled in.'

Mocky They won't stop us.
Colly Come on Mocky, dump them, you've caused enough bother.
Mocky O fuck off, I paid for these.
Joey Well don't come up with us then, walk on your own.

Mocky, somewhat outnumbered, ran on ahead saying he'd

see us in 'The Turk'. Fosser was getting very difficult to move as we tired under his weight and reluctance to go forward. It took some twenty minutes getting him into the Block. Colly discouraged the audience of little kids as we climbed the landings before finally dumping him on his bed. The three of us walked down to 'The Turk' to join the others. No sooner had we got in the door than a fight broke out at the far end of the bar. Mocky was fighting with Mr Suddy, a local man he'd bumped into on his way to the toilet. The fight was broken up quickly and Mocky brought down to The Boys' end of the bar, ruffled and dazed. To add to the chaos Titch and Emo appeared, Emo with a cut forehead where he'd fallen down. Joey took this chance to make his sermon. 'I'm not going out with you lot again if you're going to start taking pills all the time. What good are pills, they've fucked up the night out and got mates fighting with one another.'

So ended one of the few experiments The Boys have had with drugs other than marijuana. Another similar experiment is unlikely, for a few months at least. Passing out, feeling sick all night, fighting with friends were all negative effects and, especially when compared with the usual fun, pleasure and excitement of a normal night out, the moral was well drawn. Drug use is still an innovation for The Boys, a new addition to the pleasure armoury, and through trial and error marijuana has for the majority proved the most successful aid to alcohol in defending hedonism against the routinising and de-fusing effect of day-to-day existence. Since it is seen as a positive device it will almost definitely be passed on to the young pretenders, The Boys of tomorrow. Evidence of this is already apparent in the form of imitation joints, of grass and budgie seed, made by early adolescents around the area.

Another vital component of the pleasure principle is supplied by relationships with the opposite sex. The woman's position in Roundhouse and in the lower working class generally, though by no means specifically, is not very glamorous. Although she may run the household and manage family and domestic affairs, her life is housebound and her energy sapped through child-rearing. Her role is to keep house and bring up the children and little else. Family planning with the aid of efficient contraception is still very limited. The pill, frowned upon by the working class generally, is opposed intensely in a Roman Catholic community like Roundhouse where even social workers cannot encourage its use without fear of reprimand. Thus although some of the newest generation of married women are using the pill to put off further pregnancies, unmarried girls are still highly unlikely to consider its use.

Hence Roundhouse girls grow up in a tradition which leaves them highly susceptible to pregnancy. With The Boys' view of contraception as unmanly and mother's advice in terms of sex education limited to *don't*, The Girls' position is more often than not sealed by the pregnant marriage.[9] ('The Girls' is used as the generic term for The Boys' female contemporaries living in the area.)

Joey is almost certainly correct in his identification of the factors that impinge on adolescent sexual relationships. 'There's two reasons why the tarts round here don't all screw. They're afraid of getting humped and they're afraid of the big gobs. They can't do nothing round here without it getting round and their mates all calling them dirty arse.' These two reasons, both connected with the structure of the local community, have far-reaching effects. Since The Boys almost always see women in sexual terms, these local difficulties have to be overcome. Basically girls are divided into three categories—'somebody's tart', 'dirty tickets' and the 'not having anys'.

By the end of Year Two nearly half the network had a regular girlfriend, 'me tart'. These girlfriends were expected to remain faithful and obedient. The traditions of the community backed this up and indeed The Girls' own grapevine trapped them into this fidelity, they themselves enforcing such behavioural standards on their courting peers. Although by the end of Year Three there were signs of these steady relationships becoming more reciprocal, The Boys always commanded the upper hand.

'Somebody's tart' was regarded as reserved for her boyfriend by both sexes. The Boys could, they argued, 'have it off' with another available girl, but the respective girlfriends could not. Why not? 'That's why not, because I say so, because I'll give her a smack if she tries it.' By seeing The Girls as subordinate The Boys would thus enforce, by physical force if necessary, standards they themselves were not willing to observe. If she's not around when she should be, she'll get 'smacked': even Danny who is exceptionally good-natured mentioned this use of the 'smack' and 'dig', quite incidentally. His remark was intended to explain how drunk he'd got, that is how successful Saturday night had been: 'I drank half a bottle of whisky. I was really rotten. I went up to my bird's to bring her over to ours, 'coz everyone was out. She reckoned I threw her down the steps and twatted her and all sorts, I don't remember it like, but she's got plenty of bruises.'

'Somebody's tart', then, is a steady girlfriend of one of The Boys or other local men, basically out of the running as far as all but her 'feller' is concerned. In fact, generally, The Boys are more likely to have had sexual intercourse with someone other than their 'tart'. The 'tart' is usually someone they like and respect enough to want to carry on 'going with', and thus for quite a long period sexual relations will be limited to petting. Intercourse tends to take place only when both parties say they are willing to settle down if a pregnancy occurs.

The second category of girl The Boys identify is the 'dirty ticket', 'the randy', 'good screw', 'tear yer back out', 'little raver', designated for sexual exploitation. Although a few local girls come into this category, the intense grapevine and kinship taboos of the community are felt, and in the main sexual adventures are sought outside the area. Knowledge of such adventures is kept from The Girls, and many 'knowing' conversations are had in their presence without them fully realising what the subject-matter really is.

Les I saw you at the 'Blue Door' on Saturday, Colly, all right was it?
Colly Oh, er, yeh, yes, it was very nice, I felt much better afterwards.

Joan   Yer what?
Colly   Never you mind, big ears, I wasn't talking to you.

There is a hard core of 'promiscuous' girls to be found at certain down-town clubs, where The Boys will go hoping to 'tap one' for 'a quick shag'. Although the sexual adventures with these girls are often exaggerated, and petting sessions in the quiet side streets are romanticised into fantasies of erotic sexual practices, The Boys in this field at least get their share. Every now and then a 'gang bang' occurs, with the famous four-to-one permutation: I know definitely of at least two of these escapades and have heard rumours of others. A most memorable evening involved an energetic girl given the imaginative title of 'Ringspanner', when a grand total of five of the network queued up for their share.[10]

Local girls would simply not survive the grapevine if they behaved like this. The Boys in fact usually unintentionally destroy a developing local 'dirty ticket' by allowing her behaviour to be put on the grapevine. Hence Dot, who had no sexual hangups, was lost to them for ever. 'I should never have gone with Geordy. As soon as he'd screwed me he got up and went and told all The Boys. He told them all sorts of lies. Then they all think you'll let them have it. I wouldn't go with a Roundy Boy again, little knobs and big gobs all of them.'

All The Boys, whether they are going steady or not, will take the opportunity of sexual adventures when they arise. This distinction has been noted elsewhere, with women divided into two categories by local men—those designated for exploitation and those for 'more satisfying give and take relationships based on liking or love'.[11] For The Boys who are married or going steady, the same reasoning as Liebow uncovered holds true. Exploitative relationships can be boasted about through the conversation culture to refute any degrading possibility that a man could be seen to be 'under his tart's thumb' or 'a real fuckin' stop-in'.

The third category of women, The Girls who are neither 'somebody's tart' nor known as 'dirty tickets', includes those cautious about getting involved with The Boys and often regarded as 'a waste of time', since 'you'll get nothing there Boys'; they are 'not having any'. Most of these local girls are expecting to marry someone in their own backyard, but until that time they will keep within the sentiments of approval set them and not endanger their reputation on the grapevine. The Boys pool their experiences to classify these girls fairly exactly. Is she absolutely 'tight with it' or 'OK for a finger' or 'a wank'? With this category The Boys usually know their sexual drives will be frustrated, and enter campaigns with only limited expectations of success.

The relationships between The Boys and The Girls do seem influenced by the traditional standards of the working-class culture, with the subordination of women and use of physical violence still dominant themes. Traditional racial prejudice, partly broken down in some inner areas, is untouched in Roundhouse. Joey's girlfriend, we will recall, got 'a fuckin' good smack' for making eyes at a coloured boy. The Boys will put great pressure on any of The Girls who show an interest in coloured boys. Chrissy who particularly likes coloured boys claims she daren't even be seen with one. 'If you play Stevie Wonder records round here they start calling you a nigger-lover. I wouldn't dare go with one. Anyway me dad would fuck me if he found out and all The Boys would get at you, calling you slag and all sorts.' Yet despite this apparently unfair deal The Girls are usually loyal and tolerant with regards The Boys. Most don't consider their deal a bad one, and since everyone is from Roundhouse they must look after *their* Boys. This includes condoning their delinquency, showing great hysteria over any fights, lending them money, dressing up for them and generally accepting that it's a man's world.

Toughness and Trouble
As we build up a picture of the 'ideal' member of the net-work it should again be emphasised we are still only discussing *some* aspects of The Boys' style. Compared with the number of

times The Boys go out with their girlfriends, the illicit nights are rare; compared with the good nights out, the one that goes sour is uncommon. The search for the good times just goes wrong occasionally.

Fighting from all accounts is not as dominant a concern for The Boys as it was for their fathers. The earlier days of Round-house were more violent and 'toughness' had to be reasserted more regularly. Perhaps it is this tough identity of the past itself which exonerates The Boys from being an aggressive gang. As far as the network are concerned there is no issue to be settled, and they believe that outsiders, especially other neighbour-hoods' adolescents, accept Roundhouse Boys as untouchable. Inter-group fights with outsiders usually only occur if The Boys feel challenged in some way. They do not all concur about exactly what denotes such a challenge, and at times disagree amongst themselves as to when a fight is called for. More often, however, there is no problem and a challenge from outsiders is taken up vigorously, as I discovered on several occasions. Indeed if any group from the neighbourhood is fighting with any-one from outside the neighbourhood, questions are asked later.

Well after midnight, about ten of us were sitting in a local night club. It was fairly quiet and Boon was heard first time when he came running in and shouted 'Quinsey Royle's getting fucked outside.' We all got up and made for the exit. Everyone ran up the road to the action in a nearby side street. Quinsey was standing in a corner with his hands over his face while his girlfriend was trying to tend to his bleeding nose and persuade him to go home. There were four outsiders in their late teens just hoping to leave. They were not to be so lucky. It was not exactly established whether these four were responsible, but their attempts to leave were taken as guilt and The Boys went for them. A couple of punches and two of them were on the ground, the boot going in several times without discrimination, the ribs, the crutch and the face of the victims all receiving heavy blows. The other two were chased up the road and it sounded as if a similar encounter occurred there. Some of The

Boys returned, having 'fuckin' murdered them' and with 'blood on me boots' to prove it. The whole episode was over in five minutes and everyone returned to the club leaving the outsiders to tend their wounds the best they could. (Two were taken to hospital for treatment.)

On returning to the bar The Boys discussed the incident. Firstly there was some sounding to establish who had done what, who had been the most daring and efficient victor. Then followed a justification for the 'massacre'. In brief the outsiders belonged to a group of 'greasers' from 'The Lanteen' who had caused trouble before. They needed to be taught a lesson, they had rightly got a taste of their own medicine—fighting when the numbers were unfair. There was nothing worse than that, 'specially when they've [the victims] got their tarts with them. We'd never touch no one with a bird. Even that floorwalker that done Colly [Colly was fined £20 for 'assaulting' a store security officer who tried to throw him out of Flems], we'll get him in the end but not when he's with his bird. We seen him last week, but he was with his bird so we left him. It's not right pickin' on fellers with their birds, those greasers should get fuckin' murdered.'

The most bloody and vicious 'defensive' fight The Boys have been in, to date, happened on a Sunday night down-town. Six of us were sitting in a bar in Queers' Street when a rather drunk 'bloke' on the other side of the room started 'eyeing' Colly. Colly looked back and asked the bloke what he was looking at. The reply was a beer glass which smashed on to the seat right next to Colly. It was with some disbelief I watched this, for there were six of us, including Fosser and Arno whose very appearance convinces me that I'm lucky to be on their side, sitting down quietly whilst the glass-thrower only had one mate with him. Only Colly got up at first, obviously not sure whether the bloke was looking for trouble or simply 'out of his head' and thus to be excused. A second glass broke all over his head, which convinced everybody, even me, that retaliatory action was needed. What ensued was later aptly described by Murky as 'a real cowboy fight'. The two aggressors had chairs cracked over their heads, and if Arno had actually managed to get it high enough a table would have landed on them also. Colly, who'd been sitting down examining his wounds whilst the fight was in progress, picked up a Guinness bottle and broke it over the glass-thrower's head: this was a signal for retreat, and everybody left quickly amidst an uproar as the bar staff and others became increasingly hysterical. The group split into two to avoid suspicion, and Joey and I took Colly up to hospital, where he received five stitches. Extremely shaken, I sensed I was not alone in suffering from adrenalin poisoning.

According to the grapevine the glass-thrower had to stay in hospital for several days. It was also rumoured that he was a regular trouble-maker, had been in several previous fights and that the policeman who eventually arrived on the scene said 'oh you again, he's always fighting'. Everybody agreed The Boys' actions had been completely justified and the subject was soon exhausted. It was not till a couple of weeks later when Colly and I, both very intoxicated, were in the back of a taxi that the matter came up again. The 'bottling' of the glass-thrower was obviously playing on Colly's mind. Almost tearfully he went through the justifications for hospitalising the glass-thrower. He was again reassured he had done the right thing and the case was closed, at least publicly, except to be mentioned as part of local history in future debates about 'toughness'.

Whilst most of The Boys would agree, in theory at least, that fighting is only necessary as a defensive measure when one's dignity, identity or actual bodily welfare is challenged, they are not all exactly agreed about when defensive action becomes aggression. All The Boys would subscribe to the 'cult of toughness'[12] identified with working-class adolescents elsewhere. A tough appearance or style is necessary to survive if one visits downtown night life on a regular basis. However, a few of The Boys, Arno and Emo being the prime examples, read 'trouble' from much smaller cues than the others. These two are capable of emphasising their physical strength and 'hardness' to the level of provoking rather than deterring trouble. Indeed Arno's whole style of walking and 'swaggering' begs trouble and is so pronounced as to be 'taken off' by The Boys when they are in a mimicking mood. If anyone looks twice at Arno he wants to know what they're looking at and why, and if they would like to be sorted out. The Boys often take the heat out of the crises Arno provokes by making a joke of his behaviour and assuring the outsider he does not have to defend his dignity. If everyone's had a few drinks and Arno is not being adequately entertained by the conversation, trouble is always a possibility.

There was a short period (mid Year Three) when nearly all the remaining network of Boys would be out together, maybe fifteen strong, probably the biggest group in town. This show of strength tended to provoke a group solidarity and narcissism amongst The Boys, illustrated with comments like 'Round-house rules' and 'we could take on anyone tonight boys'. On one such night, near the end of the pub crawl, Arno went into action. The group had broken up into 'kitty' groups of five to help speed up the ordering of drinks, and this fragmentation had continued between pubs. Walking up to 'The Beer Cellar', the group including Arno and Emo were ahead of the others and managed to get themselves involved in an argument with three men about whose pavement it was. Fighting broke out: the men had decided to have a go, unaware of the reserve forces. Several from the rear bunch of The Boys ran up to help their mates and the men, using much commonsense, ran off up the road, pursued by about ten of The Boys. Emo returned after five minutes. 'He won't forget my face in a hurry that big feller, I worked it to him good and proper.' Gradually the others returned, talking profusely about the exact nature of the fight, a blow-by-blow commentary interspersed with technical discussions about methods used. There then developed a long discussion about the justification: Jimbo, although he can be an extremely tough character and is admired for his fighting expertise, felt the fight had been unnecessary.

Jimbo We're more sophisticated than that now. Say Gerry, Everomer and us, we're more sophisticated than that now, we don't fight like that no more. It's not hard to give it to a few fellers when there's fifteen of yous.

Emo It was one to one with the feller I give it to.

Jimbo Oh ay, but he was shitting himself 'coz he knew there were plenty more to fuck him if he done you.

Les But if there was fifteen of Dovetail (Boys) and three of us they'd fuck us.

Tank So would The Niggers.

Jimbo But those weren't Niggers and they weren't Dovetail Boys neither. I tell you those days are over, it's more sophisticated now.

This argument was not settled. Some of The Boys were convinced they'd acted reasonably. Les saw fighting as an on-going process over several years. The next fight might see three Roundhouse Boys get beaten up. His motto was 'Do before you get done by'. As we walked back up town Tank also followed this line of argument. 'I got chased into Winny Gardens by a gang of niggers the other week. They'd have fucked me if they'd got me. But sometimes there'll be a nigger on his own and I'll get him.'

This logic, especially with regards an easily identifiable outsiders' group, is widespread. Steve, relatively law-abiding and quiet, was threatened by a group of four 'niggers'* outside 'the dole' and had been lucky to get away without being robbed. His attitude when I met him shortly afterwards was '. . . but I'll get one of them, I'll see a nigger somewhere on his own and I'll give it to him'. Steve was going to 'get somebody', it didn't have to be the same person, just a representative, in his terms, of the group that had challenged him, somebody to even the score with.

A further type of inter-group fighting regarded as legitimate is the neighbourhood 'gang' fight. The Inner City contains several groups of 'Boys' identifiable by the common fate of neighbourhood. Such rivalry occurs at perhaps three age-

* In this case they were actually of West Indian and English parentage. In their own area they would be known as 'half castes', but to The Boys 'they're all fuckin' niggers'.

levels; inter-school gangs and The Ritz age-level might have their own 'agro' independently of The Boys. As Thrasher pointed out long ago, it is at times of threat that The Gang really takes shape. At such times sub-divisions and personal differences are subsumed by a mass unity against the common enemy. The so-called Toxteth Riots in Liverpool 8[13] during the summer of 1972, with considerable street fighting between white and coloured adolescent groups, happened on The Boys' doorstep. Many of The Boys and their families had relatives in the white area where flats came under attack and windows were broken. After the first night of 'riots' several of the young men from Roundhouse went up to stay with these relatives. Had their flats come under attack it is probable the Roundhouse Boys and some of the men would have become involved in the gang fights: rumour had it on the Corner that Roundhouse's reputation had been enough to protect these particular flats. 'The Niggers were on the landing but one of them said "No, leave this lot, some of the Roundy Boys are staying here. We don't want bother with them." '

This comment spread like a forest fire and The Boys in particular were well pleased that 'The Niggers' showed enough sense not to challenge their 'superiority'. Whether this statement was true or not, or whether indeed it represented the outsiders' true perspective, I cannot ascertain. What is of interest however is that The Boys accepted this statement as true, saw it as perfectly reasonable. They believe they are 'hard', 'tough' and well-thought-of for these reasons. The historical dimension, the area's identity, discussed earlier thus affects their behaviour and to some extent influences the action or lack of it. The sub-cultural theorist might well argue that this historical dimension 'provides a rationale for the members', giving them 'a sense of belonging to something with some permanence and stability'.[14] Here again it is extremely difficult to distinguish between the cultural closure, the 'tradition' of an area, and the innovation of its new members; but certainly the 'passing on' of identity affected the situation to some extent.

Such fighting of course just reinforces the down-town adolescent's bad name and further backs up Authority's claim that such areas need heavy policing for the good of the residents' welfare and property. The Boys are in fact rarely *involved* in gang fights, they usually only get as far as the verbal preparations: 'They reckon Sandy Gardens is coming down tonight boys, there could be a bit of bother.' Furthermore, unlike many newer neighbourhood adolescent groups who are still without a clear identity, The Boys actually believe they 'rule' and that there is no need to go out identity-building and image seeking;[15] since their 'territory' is very rarely invaded they have no reason to doubt the truth of their beliefs.

Moving into a more personal plane another type of fight occurs at an intra-group or 'home territory' level. Here it is expected that one must fight if somebody 'makes a cunt out of you'. This happens if one is ridiculed, has one's masculinity or dignity challenged. Sometimes 'self' is extended to cover one's mates, girlfriend or sister, so that Fatch was involved in a fight in 'Wally's' one night because 'some mad fucker' fell across his sister and knocked a drink over. On a very basic level one can get into a fight for almost no apparent reason. An accidental kick or push in a club or the disco leads to a 'butt' and a fight. Les for instance came out of 'The Cockle' one night to find his girlfriend talking to another man who appeared to be chatting her up. He simply knocked the bloke out with 'a flying head butt' only to find out it was his girlfriend's cousin. These situations are not uncommon and their particular 'solution' is again based on the need to 'do unto others before they do unto you'. Since there are no restrictions on the form of down-town fighting, one 'dig' or 'butt' can be decisive and must therefore be got in quickly.

Trouble then is always a possibility to be contended with. Miller argued that for the street gangs he studied this was a source of excitement. '. . . Since there is always a good likelihood that being out on the town will eventuate in fights, etc, the practice involves elements of sought risk and desired danger.'[16]

K

It is not possible to say all The Boys *seek* this sort of danger: some like Arno do sometimes, but in the main it is probably more correct to say The Boys are aware of the possibility of a fight because they can bump into rather than seek trouble at any time. Colly for instance who'd been fighting with 'Welsh miners' outside a chip shop during a holiday weekend returned with a swollen and cut lip. He remarked on the way downtown for an evening out, 'If I get in another fight tonight my lip'll be like a tyre.' He was acknowledging a further fight as a possibility; 'trouble' is something you simply get into.

Toughness does not just become operational in fighting however. A whole ethos of being 'hard', being able to look after yourself like a man, is displayed by The Boys and other local working-class adolescents. Language is an important carrier of this identity. The 'bad language' used by The Boys offends many a middle-class ear. The language form and content is probably the most obvious example of imitation. The 'accent', the use of stereotyped and esoteric phrases, is undoubtedly largely due to transmission. There is some degree of innovation, new vocabulary, etc, but only on the periphery. The elders of Roundhouse have a dual morality with regards language: they will swear profusely themselves but will chastise their offspring for following suit. Their lip service to 'speaking proper' has little effect, and children from a very early age will swear continuously. Sweet little girls will tell you to 'fuck off' long before they're out of primary school. The Tiddlers' use of swearing is an explicit attempt to be 'adult'. For The Boys, swearing is less important and quite 'natural'. Thus 'fuck' and its various derivations have several meanings depending on quite subtle cues such as tone, volume and word order. 'Fuck off', despite Bernstein's early explanations of public language, in fact is probably more difficult to use and learn as part of a flexible phrase than the learning of several words to cover its various meanings. 'Fuck off' can mean, to mention just a few definitions, keep quiet, go away, stop it, let's leave, *don't* or there will be trouble. It can describe a punch or blow and it can mean 'don't be unreasonable'. Used in conversation with outsiders, heavy language can suggest toughness, and a heated discussion will often take a form such as 'I'm fuckin' warning you lad, you fuck off out of here or I'll fuckin' murder you.'

Other ways of giving off 'tough' vibrations come through style and 'the look', 'looking hard', 'eyeing' and various other visual cues. The Boys hate to turn their backs on people. They will always try and sit with their backs to walls. Thus rather than group themselves right round a table in a pub they will arch in a semi-circle round two tables, which while it hampers communication internally aids communication with outsiders for whatever purpose.

This concern with toughness and trouble necessitates an alertness to potentially inflammatory situations. During my early visits to down-town pubs, what appeared to me as fairly neutral social situations were read quite differently by The Boys. What I would then see as a man coming into the bar to look for a friend he had arranged to meet was viewed by Acker for instance as, 'There's going to be bother here, that feller's after someone to settle [a score].' Or again, 'See those fellers over there—our kid [older brother] bottled their mate in 'Kate's' the other week. I reckon we'd better get off before there's any bother, 'coz we'd have no chance with all that lot getting stuck in.' (*Tommy*.)

Smartness and Fairness
Smartness, as defined earlier, involves outsmarting and out-witting others with superior mental agility. Being seen as 'smart' and 'quick' and 'funny' is an important 'concern' for The Boys.[17] At a verbal level smartness can be connected with trouble in the sense that outwitting someone can obviously involve degrading them and 'making a cunt out of' them.[18] Such sparring sometimes led to trouble within the network. One of The Boys would be losing a verbal exchange. As a strategy he would widen the tactics, and if this failed he would probably 'feel a cunt' and either back down or create further escalation.

One lunchtime in 'The Turk', The Boys were talking about interior decorating, which some of them were doing through their employment with the local workshop.

Colly Hey Jimmy Saville [Tank bears a resemblance to the TV compère), where were you this morning when you should have been working?

Tank Who's talking lad, I do more work in a day than you do in a week.

Colly Yes, one coat kid, but I do the job properly. I can paint better, wallpaper better. . . . I can wear socks better than you.

Tank O rap up ratbag and get the ale in—I wouldn't like to be in a desert with you.

And so it went on. The whole time Tank was out of approved school and before he went down again he sparred with Colly at the word game and nearly always lost. On a couple of occasions the sparring had become too intense. One evening in particular Colly and Tank had been picking on each other throughout the crawl round town. We eventually arrived in 'Wally's' where matters got out of hand. Colly, seeing two girls come into the bar, remarked, 'I wouldn't mind getting me cock up her.'

Tank She wouldn't notice if you did.

Colly OK Jimmy Saville, don't start again, come back when you can hold your ale, never mind your cock.

Tank It's a fuck sight bigger than yours.

Joey Oh give it a rest Tank, he'll only make a cunt out of you.

Tank Who'll make a cunt out of me? Come on Colly, come outside and see who's got the biggest cock.

Tank would not give up, yet the more he sparred the more it seemed everybody was laughing at him. The conflict flared up again as we made our way to a club. Tank started pushing Colly who warned him to 'pack it in or else'. Tank was rather drunk and didn't take heed. He ended up getting pushed over and banging his head. Everybody was sorry things had got out of hand and Tank was excused because 'he can't hold his ale' and told to go home, which with some help he managed.

This verbal smartness game is more often a friendly affair, however. The Liverpool dialect is itself unique and full of telling analogies and metaphors. Here people have teeth 'like a row of condemned houses', are so weak they 'couldn't punch a hole in a wet *Echo*'. Even at its best the written word cannot capture its spontaneity, flow and adaptation to suit the moment. The Girls are often subjected to The Boys' attempts to outwit them with quickfire humour. Mocky's sister walked past the Corner in a shiny midi-skirt.

It's Garry Glitter, isn't it?
Hey, Mary pull your skirt up.
Hey, Mary, pull it down.
Give us a kiss Mary, it's me birthday.
Mary You're not old enough lad, I want a man not a shirt button.
Hey Linda, do you want a nice feller?
Linda Yer, d'you know any?

Smartness means more than verbal games, however; it describes a whole style of 'attack'. It need hardly be said that what The Boys regard as smart the magistrate will regard as despicable. For The Boys it is commonsense not to pay the hot-dog man on Lime Street: firstly, he's a bit stupid, and secondly he can't leave his stand to chase you anyway. Only suckers waste 10p. If you're kept waiting in a cafeteria queue, then why not eat things while you're there; the girl on the cash till won't know you've eaten a custard tart. If you haven't got a 2p to make a phone call, ring the operator and tell her you lost your money in the machine but your call wasn't connected, she'll put you through for nothing. If you can get something cheaper, don't pay full price. The sales assistant in such and such a shoe shop is 'bent', he'll sell you a pair of shoes for £2 and forget to record the sale—you make a few pounds, so does he . . . it's commonsense, normal style and functional.

Where such infractions can be got away with they will continue. Being smart is the mild end of the morality of expediency. Even those who will not commit more serious crimes see 'being smart' as intrinsically sensible. Smartness in this sense has its counterpart in the white-collar crime of the middle classes and the job 'perks' of the affluent manual worker. In terms of pilfering employers' property there is little cultural diversity in moral terms, merely differences in the content of infractions.

Some aspects of the smartness thus tie up with delinquency. Being 'really smart' in this sense is epitomised in not being found out. You're really smart when outsiders don't even know you're being smart. However, getting found out does not always involve being unsmart, you can also be unlucky. The latter is excusable, the former is not. Being unsmart, being 'dead stupid', with regards the catseyes business, for instance, was much frowned upon. Boon once complained bitterly that he had been caught stealing a car radio because Jacko, his mate who was keeping 'dixy' on the corner, didn't do his job properly. 'He looked up and down the street but the divvy never thought of looking behind him where there was two plainclothes sitting in a Cortina. How stupid can you get?' The 'divvy' is the anti-thesis of the smart, quick person. The divvy is intrinsically un-smart. The divvy would not spot the plainclothes on top of a building or in an unmarked car.

Being caught because you're unlucky is another matter. However, fate and luck in no way translate out the way Miller conceptualises them. The Boys' fatalism is no more or less than realism. They accept that going on the cars for instance means 'you're bound to get caught sooner or later', a view based on statistical probability. Fate or luck is no more 'inevitable' for The Boys than for the motorist who drives 15,000 miles a year and accepts his life is continuously at risk. Rather than, as Matza suggested, 'to be reminded of destiny is to temporarily quit society'.[19] The Boys take their chances, aware of the risks that are involved. (The Girls are much more fatalistic and superstitious, and take on the phobias of Mum in many cases.)

Miller's final 'focal concern', autonomy, is also difficult to demonstrate as operational in The Boys' behaviour. Miller himself seems to find this category less than satisfactory. There is little in The Boys' attitude to independence and freedom which differentiates their behaviour from that of other sections of the population. The Boys' attitude to work, their rejection wherever possible of the butt-end job where 'There's always someone on your back', is more a rational appraisal of the working conditions in relation to returns than a predisposition of their cultural milieu. They often agree they'd 'do any old fuckin' job', such as clean toilets, if the price was right.

A 'focal concern' not identified by Miller but central and perhaps distinctive in The Boys' behaviour is their emphasis on uniformity and equality of effort within the network. This 'concern', which in early adolescence affected dress and appearance in the network, later demanded group narcissism, fairness and equality on involvement. For instance, whenever members of the network have to work together, whether on a camping holiday, at Sandhills, in the local workshop etc, they demand equality of effort. It is not that 'skiving' is tabooed but that no one must skive more than anyone else. If one skives you must all skive, or 'I'd work if the others would like, but I'm not slogging me guts whilst they do fuck all.'

Equality of expenditure is also rigorously enforced. On nights out The Boys insist everybody should pay their way. Here again they have a living stereotype to illustrate what is regarded as unacceptable behaviour: Murky is the deserved scapegoat here. Although he is not excluded from going out with The Boys, mainly on traditional grounds that despite his behaviour he has always been 'one of The Boys', he is talked about regularly behind his back. Murky is 'as tight as a duck's arse', a 'fuckin' miser' and the living example of Mr Scrooge. By talking about Murky in these terms The Boys emphasise to themselves the importance of being scrupulously fair when it comes to spending money on nights out. An innovation during early Year Three was the installation of a kitty system. When there were more than six in a 'night out' group, it became standard procedure to appoint a 'banker' to take £2 from everybody to pay for the evening. This procedure guaranteed everybody paid up.

Linked with this concern for equality are the fraternal senti-ments of the network: everyone should be able to enjoy themselves even if they're skint. So they will always 'carry' someone. 'If you're skint you don't have to sit in, The Boys will always see you through. Then when you've got poke and they're skint, you'll do the same for them.' (*Fatch.*) Such a system breaks down of course if everybody's skint, or a few are skint all the time. At the end of Year Three, people like Fosser, for instance, were nearly always short of money and felt obliged to stay in rather than be continually carried by their mates.

Formal Overview

Going down-town for nights out and searching out the good times is a practice of great importance. Going 'on the ale', 'doing the clubs', and all that these evenings involve in terms of fun, friendship and pure enjoyment do suggest The Boys seek specific goals and utilise a specific style. As we have seen, it is at these times when The Boys break out that heavy drinking, pot smoking, occasional punch-ups, trouble and action[20] all become possibilities. And it is when these possibilities become actualities that The Boys' behaviour (along with their delinquent activities) gives them the appearance of being different, radically different from the more controlled, routine elements of society.

It is now time to meet the lower-class culture model head on and inquire into its validity and utility in *this* case study. The poor are certainly different from the rich: they have less power, material possessions and life chances—this is not in question. What is in question is whether The Boys' style is due to these structural differences, or to their socialisation into a significantly different normative and cultural milieu, or to their lack of commitment to any standards at all. Are the traditional themes of an unskilled working-class neighbourhood transmitted from one generation to another, and does the adolescent's acting-out of the emphases of this milieu predispose him to appear 'deviant' to non-lower-class society? Given that smartness, toughness, the expectation of trouble and demand for excitement do appear important aspects of The Boys' style, several points seem pertinent.

Firstly the cultural-transmission model fails to differentiate between expectations and wishes as regards values and 'focal concerns'. I have already suggested that the parents and elders of Roundhouse, rather than emphasise the 'focal concerns' already identified, in fact aim to promote, through child-rearing practices, their children's respect for the rules and goals of the dominant ideology. They accept however that because life as it is, what they hope for their children and what they actually get, and the way they turn out, may be somewhat different.[21]

The Boys often view 'trouble' in the same way. 'Trouble' is more often than not something you get into through no fault of your own. It only needs 'one bloke with a nark on' and you may be in a fight before you know it. Most of The Boys, most of the time, prefer not to fight, but again what you hope for and what you have to expect are often different and there's a point when your face and dignity have to be defended. 'Trouble' with Authority is, as we shall see in the next chapter, a complex matter and again something The Boys come to expect simply because they are who they are, rather than because they've broken the law.

I am suggesting, therefore, that these emphases on certain behavioural themes are consequences or functions of The Boys' situation rather than traditional concerns that are simply transmitted to them.[22] Toughness and masculinity, for instance, are concerns of most men at all levels of society. The tendency for the down-town adolescent to express this concern through physical combat may well be related to his lack of control over resources and power to demonstrate it in other ways such as competitiveness, ruthlessness and other 'middle-class' modes.[23]

Likewise 'smartness', being quick, witty and articulate in an esoteric way, is as The Boys show hardly a prerogative of middle-class intellectuals. And at its extreme, 'smartness' which leads the down-town adolescent to view work sceptically and as a doubtful activity is not something he was taught in the cradle; it is something secondary school and his early work experience brought home to him. The Boys found out for themselves that butt-end jobs *are* bad news. The wages *are* 'crap'. Why should The Boys do the boss any favours? They have to wash his car and pack his soap for £12 a week. He can lay them off or sack them when he wants. Job satisfaction for The Boys is knowing you're being paid at the end of the week. They would 'clean toilets' if the price was right, but it rarely is, and their smartness and deviousness are needed if they are not to be exploited even more. Politicians, lawyers, advertisers can all be smart and devious and they get paid for it. The Boys get the sack.

Nor are the pathways to excitement—alcohol, marijuana, big spending—class-bound. The 'good bloke' who drinks, likes his women, gets stoned, can look after himself and is quick-witted is as much a middle-class man's hero as a working-class man's.[24] In fact going on the town is one of the few ways The Boys can expurgate the routine of the butt-end job and the limitations of hanging around. The action they become involved in, their glorification of immediate pleasures which prick the senses into motion, creates the better life and represents the world as a happier place. Being one of The Boys and going down-town matters. The good times matter. For with who else and where else would the down-town adolescent break out and switch on? He can't stay in the flat or stand on the Corner for ever, or play football in the dark. Facility-wise the pubs, with their drinking and socialising, are the only real leisure centres regularly and readily available.

Although the emphasis The Boys put on immediate gratification is a way out of and solution to the constrictions on them, including the lack of a place to go, it is more than this, it is a much greater demand. The Boys *aspire*, they aspire to be optimistic, to enjoy themselves, to be in control. Their style and their search for the good times provide the ingredients. Sometimes of course things don't turn out and unintended consequences ensue—the bread gets burnt. But this is life, and life is sometimes competitive; there is not always enough space and facility to accommodate everybody in the down-town world.

The lower-class culture model fails to allow for the universality of this search and so fails to see style as an adaptive response. Roundhouse is not a self-supporting and distinct cultural system. It has been viewed as an accommodation of the dominant normative system. Certainly the transmission of traditions and the continuation of 'focal concerns' are quite real. But this process is not only basic to any social entity, it is also a complex and partly functional response to structural constraints. For Roundhouse it is more the structural problems than the solutions that don't change. Further, even if we accept some degree of repetition and imitation in down-town adolescent behaviour, as Liebow points out:

> Many similarities between the lower class ... father and son (or mother and daughter) do not result from 'cultural transmission' but from the fact that the son goes out and independently experiences the same failures, in the same areas, and for much the same reasons as his father. What appears as a dynamic, self-sustaining cultural process is, in part at least, a relatively simple piece of social machinery which turns out, in rather mechanical fashion, independently produced look-alikes.[25]

Yet Liebow's deterministic pessimism is unnecessary in The Boys' case. They are not reproductions of the past. We have seen extensive evidence of their involvement in an on-going realignment and modification of solutions to their position in society, some of which are proscribed, others simply frowned upon. Adolescence itself, in whatever social class, is nearly always more radical, less compromised and routinised than the parental example. The Boys have a few years between leaving school and taking on family responsibilities. During this period they are answerable only to themselves and perhaps each other. Their search for manhood, their confrontation with inadequate jobs and prospects, their solutions to boredom and being skint are all part of the picture.[26] The good times provide some of the answers, and in their search for this ethos the styles portrayed by Roundhouse adolescents are full of innovatory energy. The Boys are the first adolescent group to use drugs socially, they had institutionalised a new pastime. The Tiddlers have introduced joyriding to the neighbourhood, and this is now being passed on to their juniors. There is less fighting by Roundhouse males, who no longer deem it necessary to have a scrap 'every time someone steps on your toes'. These changes have been created through decisions and choice by individuals and groups. We have heard arguments about the necessity of street fights, discussion about the utility of the catseyes business; these incidents and decisions are typical of the on-going process whereby transmissions from all parts of society are digested and if necessary transformed, whether they are the antics of a local folk hero or the effects of the motor car, pop culture or the post-war arrival and recent expansion of late-night drinking clubs.

The exuberance of the breakouts and the search for the good times must be seen as antithetically related to the not-so-good and the bad times. Life goes on. The good times are more than a luxury, however, they are a part of the whole, they are necessary, fundamental to carrying on. The Boys regard those who accept the bad deal, and never attempt to alleviate the situation meaningfully, as 'divvies'. The catseyes business was one such alleviation attempt. As a *coup de main* it finally failed; it was never intended as a *coup d'état*.

It is with this modified and more fluid view of the social processes involved in The Boys' style that we move back into the conflict. The centrepiece of this collision is the prosecution process—society's stock answer to a regular defiance of its rules. The mechanics of the prosecution, whilst they might seem unimportant to those who find the rules convenient, are of vital significance to The Boys. It is not the validity of the law that the down-town adolescent most often questions but the way the law is administered. The resentment he feels is yet another reason why his neighbourliness, politeness, fairness and honesty stop so abruptly at the edge of home territory.

Notes to this chapter are on pp 229–30

5 *The Authority Conspiracy*

The law's on the law's fuckin' side.

In their search for things they want Authority is the greatest barrier The Boys meet. Authority, as the on-the-spot representative of the structural constraints of society, limits their movement in diverse ways. This chapter is concerned with the outcome of The Boys' contact with the officials of the law and how they view this continuous encounter.

The student of deviance is now highly aware of the possible consequences of this encounter, emphasised in the recent switch towards viewing deviance as a transactional or processual phenomenon. In much of the recent literature the concern has been with the *transformation* of a person, or group, that may have committed a particular act, into a recognised deviant (secondary deviance). An important aspect of this transaction between accused and accuser is the possibility of amplification—that is making the accused more devious and deviant. So far studies supporting this amplification of deviance[1] have tended to deal with the more colourful, 'shocking' and therefore media-worthy forms of deviance, such as drug-taking, homosexuality and mental illness. Numerous studies have shown how these deviant acts are symbolically attached to individuals and groups, and how this attachment or labelling has consequences for the type-casted person's subsequent deviation.

157

To be able to substantiate the functioning of such a process as regards juvenile delinquency would, in a sense, be a satisfying achievement, in that it would fit in nicely with ideological perspectives held by many sociologists including myself. Identification of such a process would make possible profound statements about the futility of coercion, and the repressive nature of the capitalist state that gets the criminals it deserves. I mention this because I feel it important with such a study to point out that my apparent under-emphasis of the amplification process is based on empirical grounds. Thus from early in Year Two the 'identity problem' was brought home to me by a series of new experiences, such as being thrown out of department stores, stopped by the police, asked to leave pubs etc. If anything I was over-ready to spot any identity changes in The Boys related to the various persecution processes they regularly encountered; yet I have not been able to untangle satisfactorily any significance or lack of it. Though my own technique and personal ability may be faulty, there are 'scientific' methodological problems about measuring identity change which social scientists have not yet solved.

Even further difficulty arises from any perspective which predisposes a particular reaction from accused–accuser confrontations. The diversity of The Boys' reactions to social control leaves Taylor, Walton and Young's view as the most sound: 'The fact of social control is always problematic; it may deter some, it may also propel others into action to change the nature of control, or it may engender self-conceptions in those affected by social control in such a way that "amplification" does in fact occur . . . the effects of social control cannot be assumed to be determinate, but must be left open to study in individual cases.'[2]

My second point of caution is also related to methodology. Whilst this case study tends towards an 'appreciation' of The Boys' view, their view need not always be correct. Reasons for them may be seen as rationalisations by others and vice-versa. This chapter in particular is aimed at presenting The Boys'

view of Authority without much counter-discussion. Their un-
animity in viewing the prosecution process as unfair, unjust and
often conspiratorial is very important to understanding their
life style and its deviation from what society expects of them,
and I have represented it as best I can, trying to keep their
mood of cynicism alive. This means that the problems the police
and Courts face, whilst they receive some mention, are not fully
represented. If Authority comes off badly in this chapter this
should be seen as an indication of the kind of feedback from my
observation and participation with The Boys.[3] It is up to the
reader, in part at least, to put The Boys' view in some wider
perspective beyond the bounds of this case study.

The Police

For adolescents living down-town, 'outsiders' include most of
society. 'Them' include the 'aristocratics', the middle classes
who are 'stuck-up' and 'toffee-nose', and even those members
of the upwardly mobile working class who give the impression
that 'they think they're better than us'. As already suggested
'dissociation' is an apt description for the 'us' and 'them' relationship. Although I have argued that there is an important
dialogue between the area and the wider society which makes
explicit the 'correct' values, norms and attitudes one is supposed
to hold, this dialogue to a large extent takes place through formal agencies. Hence 'their' way usually comes over through the
schools, social services, probation services, employment services
and employers, police, Courts, the Institution and the media.

Although the residents of down-town areas have considerable
social contact with 'respectable' working-class families, they
have little informal contact with the middle classes since the
two sides move in different social space and territory. With this
link between the 'two societies' thus left to formal agencies, it is
the officials of these agencies that are burdened with the 'cor-
rective' donkey work. For The Boys these agencies are generally
seen as authoritarian and representing 'them', and at this level
dissociation changes to *alienation*.

Neither The Boys nor down-town residents in general would claim the police were unnecessary; on the contrary, down-town areas like every other neighbourhood demand police patrolling. Often residents expect extra policing to protect them from 'mugging' in one inner area and from 'football hooligans' in another. Many residents' associations have asked for more foot patrols to reduce vandalism. The necessity of Authority is thus not in question by either side.

What is constantly in question is the behaviour of the officials who represent Authority. The Boys don't have one special term for 'them'; they use a series of terms, mostly derogatory, which when analysed can be placed under the umbrella term Authority. Authority includes anyone who has the ability to impose rules from the outside and most especially anyone involved in the prosecution process; officials directly connected with the administration of the law make up the most important part of Authority.

Authority for The Boys has strong connections with conspiracy. Their dislike and distrust of it are centred round an embittered and perhaps occasionally exaggerated sense of injustice. This injustice is argued at several levels, for instance whilst middle-class outsiders break rules and generally get away with it, Authority officials break the rules continuously and get away with it. The fact that so many respectable and influential outsiders are so naïve as to refuse to believe that the policeman has two distinct sides to him is a prime source of irritation. 'A lot of people think coppers are all right ['Who, like?']. People from posh areas and that, doing a good job and that, but round here they're not doing nothing, just smacking people up and trying to cause trouble.' (*Bone.*)

Bone might also have said something like this when he was only nine or ten. He would have heard older kids say things about policemen and imitated their style. Today he has his own authentic examples. 'His knowledge of local history supplies him with an initial set of incidents on which he may subsequently build a memory file that collects injustices.'[4] Before

elaborating on how this sense of injustice operates, one particular point should be made. Although The Boys will always
discredit Authority in general, they do at the same time make
distinctions between and assessments of individual officials.
There are some fair policemen. Joey helped a police sergeant
pull an old lady out of her burning flat: 'He was a good bloke
and really cut up that she was dead and living all alone and
that.' Jimbo had made friends with his guardian during a
weekend remand pending a court appearance. 'He was all
right. He gave me a few ciggies and some comics and mags to
read. When me old lady brought some grub I shared it out with
him and a couple of plonkies.'

All officials will receive individual assessment if they seem to
affect the prosecution process. Thus 'judges' (magistrates)
range from 'At least he listens to your side of the story' to 'If
you get her you've had it, she enjoys sticking people down.'[5]

In a sense it is because The Boys and down-town adolescents
generally know officials can be friendly and reasonable that
they find the more usual 'objectifying' or degrading approach
they most often receive so distasteful. The best that is usually
said of policemen is that 'One minute they're talking to you all
right, then the next time they're slagging you.' The feeling
amongst all The Boys is that the police refuse to treat them with
any respect whether they're 'up to no good' or simply walking
around.

> *Murky*   If you're coming back to the Block after being at the club it's
> odds on you'll get stopped.
> *Danny*   Remember the other week, we was walking back up Derby
> Road and that copper stopped us? We was all walking up when he
> swings over and drives up the wrong way. He called for assistance,
> then got out and started acting hard. A jeep comes up as well and
> they all got out and searched us, then they slagged us and sent us on
> our way. There's no need for it, slagging blokes for no reason.

'Slagging', 'bringing down', hurts The Boys' pride. To be
called 'dirt' and 'yobs' pierces their identity, especially when
they can't answer back without adverse consequences. As

L

Woodsey has learnt, 'You can't answer them back, you can't have *your* say without them saying shut it and giving you a smack.' So often are The Boys stopped, questioned and searched that the procedure, which would aggravate many other citizens, does not unduly upset them. Being under methodical suspicion is simply routine. An ordinary stop is hardly worth a mention; it is when the policeman steps outside his rights that the injustice is felt. The persecution of 'well-known faces' is greatly resented. 'Ever since Tuck's come out [of borstal] he gets stopped for just standing on the Corner, anywhere, and they come up and say, "What have you been up to today Tucker?" ' (*Streak*.) 'You can just be walking down-town with millions of shoppers and they'll still stop *you*. If they know your face you're fucked. If they know you've done a bit of robbing and they don't like your face, that's it.' (*Arno*.)

When 'straight' lads are stopped and the police 'try it on' resentment is particularly strong. Mocky and Murky, generally law-abiding young men, came on to the Corner (end Year Three) outraged. They had been to buy some football boot-laces ready for the afternoon's match.

> *Mocky*   They're fuckin' cunts, those jacks. I fuckin' hate coppers. They've just tried to do us for robbing some fuckin' sword or some-thing. Murky and me were walking up the hill. Up they screeched, pulls us into the back of the car and start acting hard.
> *Murky*   We was dressed like this, no coats on or nothing [to hide things under], and they says, no one of them says to the other, what have they got there? There was this sword in the back by us. A hard-faced feller he was, starts trying it on, trying to make out we'd robbed it. The other copper says, oh, it must be off the other beat and says, 'You didn't put it there did you boys?' They let us out then but they was trying it on, seeing if they could get us for something like.

At the beginning of Year Three a week rarely went by when The Boys didn't have a tale like this. Most of the research done about police work is American, but in many ways the face-to-face contact between police officers and juveniles seems to be based on the same cues in both societies, as two recent British studies tentatively suggest.[6, 7] According to Piliavin and Briar important police cues involved in the stopping and possible arrest of juveniles include the way the youth looks and carries himself, his manner on questioning and his group affiliations. But, '. . . it is not unlikely that frequent encounters with the police, particularly those involving youths innocent of wrong doing, will increase the hostility of these juveniles toward law-enforcement personnel.'[8]

The policeman, then, because he rarely actually witnesses crimes starts his investigations by using cues which have shown to pay off in the past. The down-town adolescent thus suffers the fate of being under methodical suspicion. The policeman involved in this type of down-town patrolling must not only endure an isolation from his public but encounters the continuous look of hatred and senses an element of danger to his personal safety. To counteract such feeling he learns to put on a front. This front is articulated by the size and demeanour of the officer, his fast car, the inevitable jeep, the truncheon, the alsatian dog. However, when it comes to face-to-face work with the 'bad boy', more intimate cues are utilised. The youth is made to realise, 'You'll get no change from us, sonny.' There must be no cracks or chinks in the armour when youths are apprehended. These yobs must realise who really rules the roost.[9]

The Boys encounter this front in the 'arresting' policemen, who are noted for their attempts to intimidate and imply strength. A pub conversation one night (mid Year Three) saw a pooling of such experiences, many of which I remembered from their original source.

> *Les* They made us sit on the floor of the jeep, one feller, that red headed one, he puts his foot on me back like. Not hard, not a dig like, but just to scare me.
> *Joey* It was like that when we got caught, the coppers trying to scare you. This cunt was like that, pushing his glove down dead tight [on his hand, emphasising the fist action]. I felt like turning round and saying if you're going to fuckin' dig me, go on then, dig me.

Although it is the suggestion or threat of physical force which is employed most often by the police to try and put fear into their suspects, The Boys know that it doesn't always stop at that. Most of The Boys apply commonsense rules to avoid getting 'pulled in' or, if already arrested, being beaten up by the police. Firstly you should never try and make a getaway unless you're sure of escaping. If you do run for it to avoid arrest or questioning and you are caught, 'They can knock fuck out of you and get away with it, saying you was resisting arrest and they had to use force to restrain you.' (*Holly.*) These rules are derived from concrete examples passed on in the conversation culture and stored in the memory file. A second rule of thumb involves the expediency of answering questions straight. If you try and be clever and 'shoot your mouth off' with the police, you'll probably 'get a dig'. Pablo and Dave passed on this point after they were arrested on a drunk and disorderly charge (end of Year Two), and taken to the station.

> They asked Dave where he lived and he said in Roundhouse, and just for nothing this copper went fuck off [imitates punching action] and punched him right against the radiator. [It was not regarded as an adequate reply. Dave later claimed he was not trying to be clever.] My fuckin' heart went boom, boom, I fuckin' shit myself. Then they put him in a cell. This copper that had digged him says to the sergeant that Dave had been shooting his mouth off like, you know lies, and the sergeant was writing it all down. And when I was going to the cell this other copper gives me a ciggy and matches to have a smoke like, he was all right like, he could see I was shitting meself. (T.)

As said above, it is the fact that the police themselves break the rules that makes the sense of injustice so profound. The Boys do not deny they steal or that there's such a thing as a 'fair cop' in the sense of being caught red-handed: that is an occupational hazard in the given rules. But The Boys demand scrupulous fairness. Streak was actually caught in a car unscrewing a radio bracket (end Year Three):

> I looked up and saw the side of the jeep, I knew that was it like, so I just sat there and said nothing. This copper said, 'You know you're copped lad, in the back.' I got in like, and this other feller went 'whack' and gave me a beaut right across the ear. He said, 'Leave other people's property alone.' That was fair enough like. What got me was in Court

they told all lies. They was saying when patrol so and so was proceeding down some street it saw the accused booting in the window of the car. Well that was lies 'coz I used a punch to open the side window. Then they said I tried to make off which I never, I just sat there. They tell all sorts of lies.

If The Boys are being punished for rule-breaking their accusers must be without blemish, or else their authority is negated. Thus Fatch was incensed about a loitering charge that was 'stuck on him' for 'fuck all'. Fatch admits he was pipe-ing cars but he thinks 'there's no law against that' since he was only looking for interest and had no intentions of screwing a car.

I hadn't done nothing I was just walking around like, but these plainclothes busies, they pulled me in. They made up all sorts of lies in the station and said I was trying door handles and that. But they give themselves away. They kept saying, 'Plead guilty, plead guilty.' You'd have thought I was up for murder. They gave it away doing that, they had nothing on me so they made it up. [This charge was finally dropped.]

The police operate in increasingly devious ways. They cannot stand the frustrations of missing the chance to charge somebody they '*know*' is a car-radio thief (ie, a reputed thief or suspected person) even if not at the particular moment they observe him. They will tend to move over-quickly and without adequate evidence to the situation where they feel they can prosecute a suspicious person as a suspected person loitering with intent to commit a felony.

Completely false arrests are used by the conversation culture to back up stories of how inaccurate and malicious the police really are, and The Boys make a meal of such affairs. One particular case I witnessed involved about ten of us standing on the Corner one Saturday afternoon. Saturday shoppers park their cars all over the area till it becomes hard to cross the road. The Boys were standing in their usual spot, a few of them leaning on a parked car. What turned out to be two plainclothes policemen walked up the road and stood opposite. They were soon recognised as policemen, and Colly decided he was

not going to wait to pass the time of day with them. He suggested we all go for a cup of tea. Just as we moved away the
policemen came over and stopped Joey and Emo. The rest of us
stood back watching, no one wanting to get involved and expecting nothing to come of the incident anyway. However, Joey
and Emo were 'pulled in' and later charged with loitering with
intent. At the Court case, one of the arresting policemen gave
his evidence in such a way as to deny the presence of a large
social gathering at all, so although he did not lie at this point
his evidence suggested the 'two accused' were on their own—
and thus it was implied they were loitering with intent. It was
also claimed that the car in question was rocked to test if it had
an alarm, which again was inaccurate. The only completely
false piece of evidence involved 'the accused trying the door
handles'. The case was dismissed, the police perjury ignored and
Joey with great indignation gave the policeman involved 'a
beaut look, must have made him feel a right cunt'. Joey also
went to try and collect his 'dabs' (finger prints) and have them
destroyed. Joey is smart.

Mal was also subject of a false arrest, but was less fortunate at
his Court appearance. In fact as a juvenile Mal had no right of
defence or a chance to call witnesses. There was never any
suggestion throughout the hearing that the police had been incorrect in their apprehension. Mal had appeared before the
Juvenile Panel only the week before on a theft charge which he
had admitted, so this phony arrest coming so quickly afterwards saw him placed under the supervision of a probation
officer. A stolen car had been left in the area close to Mal's
house. Mal and Joey were standing by the car looking into it.
As they were doing so a police car came round the corner, and
the two boys ran for it. Mal, who was well known to the police
at that time, was recognised, his blond hair and brightly
coloured pullover giving him away. He was 'called for' and
taken to the police station. His mother on hearing the evidence
of bystanders went down to the station to protest: 'They said
they saw him with his head inside the car window and he ran

away. I said that doesn't mean he took it. This policeman said that's good enough for us, he sticks out like a sore thumb.'

Fosser's older brother Al finds living in an area whose adolescents are under methodical suspicion hard to cope with. Al is a confessed innocent; he never robs, he simply 'hasn't got the nerve' in his own words. Al's peers accept his style and in a way admire him for his honest individuality. Al however looks like everybody else, his appearance, style of dress and associates all fit the policeman's 'bad boy' stereotype. So because Al happened to be nearest to the broken window of a local car-accessories shop he was charged with burglary. He was arrested by a 'young constable' who gave him 'a real smack' and took him to the station. This was not the first time Al had been charged with an offence he didn't commit, and as he puts it 'it won't be the last'. He takes his harassment fairly philosophically. He is a passive person anyway and comes from a 'criminal' family which is used to 'putting up' with the police. If anything it is his friends who make the most fuss about his unjust treatment.

Many 'stories' included in The Boys' memory file are difficult to swallow, some are undoubtedly exaggerated over time, others are simply not true. However, the majority of The Boys are aware of the dangers of exaggeration and how 'rumours get made up', and in fact take pains not to exaggerate but to discredit the fairy story and those who are always telling 'mince pies'. The incidents included here I believe to be accurate. They are all incidents I have witnessed, or just missed and heard on-the-spot accounts of, or they are incidents that have been repeated by various independent parties shortly after their execution and before serious distortions of time have crept in.

Probably the most difficult area of adolescent–police encounters to assess is what goes on during the 'bargaining period' in the police station immediately after arrest. Obviously more often than not the arrest procedure is simple, routine and bureaucratic, with the adolescent admitting guilt and being prosecuted or simply cautioned. Quite often the police will admit a mistake and release their suspects. However, there seems to be a fairly distinct line between the good boy and the bad boy and most of The Boys are now seen as bad boys.[10] The younger adolescents probably receive a more lenient treatment as they are more likely to be judged good boys. Mickey for instance was 'arrested' by a security guard in a nearby carpark (mid Year Two) and when taken to the police station could have been charged with attempted theft.

> They took my shoes off, took my kecks off and left me for ages. Then they gave me me kecks back but kept me shoes. They said, 'We've found glass [from the broken car window supposedly] in your shoes, and the security guard will say he saw you, so you might as well plead guilty.' Then they wanted to know who the others were. I wasn't saying, so then they said that if I told them, like, they'd let me off, my parents could come and get me, and I'd only have to see the JLO. If I didn't tell them they said they'd take me to court and charge me with theft. I was shitting myself but I didn't say and in the end they let me off anyway. (T.)

Youngsters from the area whose faces aren't known and who don't have criminal records so becoming 'reputed thieves' are often treated in this way; indeed juvenile offenders have a 50 per cent chance of only receiving a caution for a minor first offence. The bad boys, those who have criminal records or associate with those with criminal records, etc, are treated much more harshly. Hence Jimbo, whose case with Colly eventually saw him acquitted, was kept in the local police station all Friday night and remanded in custody over the weekend. 'They'd got nothing on me and they knew it, but they reckoned just 'coz I was a robber they could get me on anything they liked.'

Fosser actually received a Detention Centre spell on what he claims was a 'load of lies' by the police. He admits he was pipe-ing cars for radios and that if he'd seen 'a cert' he would have tried to steal it. However, he and his accomplices had got no further than trying a door handle when he was picked up by two Task Force detectives. 'They said we'd unscrewed this radio and that they could have the marks on the screws tested to show they had been made by my pliers [they were carrying a pair]. I said to this copper, "You know and I know we didn't unscrew that radio," and he says, "Yes sonny, but who's going to believe you?" ' The charge these two should have received was loitering. Instead they were charged with a more serious offence—attempted theft. This 'negotiation of reality' by the police has been noted elsewhere as 'not due to the policemen's machiavellianism but rather to their desire, in the name of administrative efficiency, to jump the gap between what I will term theoretical and empirical guilt'.[11]

The period the adolescent spends in the police station before a charge is formally made is a critical one. It can involve bargaining about naming accomplices and admitting other offences for a lesser charge, and it can determine whether the police ask for custodial remand or accept bail.[12] The Boys will sometimes collaborate with the police by pleading guilty on a lesser offence which is acceptable to both sides. They usually do this when they expect to be found guilty anyway. Pleading guilty also means you can get it over quickly, that the police won't get at you and that you can perhaps avoid a remand in custody. Arno pleaded guilty to loitering with intent in November in order to get the case over by Christmas rather than wait until legal aid had been sorted out which would have meant the case hanging over till the New Year.

The Meaning of Court

Leaving the arrest situation, we move with The Boys further along the prosecution process towards the theatricals of the Courtroom. The police of course reappear to read their lines, but they are only one link in the conspiracy chain. In the Court they link hands with other outsiders to act out further injustice and mystification of reality before The Boys' eyes. I had aimed, over Years Two and Three, to attend every Court case directly involving The Boys. This was not possible and I attended about thirty of an approximate forty cases. (Usually two or more of the network appeared on the same charge.) I always attempted to get the individual's interpretation of the hearing even if I missed the session. By attending Court proceedings, walking home with The Boys involved if they were not remanded in custody, and listening to their versions of the proceedings I too had attended, I was able to gain some understanding of how they viewed the prosecution process. I could check for distortion in their recollections for the memory file and watch for general and recurring themes in the conversation culture.

Sociologists have used a dramaturgical analysis of the Court with considerable effect. Such an analysis is particularly fitting in this case study, as The Boys themselves use several theatrical terms to describe the prosecution process. To them the pomp and rigidity of nineteenth-century justice, still retained in to-day's Court, would be farcical were it not so powerful. As we unravel their view of this crucial part of the prosecution process one thing should be made explicit. The Court's kadi, the judge or the magistrate, is trying to assess the accused's moral character. Despite whatever else is meant to be happening the whole process is seen by The Boys as an attack or denunciation of the accused's character by the prosecutors, with the defence making a pitch in favour of his honesty, self-discipline, genuine remorse or whatever particular personality trait could help-fully be emphasised at that moment.[13]

The Boys' part in the drama is usually a small one; often it is a non-speaking part, seldom is it eloquent. The more important actors will often proceed without even looking to the dock or acknowledging the accused's presence. The Boys thus continue to feel powerless and are even less willing to speak out than when arrested, believing that any attempt to do so will be taken by the bench as disrespect and aggression. This may well be the case since the whole ethos of the Courtroom is aimed at in-timidation, with the procedure quietly emphasising—you may not be guilty this time, but you're one of them, you look and speak like one of them and you'd better respect this Court and take home your experience as a warning. This attitude beams out of Court officials right down to the way the man on the door treats any 'public' who come to listen to the case and look like an ally of 'one of them' in the dock. I suffered this 'slagging' on several occasions because I was seen as one of 'them', scruffy yobs who'd nothing better to do than come and sit in the Courtroom. Like relations and uninvolved members of the network who came to particular Court cases, I was often upset at the ill-mannered and degrading attitude of, to quote Tommy's mother and sum up my own sentiments, 'that ol' bastard on the door who thinks he's fuckin' god almighty'. The Boys themselves accept this treatment, especially if they are in the dock.

> *Arno's father* Why didn't you speak up about them keeping you in nick all weekend and tell them you didn't do it?
>
> *Arno* I pleaded not guilty didn't I? It's no good shooting your mouth off. That does no fuckin' good. They'd only have kept me in till February 15th then (date of hearing proper).

The Court expects everything to be said in a highly formal and over-articulate way. The Boys' linguistic style does not fit into this nineteenth-century Queen's-English extravaganza; such theatricals are left to the paid actors. Hence on the few occasions when The Boys speak their words are likely to be dissected by one of the 'stars' and tested for grammatical correctness.

> *Prosecution counsel* When you say you didn't say nothing, do you mean you didn't say anything or you did say something?

Another form of denunciation and intimidation employed by the Court is what Fatch calls the 'stand up, sit down, say ninety-nine' procedure. The accused must act as if he's feeling accused, he must actually be intimidated. Hence right from the first 'all rise' the spotlight is on.

> *Magistrate* Are you chewing?
>
> *Fosser* Yes, sir.
>
> *Magistrate* Well get rid of it. This is a Courtroom not a coffee bar and stand up properly both of you.

Intimidation and denunciation is just as venomous after sentence. Streak recalled accurately how he had been brought down: 'This clerk of the court feller, you know the one that sits near the judge. He says have you got £20 to pay the fine and I says no. Then he says why not! Why fuckin' not, I ask you, why fuckin' not. Honest to God. He wouldn't fuckin' know why not, the silly old cunt. I should have gone . . . that's why not.' Such explicit incidents are less common forms of degradation than the on-going distortion and mystification of reality performed by the key-jangling, wigged, gowned, order-shouting and board-carrying officials. The continuous refusal of the paid actors to refer to the accused whose fate they are deciding further convinces The Boys that a plot is afoot.

> You can't even hear what they're saying half the time.
> What right have they got to talk about your home life?
> He says, 'I think we know what sort of an area we're talking about your 'onour. 'It's a friendlier place than where he fuckin' lives.
> It's a jungle out there. Twice he said it. I felt like saying well give us a banana then, Tarzan-face.

The scene is often re-enacted after the hearing, as The Boys try to regain their dignity. In the pub a Courtroom sketch brings relief.

> I have heard all the evidence and I find you guilty and sentence you to ten years' imprisonment.
> But yer 'onour, it was only a parkin' offence.
> Silence, make that life for insolence.
> Next case.
> Yer 'onour, on the fifth of the fifth at five I apprehended the accused breathing heavily outside the 'Tatler' [shows uncensored films].
> There is no excuse for this sort of behaviour, hang him.

The whole atmosphere of the Courtroom suggests to The Boys that it is a put-up job, a 'show' more concerned with bringing you down and punishing than with implementing fairness and justice. This does not of course mean that they are not intimidated. Indeed at the time they will admit fear to their own side, though do their utmost to keep face with 'them'. 'Me legs were like jelly. This jack in the dock he looked at me shaking like. I was trying to keep cool like so I didn't feel a cunt, but he knew I was shitting myself, the bastard.' (*Tuck.*)

To understand further how The Boys comprehend Court and its meaning it is necessary to discuss their view of the individual actors that come together to link hands in the conspiracy.

Probation officers and social workers because of their part in the prosecution are also classed as Authority.[14] Probation officers, The Boys presume, have power to sway the Court. The good officer should always speak up for you, the bad one will recommend borstal. While there is a general distrust of officers the discrimination between 'he's OK' and 'he's a bastard' is again made. An intrinsic disadvantage for the probation officer is that he is seen as a part-time plainclothes policeman, particularly if he takes his role conscientiously and calls to see his 'client' regularly. 'I always used to go down to his office to see him at four o'clock. Our kid [brother] said don't have him coming to the house and snooping around. You don't want them nosing around like, they're all the same—if they clocked [saw] a bit of gear [stolen] they'd blow the whistle wouldn't they?' (*Herbie.*)

Since 1969 social workers have also been expected to take part in the prosecution process, which has led to some confusion on both sides. For the early adolescents the social worker who used to bring Christmas presents and details of extra financial allowances now also brings trouble in the form of a supervision order. Thus even the most well-intentioned social worker can be rejected. Tank was extremely disillusioned to find that the social worker who had always helped out with his rather chaotic family circumstances had finally recommended him for a period of detention. The social worker had in fact not denounced Tank but made a fairly subtle 'pitch' for him because, as he put it, 'He was odds-on for borstal. I recommended Detention Centre because it was only three months. I would have been laughed out of Court if I'd got up again and said he was a good lad. If I'd rubbed old . . . [the magistrate] up the wrong way he might well have used borstal. As it was we probably got off lightly

with three months' DC.' Tank didn't see it like that. His
reaction later when I visited him was, 'He just wanted to get
rid of me so he didn't have as much work to do.'

To The Boys the most subtle help they might receive from a
social worker is not fully comprehended since neither they nor
the officers manage to break down their role barriers and explain how it really is to each other. A social worker or probation
officer is only regarded as a good bloke if he makes an obviously
successful pitch on his client's behalf. Hence Colly's PO was
OK because the magistrate, in handing out a relatively lenient
£20 fine, said, 'It was only your reports that saved you. Mr
White obviously has more faith in you than I do. I hope that
you won't let him down. This is your very last chance. You
know what to expect if you appear before us again on a charge
of this nature.'

Another group of actors not to be trusted are the solicitors—
lawyers. The Boys, certainly after their first offence, are nearly
always allowed legal aid, because their charges are indictable
and usually regarded as fairly serious. To the down-town
adolescent these distant, formal, often wigged-and-gowned
outsiders are not seen as likely allies. It is believed that defence
lawyers are in league with their prosecution mates and the
prosecutors in general are in league with the judge. Solicitors
are not seen to be fully professional. Jimbo and Colly, for instance, were interviewed by two representatives of the solicitor's
firm defending their case. As we left the offices to walk back
home they discussed their interviews.

Jimbo   I nearly slipped up once. He asked me why I was walking down
with you that morning.
Colly   What did you say?
Jimbo   Oh, er, I said, I was going to the shops and just met you on the
way.
Colly   Oh that's all right, that's what I said.
Self   Don't you trust them? They're meant to be defending you,
they've got to keep what you say in confidence.
Jimbo   You can't trust those fellers. Some of them are OK like, but
if you say you did it, like, they tell their mates who are prosecuting

you, or they tell the judge and you get done for it. It's always best to keep to the same story, then you don't slip up.

Thus on two levels The Boys tend to provide false information to their defence counsel. On one level they simply don't trust their gowned, wigged and unlikely ally. On another they find it more economical to keep to one story of what happened from the beginning to the end of the whole affair. Hence everybody involved in the bureaucratic prosecution process is told the same story. At times The Boys hardly distinguish between the truth and their defence story themselves, so that in a pub conversation they may actually find themselves practising their story of innocence to people that know better.

The Boys and The Ritz thus sense a fundamental incompetence about the Court actors. They think the defence counsels are particularly inept. Some lawyers only straighten out 'the facts' a couple of minutes before the hearing and give the impression during actual Court proceedings that even those two minutes were void of meaning.[15] Fatch sensed this incompetence in his most recent appearance, which cost him £50. 'The lawyer feller didn't give a fuck, he got half of what I told him wrong, and the other, prosecuting he'd got it all learned off by heart and made a right cunt out of the bloke defending me.'

The magistrate (or judge in the Crown Court) is the master link in the conspiracy chain. In the end it is the kadi who seems to judge the meaningfulness of the other actors' lines. The Boys are manifestly aware of this and whilst they make their own individual judgements also about the scruples and sensitivities of the individual member of the bench, they tend to distrust the kadi *per se*. Obviously any of us will dislike someone that has immense power over our very freedom and this simple hatred is to be expected. However, in their more philosophical moments some of The Boys at least are more discriminating. Magistrates, they argue, are middle-class and middle-aged and basically they simply don't know the score about the traditions, life style and pressures for down-town adolescents. Thus whilst there are some real bastards on the bench there are also fairly well-meaning, old men, who, whilst they probably aren't megalo-maniacs, act harshly because they are shocked by what the police tell them. 'They don't understand about the police telling lies and twisting things, they've made their mind up before they start.' (*Danny*.)

For the persistent offenders or those boys who feel they have been unfairly treated the explanations are explicit and dog-matic. 'I don't even like judges 'coz I think the law is on the law's fuckin' side. You know when you're in Court the way the judge listens to you it's just going in one ear and out of the other with him. But when a copper's talking he's taking it all in. He's all for the fuckin' copper.' (*Emo*.)

Fosser appeared in Court for a remand hearing in which the police requested custody. With a black eye and a cut lip ob-tained whilst being 'arrested' by two police officers, Fosser sensed the same stone wall. 'The judge said to me, have you got anything to say that could give you bail? As if he'd take any notice. He just said that because he had to, he didn't even let me finish talking, he just said I'm sorry you must remain in custody.' (Nor was Fosser informed of his right to appeal to a judge against the custodial remand and how to ask for legal aid.)

In short, then, The Boys like most 'delinquent' down-town adolescents do not accept the prosecution process as fair. They recognise there is an inbuilt bias in the Authority officials against 'our kind' and this to some extent negates the authority and meaningfulness of the prosecution. The mystification of 'how it really is' that is carried out in the Court further alienates the adolescent and obliges him to become a passive prisoner carried along by the bureaucratic procedures. For the regulars to the Court, however, there was a definite de-mystification and de-coding of the stage-craft over years Two and Three. This increased awareness did not mean very much in terms of power or freedom for the seriality however. If anything the regulars, such as Fosser, Tank, Tuck, Colly, Jimbo and Arno, realised how predictable their conviction was once they had been apprehended and the prosecution begun. A more sophisticated appreciation of verdict became part of the conversation culture. One's fate would be predicted with some accuracy. Probation officers, for instance, would make out social reports before their clients were found guilty with an air of inevitability which The Boys sensed. Yet rather than object to this pre-judgement of their guilt The Boys use it as a guide to the outcome of their prosecution. 'He [Probation Officer] says you don't have to have this report done now, but if you're found guilty it might help you get the case over quickly. He reckons I'll get a fine.' (*Bone.*)

Another cue sometimes used by The Boys involves the payment of fines. Many of them have fines long overdue. If just before a 'serious' Court appearance a demand letter for fines to be paid is received, this is taken as an omen for the worst. Fosser received one. 'I reckon this means I'm going to get stuck down and they're trying to get that fifty quid before I go. Well they've got no fuckin' chance.' (I have been unable to substantiate the validity of this particular cue.)

To some extent the increased awareness of how the prosecution process works has helped the regulars take a small amount of evasive action. For instance it is wise when appearing before a magistrate to have just got a job: since the bench is usually aware of the employment difficulties of adolescents and feels some guilt about the situation, it brings some possibility of 'mercy'. There are always a few butt-end jobs vacant because of the boring, dirty nature of the work and its bad pay and consequently high labour turnover. A 'favourite' job taken by The Boys is skinning and bleeding cows at a city abattoir. If a boy is in work, defence counsel can then pitch for leniency for a youngster also in hard times who has at last been able to settle down since his unfortunate escapade several weeks ago. Perhaps another chance, a small fine? Once in regular employment this line of defence disappears. 'If you get caught screwing cars when you're working you've got no chance. The judge will just say you're a bad man, you're greedy.' (*Murky.*)

M

Year Three, with its drying-up of the opportunities to make a good living from the catseye business without loss of freedom to the Institution, saw many of The Boys looking for employment, mainly with a local workshop. This change in direction had the added effect of making a Court appearance for stealing for 'greed' that much more unsavoury. By mid Year Three the network had come to realise just how powerful Authority could be and how leniency and 'another chance' disappeared with each prosecution.

The powerlessness of the accused to have his say ensures the persecution will come off smoothly. The memory file reminds the down-towner of the fate of those who tried. Moses (a double pseudonym for one of The Boys) was seen as a nutter by his peers for having his say. Whilst his stand was admired it was regarded as futile martyrdom which led to inevitable consequences. Moses was accused of assaulting two policemen. Although the whole affair is nothing out of the ordinary it is worth mentioning a few aspects. The 'fight' Moses had with the police caused a great deal of ill-feeling in the area. Basically, Des, Fatch and Moses had been walking around at about 1 am in the morning, nothing unusual for them. They had stopped outside a disused shop which had long since been boarded up. Moses, swinging over the doorway, had taken a few kicks at the door, presumably to try and get inside. He was not in fact quite sure why he wanted to get inside as he knew the shop was empty. However, before he had to face that decision two policemen came running across the road from their jeep which had been concealed in the darkness of a nearby forecourt. The Boys scattered and ran for safety. Moses was eventually cornered in the back yards of some maisonettes near the Block. A fight followed which, according to locals watching from bedroom windows, lasted about five minutes. Moses, well known for his fighting ability, was resisting arrest and shouting comments such as 'throw us a hatchet someone'. However, most accounts, or rather all accounts except the two policemen's, claim Moses wasn't really arrested but beaten up. 'They had him over the railings, hurting his back like and punching and kicking him.'

Moses was 'dragged across the road', 'by the hair', and when police reinforcements arrived a police dog was set loose, some ten minutes after the fracas started. All accounts from eye-witnesses both before and at the trial suggested that both sides had behaved badly and without restraint. Locally of course Moses was not blamed for resisting arrest, but praised for resist-ing his beating so ably. The two-day Crown Court hearing, in my *opinion*, because of the mountains of conflicting evidence should have led to an acquittal. Moses, however, was found guilty of assaulting two policemen and sent to borstal. The decision was, I *believe*, based on a different kind of evidence— that of Moses' attitude and approach to the proceedings. His attitude was then (mid Year Two), as it still is, highly anti-Authority. He believes the police 'cause half the crime them-selves' and that judges 'enjoy sticking people inside'. Thus when asked why he ran away from the police if he was not in-tending to break the law, he said: 'What difference does that make? They'd have dragged me in anyway.' 'Dragged in?' asked the prosecution. 'Yes, they don't care if you're guilty or not that lot.'

(Later.)

> *Prosecution* Do you usually walk around the streets at this time of night?
> *Moses* Yes, nearly every night.

(Later.)

> *Defence* Don't you think it rather foolish to run away if you've not done anything wrong?
> *Moses* That doesn't matter. I ran to safety, far away from the men in blue as I could get.

(Later.)

> *Prosecution* Had you been drinking that evening? Then why were you unsteady on your feet when the doctor examined you at the station?
> *Moses* Wouldn't you be unsteady on your feet if you'd just been beaten up?

(Later.)

> *Defence* What was happening to you when you were over this fence, how did you get there?
> *Moses* I was scratching my back with the aid of those two constables.
> *Judge* You realise your attitude is not helping your case.

Moses went to borstal 'for some proper supervision and discipline'. He had a 'chip on his shoulder' and needed to learn 'more respect for Authority'. Moses called the judge 'an ol' bastard' and disappeared for nearly a year. His defence counsel was convinced 'he sent himself away': he made the deadly mistake of attacking the Court's officials.[16]

In summary, Court for The Boys means trouble. Court is part of the Authority Conspiracy where 'they' come together, holding all the trump cards. Court is where the police change their style from the street corner slagging to a subtle word game with the other actors to create a more potent and mysterious degradation. Court is where the 'truth' is fornicated so that 'their side' is over-emphasised through 'lies' and 'twisting things'. Court is where a whole collection of middle-class officials can say what they want about you and you can't do anything about it. Court is a circus which leads to the zoo.

When Authority Becomes Power

There are two sides if you're a down-town adolescent, your lot and theirs. Their ideas about what's right and wrong aren't always yours. The conflict of interests between many adolescents from the area and Authority is an open contest, a cold war which sometimes becomes a guerrilla war. The polarisation of interests is in fact exaggerated by structural factors quite beyond the control of the grassroots actors on both sides. The State demands, the public demands, the police do their best more often than not, but their action leads to almost inevitable unintended consequences and animadversion from some quarter.

Policing strategy in the form of the unit beat policeman has not been workable in the Inner City. The original concept has been diluted or actually rejected in favour of the 'three-shift' system. The Roundhouse area on paper has a 'neighbourhood copper', but in practice is mainly policed by three shifts, morning, afternoon and night, of outside officers. In terms of community relations such a system has distinct disadvantages. To the neighbourhood concerned, and particularly its youth who spend so much time on the streets, the three-shift system gives the impression that large numbers of anonymous and potentially troublesome strangers are patrolling the area in strength at all times. The chances of a positive relationship developing between the police and locals is even more remote than with unit beat.

The police officers for their part are also unlikely to develop any sense of loyalty or attachment to 'their' neighbourhood. The introduction of a nominal 'neighbourhood copper' into the area is in practice little more than a public relations set-up to try and smooth over some of the basic antagonism. Consequently a local paper's front-page story of a community-relations success, showing two friendly bobbies and a few smiling Roundhouse infants, was published the same week as the police station was pelted with stones. The 'friendly' neighbourhood copper had thought it tactful to say in the report that 'the people seem to have taken to me, especially the kids'. The officer was doing his best. Younger, less embittered kids will certainly take to the person behind this uniform, especially when he's not in it and helps organise a day out to the seaside. But, in uniform on the beat, the personality disappears behind the front, and the copper can no longer be a friendly 'good bloke' social worker. His training, his style, his job requirements, will not allow it. If people break his rules he will become an Authority figure. A conversation in 'The Cockle' one night involving The Ritz was not really a good advertisement for the neighbourhood copper. Woodsey had been told off for using bad language and concluded 'he's not so friendly anyway'.

Boon   He's just there to suck'ole the kids, to pump them about who's
got stolen gear and that.

Bone   You can't tell me he won't pull someone if he clocks them with
a catseye or something. He'll run them in, the same as all the other
cunts. He's nothing special.

The officer picked to be the neighbourhood copper in a
'delinquent' area is in a conflict situation. However tactful and
skilful, he is doomed to considerable failure. His role involves
conflicting demands, and each action leads to an unintended
consequence in terms of someone's interpretation of his action.
If he is lenient he is soft, if he sticks to the rules he's just like the
rest, if he breaks the rules he might as well give up. The only
pressure that is not so intense for the neighbourhood copper,
with his PR brief, as for his colleagues, is the demand for the
containment of crime and apprehension of law-breakers. With
the 'three-shift' outsider policeman, this goal supersedes all
others, since the area is simply a place to patrol rather than a
neighbourhood which is his beat. Consequently, keeping inside
the rules and being sensitive to community sentiments are not
of great consequence. If this is true for the uniformed constable
it is even more so for Task Force. This police section tends to
work in problem areas and has, to quote one senior officer, 'a
phenomenal clean-up rate'. Task Force tends to follow the
statistics of reported crime and consequently 'the squad again
concentrated its main effort in the city centre and continued to
be a most effective measure in combating crime and disorder'.[17]
Most of the 'heavy hand' which has alienated The Boys has
come from this squad. Working as a fairly 'closed shop', Task
Force has, given the goals, necessarily resorted to devious
methods. This concentration on the area built up particularly
during early Year Three, when look-outs with binoculars hid in
warehouses and on the roofs of tall buildings to survey carparks.
Plainclothes officers in unmarked cars patrolled the area and
nearby concentrations of parked cars. A 'widening of definitions
of delinquent behaviour' noted elsewhere took place.[18] Thus
there were more stops for questioning and search, more loitering

charges and more 'slagging' than before. Car attacks have become an increasingly serious problem in 'crime statistics' terms, and although compared to mugging and violence these receive little publicity they are none the less treated as in need of concerted police attention since, 'Offences involving theft from or of motor vehicles are a considerable problem in the force area. In 1950, 8·3 % of crimes known to the Liverpool City Police concerned these offences, in 1971 this proportion had risen to 31·2 % of total crimes known.'[19]

More immediately a 'delinquency area' which needs 'clearing up' is defined by a grid-square reference of reported offences. Such statistics are fairly accurate since most people will report thefts from their cars to the police. Figure 4 (page 184) shows just how sore a thumb the area is, and thus demands a police offensive and saturation. Obviously the statistics indicate in what parts of the city car parking is concentrated, but they are none the less created largely by activities of residents in the area as well as visiting outsiders.

The police position is thus quite clearly defined. The area is a problem and should be treated as such and cleared up. This basically means deter and apprehend local adolescents and their older accomplices. The police are the on-the-spot representatives of Authority, they know what they have to do and how their performance is judged. They must contain crime and apprehend offenders.

Quite obviously the police do other things, as it is equally obvious the down-town 'delinquent' adolescent only breaks the law a small fraction of the time. However, The Boys' attitude to Authority and to society itself is judged where conflict arises, and it is at such friction-points our comprehension must lie. As we have said, the idea of the law being fair and just and consequently meaningful is disputed by The Boys. Authority does not come up to the standards it sets itself. The sense of injustice felt by down-town adolescents arises from answers to the following demands which Matza puts on behalf of his subcultural delinquents.

It is only fair that some steps be taken to ascertain whether I was really the wrongdoer (cognizance); it is only fair that I be treated according to the same principles as others of my status (consistency); it is only fair that you who pass judgement on me sustain the right to do so (competence); it is only fair that some relationship obtain between the magnitude of what I have done and what you propose to do to me (commensurability); it is only fair that differences between the treatment of my status and others be reasonable and tenable (comparison).[20]

The Boys as we have shown make all these demands indirectly. The law of the State will only command authority if it is fair and just and likely to be seen as meaningful. As we have suggested earlier The Boys have never come to find the law particularly meaningful even in terms of expediency; and this minimal meaningfulness will be further reduced if it is seen as biased or unfair.

Grid Square Mile	No of Offences 1971	No of Offences 1972
The Area	1,096	1,527
	702	872
	370	397
	310	273
	236	274
other	134	122
central	107	211
areas	107	236
	106	110
	90	111
	90	92
	84	85

Figure 4. The grid-square areas of Liverpool and Bootle having the highest concentration of offences of theft from unattended vehicles during 1971 with the equivalent figures for 1972

So far we have used Authority as an umbrella term to encompass a diverse group of officials whose job it is to process the accused delinquent. On a more analytical level, 'authority' means something else. Dealing with the 'authority' of the State, Michael Banton suggests a distinction should be made between 'authority', 'power' and 'might'.[21] This distinction rests on the idea of rules becoming less meaningful as one moves towards 'might' as a form of control. Hence 'authority' is associated with these rules which are willingly complied with by the majority of society. Accordingly, a meaningful law has 'authority' in that it is a particular type of rule which the bulk of the members of a given political community recognise as binding upon all its members. If the law is not meaningful at a voluntary level we move into the realm of 'power', which is associated with a more reluctant compliance when citizens accept the law in general as something they must accept, even if they dispute the application and administration of some aspects. At this level, social order is obtained through expediency; for most people most of the time it's worth playing ball. 'Might' comes into the picture when the rules are not themselves meaningful or complied to voluntarily, but have to be enforced, usually by the deployment of coercion.

The Boys and Authority usually conduct their transactions in the milieu of 'power' and 'might'. In earlier chapters we discussed ways in which the law was not grasped as 'authority' by children growing up in down-town areas. This chapter has added a further reason why this meaningfulness has not been remedied by the intervention of Authority: the Authority officials are not seen as exercising 'authority' but 'power' and 'might'. They are seen as unfair and unjust, and as manipulators of the prosecution process so that it becomes a persecution not intended by the law.

This does not imply that if Authority became scrupulously fair and just The Boys would no longer break the law. This is obviously not the case; we have already shown there are more fundamental reasons why The Boys do not find the rules of the wider society expedient. However, the genuine sense of injustice the down-town adolescent feels does reinforce his lack of commitment to the law, and provides him with a secondary reason which neutralises what little moral bind the law had and amplifies his dissociation from the expectations of the wider society.

It may be useful to leave the world of the concrete for a moment and look at The Boys' 'process' in Sartrian terms. The Boys live *dans un monde de la rareté*, in a world of scarcity. In such a world need arises. But as needs are satisfied new needs are created. The Boys grow up with less than they need. In the world of *rareté* they are *given* less than their share. They act against this scarcity and deprivation, because, as Laing puts it, 'If you steal what you want from the other, you are in control, you are not at the mercy of what is given.'[22]

When taking from the other involves breaking the law then one is taking from no less than the State. The State, dismayed at the failure of its conditioning agencies such as the school, the church, the social services and community development projects, resorts to coercion through 'terreur'. Thus for the poorer working-class 'delinquent' boy, who grows up in the city, adolescence is a period of coming to terms with Authority. The unity which seems to occur between the State, its rules and The Boys is a false unity. It is an imposed acceptance based upon the impotence of the 'seriality' to resist the State's demands presented through coercion. For the seriality the unity goes no deeper, their commitment is only a 'serial acceptance' in that there is nothing distinctly legitimate or illegitimate about Authority, it is simply a fact of life: 'I am obedient because I can do nothing else and that gives pseudo-legitimacy . . . to the sovereign.'[23]

This pseudo-legitimacy is consistent with what Alvin Gouldner calls 'normalised repression'.[24] If The Boys accept less than their share it is because they are impotent to get more. If they steal less today than yesterday it is because even the delinquent solution has become blocked to the extent that they will choose to be skint rather than incarcerated. They are the losers, because they remain separate and isolated from the larger 'totality' even of the city. Because they live in a confused social space and because that space is saturated by Authority, they believe 'there's fuckin' coppers everywhere'; they do not fully comprehend that they are selected for persecution because they are different from the Others.

At a parochial level The Boys also remain separate and 'serialised'. To try and resist as part of a collectivity is to go beyond comprehension and to get oneself too deeply involved in the contest. A practical example of this comes in terms of the reluctance of down-towners to become witnesses in Court. Moses should have had six defence witnesses for his trial; only three appeared. The reluctance of the seriality to support each other on alien territory is widespread. Hence the prosecution process is not just furthered by the more efficient closed shop of the prosecutors for the State but by the fear of the defence to organise itself. 'If the coppers see you down there trying to get your mates off they'll make trouble for you.' (*Murky.*) 'If they get to know your face like, and those fellers you've spoken for get off, they'll make sure they get you instead.' (*Tuck.*)

Bone, whose conviction relied on whether he could show he was mistakenly identified and was in fact in the 'club' at the time of the alleged offence, was not disappointed that his mates would not help him out. 'You can't blame the lads for not wanting to give evidence. Like Mal and Jaw who saw me in the club, they've both got to keep out of trouble or they'll go down.'

'Trouble' is extended here to include actually being seen by Authority. To keep out of trouble involves disappearing—out of sight, out of mind. This restriction of freedom suffered by the down-town adolescent, with the face that fits, can be seen in other ways. I remember walking across town with Jimbo and Colly a few days after one of their convictions. We were taking a short cut across a carpark.

Jimbo I'm not walking across no carparks and getting picked up for loitering. Come 'ed this way through Hall Street.
Self Oh come on Jimbo, you can't get done for just walking through.
Jimbo You can't, but I fuckin' can, they know my face, they're just waiting to stick me down.

Problems of Identity

In a sense Jimbo was admitting a soiled identity. He was admitting others see him as deviant, he was admitting a restriction
of his freedom to move through public territory and in 'normal'
society. Transactional theorists might argue that a person's
awareness of the society's negative evaluation of him is likely to
accelerate his commitment to delinquent or criminal roles.
Leslie Wilkins, following Kitsuse and Dietrick, has described
this circular chain as a 'positive feedback loop'.[25] Basically the
loop involves the individual learning the values of the delinquent sub-culture through participation, which may occur for
various motives. The deviant behaviour is met by formal negative sanctions and rejection by middle-class society. This means
that all members of the sub-culture of delinquency suffer
similar problems, and counteract their rejection by themselves
rejecting the standards of 'respectable' society, turning inwards to achieve identity and status. Such alienation on
both sides hardens feelings and 'while such a loop continues
the situation will continue to get further and further out of
control'.

Such a positive feedback loop is now regarded as basically an
'ideal type' unlikely to be encountered in the field. More recent
theoretical formulations are much less deterministic, emphasising the problematic nature of social control. Certainly Downes
and Rock's discussion is more pertinent to The Boys' position
when they suggest that,

> It is not simply that the deviant seeks to evade the impact of control
> and apprehension. It is that control helps to shape the forms of deviance
> available, the degree to which they are seen as deviant by the deviants
> themselves, the extent to which deviants have taken to transparency,
> deviousness and collaboration (Matza) to cope or collude with the type
> and level of social control against them. It is in this sense that social
> control operates to transform rather than cause deviance.[26]

The amplifications that did occur through The Boys' contest
with Authority was, as discussed in the last chapter, peripheral

and temporary in relation to the more general deterrent effect of coercion and the threat of incarceration. Theft behaviour became 'bad news', the reduction of delinquent action became a chosen reaction. At the level of personality 'amplification' becomes a different matter however and discussion comes upon identity change. To this matter of soiled and spoiled identity I now turn briefly.

If the theoretical problems we are set concerning the transformation process into secondary deviance are complex,[27] the methodological problems of answering the questions posed are monumental. Social scientists' ability to discuss meaningfully what motivates actors into particular behaviour cannot be taken as read. When we start talking about unintended consequences and the effects of identity challenge, face work and the like we are probably out of our safe depth. One thing a case study of this nature with its emphasis on the little 'ifs' and 'buts' can tell us is that we must be modest about our ability to describe and analyse social reality. Even at the level of personal friendship, which will nearly always elicit honest responses to questions, there are still severe limitations for analysing motives behind social action and the 'becoming' of personal identity. Sociologists have an almost uncontrollable urge to tidy up the data they collect, to generalise, to fit the facts into logical pathways. We feel our own ability as social scientists is judged on whether we can present a profound yet parsimonious analysis of social action. If we cannot tidy up it appears we've failed. Yet if we tidy up what is untidy we have been dishonest to ourselves and our discipline, we have led ourselves astray. At the level of a one-man case study of this nature, the lack of ability to tidy up may be with the researcher; but since he has a monopoly on the data neither he nor others have any real way of ascertaining where the problem lies. The evidence from my participation in and observation of the network's response to the Opposition of Authority leads me speculatively to suggest that amplification of deviance in relation to the taking on of a soiled or spoiled identity was negligible. Whilst most of the interpretative points I have made throughout the book have been based on recurring incidents and conversations which have built up over time to give me some confidence as to their validity, I can say little about identity change.

One much-written-about consequence of social control is based on the idea that the concept of self is anchored in the social setting of other: 'Through the use of language, through the use of significant symbol . . . the individual does take the attitude of others especially [those] common attitudes, so that he finds himself taking the same attitude toward himself that the community takes.'[28]

This sort of transformation may well occur; it could have occurred in The Boys—they could have taken on self-conceptions of themselves as deviant. Indeed from time to time isolated incidents during the field work could be interpreted in these terms. Yet in the end I have not gathered sufficient evidence to justify talking about transformation at the level of personality. In terms of amplification this case study has been able to point to an increase of dissociation from 'normal' society, but with no evidence that even at a group level this dissociation then leads to the strengthening of deviant motivations and the re-affirmation and increase of deviant activities.

There are several forces within The Boys' socio-cultural milieu which protect them from taking on a soiled or deviant identity. Whilst the down-town, delinquent adolescent certainly cannot be indifferent to the forceful attentions of Authority and other social control agencies, he may well be able to avoid taking on the sentiments of the degradation imposed by outside typecasters. As already illustrated, Roundhouse is in practice a 'condoning community' as regards its general attitude towards most kinds of delinquency. Thus whilst there are certain internal taboos on deviant activities, theft is regarded as acceptable if it is from outsiders. The hatred of Authority is implanted at all age-levels. In their own way parents and sons feel the same way and protect each other against officialdom.

Our house has been turned over a couple of times. They knocked on the door and said we're detectives. Me dad says fuck off and get a warrant. They came back with one and he let them in. They said they'd been tipped off but they wouldn't say who by, like. They went all round the place, turned the house upside-down. They was just going 'coz they hadn't found anything, like, when me mam says, 'Don't think you're leaving them beds like that, you make them like they was before.' This copper went all red-faced like and starts making the bed properly. Me old feller went down to the Citizens' Advice Bureau to see what they could do about it. They said you can't do nothing about it unless they do it again and again, then you can do them for persecution. Our kid's got a record as well as me, I think that's why they did our house. (*Mal.*)

With down-town families in agreement that they are harassed, and agreeing that community sentiments are important enough for the blind eye to be turned, the protective social compact summed up by the philosophy 'good for them if they can get away with it' operates nearly all the time: 'Say nothing even if you "know the score".' Hence the 'delinquent' living in the area, as long as he doesn't offend internal standards of behaviour, knows he's pretty safe from traumatic accusations and attacks on his face since 'everybody's together in the Block'.

Labelling attacks will only come from outsiders. The most deliberate campaign, as we know, comes from Authority. As already said these typecasters are regarded with sentiments ranging from suspicion and distrust through to, in The Boys' case, hatred and a profound sense of injustice which facilitates a rejection and refutation of anything Authority might claim, wherever that is possible. Authority is accepted through its power and might, it is accepted through fear. However, we can in no way assume compliance is synonymous with the taking-on of a deviant identity.

Throughout the book we have noted a steady transformation of down-town adolescents' delinquency patterns due, in part at least, to the attempted control of Authority. We have identified several changes as the 'young delinquent' appreciates risk, undergoes apprehension and conviction, begins to dread the Institution, comprehends fear and perhaps loss of nerve. We have noted increased deviousness on The Boys' part to avoid apprehension and some sophistication in their 'front' during the prosecution process. Most importantly we have identified the fanning out of the network's solutions to each new contingency. Some of the network have finished with law breaking, others have become more covert and cautious, others again have carried on regardless. Some have side-tracked into another social group of 'non-robbers', some have changed their direction and doubled back.

In terms of curbing a delinquent or criminal career the prosecution process has had in a rather pathetic and distasteful way a deterrent effect for most of the network (negative feedback). Yet for others, such as Fin, Tuck and Tank, delinquency has continued and has cut through any barriers Authority has been able to offer, including the Institution. Such indifference to coercion is not easy to explain, nor would generalisation from so few 'processes' be meaningful. The other Boys themselves perhaps have the key when they role-type such individuals as 'mad', 'never learns', 'just wants sympathy'. Tuck for instance, as his brother pointed out, 'doesn't seem to be able to take it in, he listens to you and says you're right, then he goes back on the rob again'. It seems likely that the Cleptos, Tucks, Tanks and Fins of this world are less well adjusted and less able to comprehend the world in the same way as others. These adolescents have been identified for many years by locals as 'bound to end up in borstal', and seem to be moving doggedly into a life of crime. What does seem evident here is that the measures used by social control agencies, which become increasingly coercive, as warnings run out, have almost no success. From what we know about the effects of inmate cultures in total institutions, it does seem possible such measures could amplify deviance.

For the majority of the network things don't go this far; where amplification does occur is at the level of dissociation. The Boys find their freedom of action and movement in middle-class society is limited. They are to some extent excluded from what should be public territory: Jimbo won't walk across car-parks, The Boys won't go to Court as witnesses for each other,

they will leave the Corner to avoid policemen, they won't
carry certain goods from A to B in case they are stopped and
accused of theft. More generally they may have to leave a
camping site not used to their life style, they won't eat in certain
restaurants where there's been 'bother', or drink in pubs where
they feel socially uncomfortable. The Boys will not stray into
outsiders' territory because 'they'll throw you out'. One example
in Year Two brought this point home to me—in fact I suffered
a small identity crisis myself. It was during the street-corner
days when I was hanging around like everyone else. We had
been in Flems having a cup of tea and we were walking back
through the store looking at the shirts. The next moment a large
security manager appeared having made up his mind to remove
us.

> Come on you lot, the door's that way.
> *Fosser* We're not doing nothing wrong.
> Listen lad this is private property you're trespassing, now out before
> I have to throw you out.
> *Colly* Come on boys, let's go, this place isn't worth a wank anyway.
> Come 'ed Fosser (pulls him by the arm).
> *Self* You can't just throw people out for no reason, you didn't mind us
> spending money in your café five minutes ago. I'll see the manager
> before I go.
> I'm the manager as far as you're concerned, now out.

I wasn't convinced, so walked off and found the store
manager's office whilst the rest of the group left. I complained
bitterly that I had been mistaken for someone I was not.
'Whenever, for instance, a person finds himself mistaken for
someone else, he gets a glimpse of how important such classification is . . . If people mistake him for a disgraced person, he
will be quick to deny the identity and point out the mistake. To
do this, he indignantly produces his social credentials, showing
signs that prove conclusively (he hopes) that the other people
are mistaken.'[29]

I had given up the role of participant observer that day,
backed down and stepped out. I had argued with the typecasters and in fact received a promise that such indiscriminate

N

'barring out' would not continue, which was actually the case for a few weeks. In The Boys' eyes I had been 'a good bloke', I had shown whose side I was on, so they thought. But really my actions had reminded me that I wasn't even a very good imitation street-corner boy. I had not been willing to accept the pointing finger. The Boys had accepted a label I had refused. I was lucky to have learnt a lesson so early on.

Why had The Boys left when they 'hadn't done nothing wrong'? Was this yet another example of their acceptance of a soiled identity and an implicit agreement with the typecaster's diagnosis? I suggest not. The Boys left because Colly had been convicted of assault and fined £20 for refusing to leave the same store a few weeks earlier. The Boys accepted they were up against a stone wall—the law's on the law's side. It was not worth arguing, so they try another café, perhaps one where they were barred out a year ago and their faces long forgotten. In the same way, renovation of the pubs of call takes place, with pubs where there's been 'bother' avoided for a while and a new haunt found. Social control impinges on The Boys' circuit of social space, it partly defines territory for them. At times it causes them to withdraw, to reduce their horizons. They choose between confrontation and dissociation. Usually they withdraw into their renovated circuit of space where they are accepted and where others will agree that the outsiders, 'they', aren't 'worth a wank' anyway. In a sense The Boys are the losers, but they only lose battles, not the war; they refuse to be objectified and labelled as 'no good', because their side is still united in the sense that 'they' are 'no better than us'. 'They' are just as bad, and who are they to talk anyway? Isolated and with little power The Boys may be, but objects, accepting definitions stamped on them, they are not.

Notes to this chapter are on pp 230–1

6 On the Edge of Society

I don't really understand all of it, how it works, I'm trying to work my way up from the working class to see, like. We work and the money they take off us goes somewhere to these fellers who've got really flash cars and change them every year to keep up with the style. They're the bosses like, I don't like any kind of bosses . . . I'll have no bosses. (Titch, T.)

Understanding how it works is very important. Their failure to understand fully how it works is The Boys' biggest handicap. It is their immersion in a community living from day to day which prevents their full comprehension; and their failure to comprehend subsequently perpetuates their situation. It has been argued throughout that the meaning system operational in Roundhouse contains large doses of the dominant ideology, with conflict arising more out of necessary adaptation rather than distinctive norms. Differences are related to local contingencies and occur through adaptation to and dissociation from the stricter and more dogmatic elements of the dominant normative order.

As we have shown, for a whole series of reasons The Boys grew up on the Corner and in the Block where they could not fail to be impressed by the concerns of the street's youth—smartness, toughness, excitement, a contest of wits, etc. Parental influence, although theoretically opposed to aspects of the street lads' style, was usually only able to make a verbal counter-attack. Parents could not offer a real alternative environment for their children and thus tended to acquiesce, making only spasmodic stands when the kids got 'in lumber'.

School on the other hand did initially make a consistent attempt to show youngsters what society expected, what was correct and what was to be worked for. By the time they got to secondary school The Boys were realising that what school demanded and what mattered back in the Block could be different. They all went to Catholic schools and it should be remembered that over a third of the network and most of those who became the core in Years Two and Three passed the 11 + and went to grammar school. Here dissociation and adaptation started in earnest. With the exception of Murky and Emo, all the 'scholarship' boys were back at St Patrick's, the local secondary modern school, within three years. Fosser didn't last a year.

> The first day I was there I came home with homework. I was reading a book on the bus on the way home and I shit meself 'coz I couldn't do it. The first day, boy. I was always getting lines for not doing homework and sagging.
> One day me old man saw me sagging and when I got back home he battered me and said I either got back [to school] or he'd take me down to the probation officer. I said the probation officer, and me old girl shit herself and said get him out of there, so I went to St Patrick's on the Monday after. (T.)

Danny, Fatch, Pablo, Colly and Streak all followed suit before long. They felt uneasy and out of place at grammar school and resented the treatment they received. Streak got off on the wrong foot right from the start.

> It was a bad place. For one instance, we'd only just started there and this one teacher Rizzole had us when we'd only been in the school a few weeks. He was going round all of us like and saying what's your name and where do you live? I said Jute Street, Roundhouse Gardens. He went Pooh! and pulls a face and says, 'One of the Roundy Boys eh?' Just like that, in front of the class. Me and Fatch said nothing, like, but he was a fuckin' bad man. (T.)

When the 'scholarship' boys got back to St Patrick's they saw grammar school in an even less favourable light.

> It was when we got back to St Pat's that we realised how bad the teachers was. Like in St Pat's there were a few bastards, but most of them was OK, you could talk to them and joke with them. But at grammar school they seemed just like zombies, they'd come in, do the lesson and go out, you couldn't say a word out of place. (*Fatch*, T.)

St Patrick's was not regarded as a 'bad place' by many of the network whilst they were there. Individual teachers became identified as 'good blokes' with whom attachments were made and who could be trusted to act reasonably and consistently.

> Now Miff was a good bloke, he was the best teacher there. You know I'm a Liverpudlian, well he's an Evertonian and say Liverpool had played the night before and won. The first lesson he wouldn't look at me or nothing and I'd be grinning and giving him the thumbs up. Then when Everton used to win he'd come in and go hello Streak, letting on to me they'd won, like.

Despite their appreciation of some of the teachers' efforts and desire to 'make something' of them, The Boys treated school as simply a process they were involuntarily put through. The dialogue on both sides of the desk had its own priorities, refusing to give way and be what the Other wanted. Hence The Boys' intellectual potential was exercised voluntarily more out of than in the classroom.

> I used to be sagging a lot before I should have done CSEs. And there used to be this sly teacher and every time I used to stay off, whether I was sagging or not, he'd ring up me old man's works and tell him. I thought it was dead sneaky then, but I suppose he was doing it for my well-being. (*Fatch*, T.)

The network indulged in truancy a great deal, especially in their last two years when the school had to go to considerable lengths to check it. The Education Welfare Officer was simply not able to cope with the situation, and since he did not have the necessary 'gun on each hip' left The Boys to their freedom and concentrated on the juniors of the neighbourhood. The Boys simply didn't expect or wish 'to do well' beyond a few

CSEs. They weren't going anywhere new or breaking out of Roundhouse, they didn't need anything school could offer in academic terms.

> You know all the boys that passed the scholarship, when they came back to Saint Pat's we all got put in the A stream and Miff used to say, 'You lot you're the cleverest in the school, but you're idiots as well 'coz you won't put it to your own well-being, you just like being one of the lads instead of working hard.' (*Colly*, T.)

Coming from a Roman Catholic community and attending Catholic schools, where considerable time was given over to religious instruction, The Boys were fully aware of 'them's' ideal Christian standards. By the end of Year One, looking back on school and the church, The Boys tended either to disbelieve in or only to pay lip service to God or his message. Whilst they 'had to go' to mass and school as 'kids', they now 'saw things better'. Most of the network derided the doctrine and ritual of the church and associated it with 'superstitious old women' and The Girls who 'believe all that stuff about bad luck if you put your boots on the table and that'. Jimbo's comment summed up the common view of the network: 'The church has got nothing on the boys today . . . most of them would lie standing on a stack of bibles.'[1] When they first left the school and church atmosphere (Year One) The Boys were less articulate about what they resented than they are now. Their consciousness of the process they went through seems to have become clearer only recently.

> *Titch* It was only after I'd been away, to London and that, that I started realising things about school and teachers and that. Like when I was at school I was one of the first to start letting my hair grow long. I started getting criticised for that, getting called a yob by one teacher. This really happened, like, we were all on one side of the classroom and he comes in and says I see all the respectable ones have got their uniforms on and you lot haven't. You're the long-haired yobs. That was in the third year. I've got more sense now, I'd have said who are you calling yobs and saying what we should wear.
>
> *Fosser* The things they could do to you boy. We was all in the art

room and a teacher came in and says all you lot sit down. But I had all soap on me hands and I wanted to wash it off, so I stayed at the tap. He came over and digged me on the ear, a real smack, and says sit down when you're told. If I saw him on the street now I'd fuck him for that, he made a right cunt out of me.

Having grown up and gained their autonomy and their own standards of acceptable behaviour, the more thoughtful of the network look back on much of the discipline at school as unnecessary denunciation.

> *Emo* If I went back to school now I wouldn't last five minutes. I'd get expelled. You'd got to go in and sit down for forty minutes, don't talk, don't eat, listen to me. Now if I wanted to talk to the next feller I'd talk, if I wanted to chew I'd chew and I'd refuse the cane.
>
> *Titch* Right, so would I man, what good's the fuckin' cane, it doesn't stop you talking, you just start talking again. You don't think 'I won't talk again, in case I get the cane'. You just carry on, it's natural.

The 'indoctrination' of the church is also condemned as 'just power over the kids' and hypocritical in its outlook.

> They're always coming round for fuckin' hand-outs, expecting you to give money to the church. Look at the Pope, he's got a ring on his finger worth £200,000, and look at the mansion he lives in, yet 12,000 people a day die of starvation. (*Streak.*)
>
> When I was a kid me mam used to say do this or do that and I'll tell the priest of you. Now, I'd say so fuckin' what, what does he know? Turn the other cheek here boy and you'll get fucked. (*Titch.*)

These attitudes usually only came from a few of the network, however. For the most part The Boys talk about neither the church nor school. Some things were bad, some OK, often you actually had a good laugh, but such days in retrospect weren't very relevant to how things are here and now. Certainly neither had helped The Boys develop a comprehension of their position in society or what they could do about it if it offended them. On the contrary such agencies defused any potential explosions, and made the distribution of wealth and lack of facilities and opportunities a non-issue. That a few of the network have in retrospect realised such agencies were a denunciation of their autonomy is to their credit, for more often Danny's diagnosis is in keeping with the down-town adolescent's attitude to under-achievement.

> The schools are there like and the lads have got their own minds. If they wanted to get on it was up to themselves, things were provided like, even St Pat's had the grammar stream. If they wanted to pay attention they did, if they just wanted to mess around they did. I had the choice like, and I didn't take it and I'm glad. I'm better off where I am. Anyway even if you've got O levels now you don't get any better jobs, apprenticeships aren't so marvellous.

So the education The Boys received, despite its theoretical ability to develop their intellectual potential, which is un-doubtedly there, had little effect. The grammar-school style, so articulately geared to middle-class standards, took The Boys out of their stride so violently that they recoiled and dissociated from its ethos. Back in the comfort of the familiarity and friendliness of the Block, middle-class kids were judged un-fortunates rather than super stars.

> Like they've got pushy parents who make them stay in and do work and have extra tuition and all that. Say after school it was dead hot, we'd say let's go over the water to New Brighton baths, and we'd just go. But the posh kids have to go home and play in the garden and that, they don't get to just do things 'coz they want to, like The Boys do. (*Danny, T.*)

So what was familiar was celebrated and what threatened their autonomy rejected. St Patrick's was a better alternative and leaving school as soon as possible an even better one. They left school and, as we have seen, found out that butt-end jobs, after the initial attraction of having 'a few bob in your pocket', were only more wholesome in that you could pack them in without breaking the law. By the end of Year One the majority of the network did pack them in. We know the reasons why, at the end of Year Three, they were gradually and reluctantly returning to them.

They have experienced for themselves over their first three

post-school years how dispensable society finds them. They are offered very little except indifference if they say nothing, and punishment if they become a recognisable problem. The Boys are left uncommitted to a social order of which they are meant to be part. For once out of school they found official agencies unable to offer any legitimate careers worthy of their commitment. Youth Employment had no jobs, social services had neither time, resources nor expertise to reach The Boys at a 'preventative' level. Social work is crisis not case work. You have to be a juvenile crisis before you become a reality, only then will you be considered for processing.

Although The Boys have never received much 'help' or even a reciprocal contract from outsiders, they have received, through the media, plenty of noises suggesting what should be done about them. For the do-gooders The Boys are part of a 'social problem', they are talked about in a way they resent. The liberal diagnosis, 'underprivileged' and 'deprived', is refuted by Roundhouse youth.

> They say in the papers the area's deprived and that the kids are underprivileged 'coz they live in blocks of flats and that they haven't got luxuries and grass and trees. But we're not underprivileged, we have enough food and clothes and blankets and a few bob for a bevvy. It's not like the poverty in the old days or like families where the bailiff comes and turfs them out. (*Tommy*.)

Whilst The Boys are aware of the affluence of the middle classes they tend to judge their situation in relation to more 'respectable' and aspiring working-class families. As the social drainage of 'successful' families to the more salubrious estates continues, slowly but surely,[2] Roundhouse takes stock. The majority of the network consider their situation as superior.

> We could have a house in Childwall or Netherley and that, but the kids don't want one. You've got your mates round here, you've got all the old faces, you can have a good laugh, you're guaranteed a game of football every weekend. And you're on top of town if you want a good night out. There's nothing like that in Netherley and it costs a bomb for a taxi back if you do come in. (*Tommy*.)

By celebrating their community and the advantages it holds in relation to conceivable alternatives, The Boys reject any suggestion that they are deprived. Objective and subjective measurements are not always compatible.[3] The Boys' awareness is parochial and their world view localised. Rather than complain about their deal or rally round the local neighbourhood residents' association, The Boys play football in the Block. Rather than complain about the condition of what 'objectively' could be seen as a slum ghetto, they accept the conditions with little comment. Such matters do not yet concern them.

This view does not mean that agencies which work under the help or support banner are rejected *per se* by The Boys. Genuine people whose consistency and stickability speak for them will probably find acceptance amongst Roundhouse youth at some level. The probation officer and social worker can be OK if they are able to form attachments and comprehend the context in which their reluctant clients live. The employer who shows concern and pays a decent wage and gives his staff 'a chance' will find some reciprocity.

The youth club, because it doesn't make unreasonable demands and create impractical rules, is rarely seriously abused. Sandhills is another 'agency' which is enthused over and receives attachment and commitment. Yet in relation to The Boys' total life style such agencies are of negligible significance. All these social services are caught in a dilemma. The holiday away, play schemes, discos, help to get a special allowance, a long chat about 'things', are all overtly positive and useful services. But such improvement to the Roundhouse lot is *minimal*. The youth club holds interest only transiently. Sandhills as a holiday centre is unable to change anything. In Year Two, for instance, The Boys would go on the cars in order to get enough money to pay for their weekend away rather than go to Sandhills 'to keep out of trouble'. No doubt the detached youth worker can 'get through' to down-town adolescents. There is no great mystery in such a liaison: many outsiders like myself have done this. But what does the detached youth worker do, what does he say to The Boys when they're skint—'Let's go and have a cup of coffee or play table tennis'? They can do that without him. The inter-personal relationships between social worker and adolescents may be fine but they change nothing.[4] Even if social services and community projects were financed properly their attack would need to be at the level of education, economic development and a rearrangement of political machinery before The Boys for instance would notice any difference in their life chances—and such a development is highly unlikely anyway.

More often, do-gooders are not simply impotent but harmful. If the do-gooders are suspected—'What's in it for them?'—they should not be surprised, for the question is a realistic one, the paranoia justified. The Boys have seen nuns, middle-class housewives and social-work students by the score appear for a few weeks, never to be seen again—they were just pretending, it appears. A more critical example of do-gooders being dobadders occurred in Year Two. An 'appreciative' TV documentary about youth unemployment was made near the area and involved some of the network, who were willingly 'hired' to act in the film on condition nothing was shown or said about their delinquent activities or indeed anything that would 'get the place a bad name'. As an assurance it was agreed by the production staff that some of the adolescents involved should go to London to help edit the film. The film crew came, filmed and left, but their promise was broken. Not only was no one consulted about the editing but the title was changed from a provisionally agreed 'After School, The Dole' to 'The Dead End Lads'. The Boys were disgusted and angry. They felt genuinely cheated, dishonoured and labelled something they were not. After the anger came the philosophic view. 'It was our own fault, we should have had more sense than to trust those twats, they're only interested in making fuckin' money.' (*Joey.*)

If many of the 'sympathetic' do-gooders are not to be trusted, and their attachment is spurious, it is not resented as much as the more common view The Boys receive concerning their life style. To most outsiders The Boys are not deprived but depraved. If they trespass on the gin and tonics' territory, the abuse comes thick and fast. The repetitive camping-site sagas provide extensive examples. 'You're not leaving that [wash] basin in that state, young man, other people have got to use it after you . . . Have you got permission to use these facilities?'

Another condemned Roundhouse language as 'a disgrace to Great Britain, you should all be ashamed of yourselves, especially you girls'. The Boys for their part reject the typecasters 'who think you're lower than them' as 'stuck-up twats'. The typecasters are told to 'fuck off' which merely consolidates the 'correctness' of their original diagnosis. So both sides stand back and throw from behind barricades.[5]

The typical middle-class outsider's response to The Boys is that 'they', the 'delinquents', the 'muggers', the 'vandals and hooligans', are incapable of consideration for others, are without acceptable standards of decency. It is this sort of conclusion that some psychologists also reach.

> To act responsibly, both personally and socially, man must repress
> impulses and tolerate frustration. This is ego control, an area in which
> delinquents are deficient . . . The problem with many delinquents and
> criminals is that they are still seeking biological, primitive, animalistic
> pleasure rather than realistic, responsible, fully human pleasure.[6]

The Boys are not impressed with such judgements. The middle-class outsiders are like the 'judge': they don't understand that morality isn't some universal code which can be administered for everybody to live by, no matter what their situation. Such demands fail to show an appreciation of what 'realistic' and 'responsible' mean in somebody else's shoes. Certainly reprimand is sometimes due, certainly individual personalities behave unreasonably in whoever's shoes you are in. Such was the diagnosis of the network in its role-typing and exclusion of Clepto, for instance. Indeed The Boys would agree that they find self-discipline difficult at times, to the extent that when a 'reasonable' job does come along they will still 'skive'.

Hence a few of The Boys told their new boss, who was offering them good wages, 'You've got to keep at us 'coz we'll skive again. You just get out of the idea of working all day. You stay in bed and say "I'm not going into work". We want to work really but we need a hard boss to keep at us 'coz we're lazy.' (*Tank.*) But the self-discipline needed to hold down an un-skilled manual job is for The Boys related to motivation and practice rather than 'ego control'.[7] Motivation comes in the pay packet and practice comes in learning to accept a nagging boredom. Since The Boys have rarely encountered good legiti-mate opportunities with people who are willing to form attachments and nurture commitments in them, they tend to 'mess up' the occasional good chances. Their problem is thus related to the scarcity of good chances and practice, not pathology.

We have seen a little of The Boys' initiation into life at the edge of society. They have tried to get 'their share' both within and outside the rules of society, as their neighbourhood has had to do in the past. Both methods have proved hazardous and limited. Both styles have left The Boys with less than their share of both goods and control of the future.

Where will they go from here? We should not pretend to predict their future process too accurately, but certain struc-tural constraints seem to hem, if not hammer, The Boys into the place they are expected to occupy. Their freedom to choose is limited by structural limits which not least affect their com-prehension of the very nature of social stratification. Concern will continue to be for the present and the satisfactions that *can* be achieved. Future planning is not the reality it can be for those with 'enough'. 'The future orientation of the middle-class person presumes, amongst other things, a surplus of resources to be invested in the future and a belief that the future will be sufficiently stable to justify his investment, at a time, place and manner of his own choosing and to his greater satisfaction.'[8]

Perhaps a few of The Boys will refuse to modify their delin-quent style and will continue to challenge, on their terms and with tactics best suited to their locale. Crime will become a business. It will be talked of and seen as a business enterprise with occupational hazards. Such 'business' may or may not pay for these men, though with their intelligence, initiative and thorough apprenticeship some will, despite occasional imprisonment, become 'big spenders' and perhaps even move out to a 'better area',[9] a process which like the argot of the 'full-time miscreants' is a compliance with rather than an attack on the system. ('He's doing OK', 'He's got a nice little business going', 'He's got a job lined up'.)

That most of The Boys will not even break out to this extent nor deviate from what they know to be *the* rules,[10] can be explained only by a subtle blend of time, experience, coercion, compromise, mellowing and acceptance of other conventional roles such as husband, father, breadwinner. And this compromise of adulthood, this acceptance that the neighbourhood's 'adult' version of the dominant ideology is safer than the street corners means what? It means compromise, but not one made out of choice in the true sense. The choice is to comply rather than be coerced, to accept inequality, to cease resistance to the bad deal; the need for another line of attack is not comprehended. The Boys grasp little of their persecution as they contest with Authority. They direct their opposition to the baton that beats them rather than the strings that hold the hand. As Mann points out, 'There is no need for working-class people to develop beliefs which legitimate or illegitimate society, as long as they recognise the *factual* need to comply with its demands. Only those who seek to change society need encompass it intellectually.'[11]

The Boys firstly want their immediate share of the good times, they are in no way ready to comprehend structural change. What adolescence has taught them, and they have the scars to prove it, is that they are not destined to receive such a share. And since the baby, the wife, the rent, all have to be taken care of there is no time to argue. One simply makes do with the inequality which becomes ingrained into Roundhouse life style as a permanent feature. Resentment is only spasmodic, being washed away by the celebration of what the neighbourhood has. The reputation, 'the boys', the family, football, nights downtown—all that is tangible, obtainable, personal, local and beyond the reach of the outsiders—comes to the front. Life after all is acceptable if you stay close to home territory, where you're one of The Boys.

Notes to this chapter are on pp 231–2

Final Words

The writing is over and we are now several months into what is the equivalent of Year Four. A great deal has happened to The Boys since the end of Year Three and many personal situations have changed. At the risk of distortion, the story of the 'delinquent' down-town adolescent as represented by The Boys has been as follows. The adolescent out of school and hungry for the status of adulthood looks around him, weighs up his situation and sets off in search of finance to purchase that manhood. He soon concludes, as he suspected he would, that 'making it' and 'having a few bob' is not all that easy. He is at the mercy of economic growth. When casual work dries up there are only butt-end jobs and low wages to compete for. He packs it in and hangs around. Having grown up where he has and knowing what he does, the adolescent, if the circumstances are right, and because of his limited commitment to the dominant social morality, may try to cut across the rules. He knows he is deviating, he chooses to do so. Why shouldn't he be delinquent?

The Boys wanted their share, not just of the finances of a reasonable living standard but of the good times and being in control. How did society's appointed agents greet such a demand? Did they say, 'OK boys, that's fair enough, we all want our place in the sun, there's a gap over there, take this road—

it's straight, you can't miss it'? No, instead and because of the cost of widening the road, The Boys' demands were ignored until they interfered with other traffic. At this point The Boys were firstly warned against and then punished for making their own route. They were returned to their enclosure and threatened with expulsion from society. Human enterprise being what it is, The Boys tried again. But again they were forced to retreat and some of their number put in confinement. At this point The Boys reconsidered in depth. They greatly resented this treatment but nevertheless most felt that continuing proscribed behaviour in the face of such opposition was irrational. So the majority, for a while at least, capitulated and complied. They sat down, looked around at what facilities they had and tried to make themselves as comfortable as possible.

Now, a year later, the heat is off The Boys. Others elsewhere are breaking out and resources are diverted to retrieve obedience there. The Boys remain divided about delinquent action. Fosser looks back on the catseye days with astonishment. Now he's working and keeping out of trouble and those days seem rash and dangerous. 'We were fuckin' mad then, boy, the things we'd do for a few bob.' Arno is the antithesis: he has recently seen Detention Centre and a crew-cut come and almost go. He's still 'on the rob' to try and pay off fines which threaten his freedom. Fatch, who'd been out of 'business' for so long, awaits an important Court appearance for car-radio theft. Colly, Tommy and Jimbo are still taking their chances occasionally and even Danny has joined such escapades.

For the rest things have quietened down. They have turned to the jobs created by local economic expansion and are, for the time being, not short of money to buy some good times. The Boys are continuing to get married. Herbie thinks it must be catching. Mocky, Holly, Des and Pablo have joined Streak, Jimbo and Joey in the acquisition of a wife and a flat. Most of these couples want to live in the Block but have had, in the short run, to move into nearby high-rise flats. The waiting list for these flats is to move out, not in. However, it is likely that

o

plenty of vacancies in the Block will soon crop up. With the modernisation programme (discussed in Chapter 1) well under way, Mum's housing priorities are changing. As sections of the Roundhouse tenement complex are emptied for renovation, families are being offered alternative accommodation temporarily, and permanently if desired, in new maisonettes on 'better' estates on the city outskirts. Mum is often impressed by this upward mobility, the space, the central heating, the 'real' kitchen and garden. She is now, in keeping with her basic acceptance of society's goals, reluctant to return to 'that dump' down-town. She realises she's changed her tune, but it isn't as though she's stuck up, she argues, she can go and visit and stay with friends and relations still down-town.

With some families choosing to stay in their new houses and not return to the Block, when modernisation is finished the Roundhouse population is liable to change. These vacant and newly decorated flats will go to the less immediately mobile, married couples, with small families perhaps, who will be attracted by lowish rent. The young couples are of course, Des and Jean, Joey and Mary, Streak and Moira, Jimbo and Pam, with others soon to follow. The Boys are staying close to home and appear to be accepting the roles of husband, father and wage earner. Their marriages are not without stress and drama, but possess a certain stability in their instability, a predictability in their explosiveness. And what of The Boys' boys? They too it seems will grow up in Roundhouse as tomorrow's street kids, but unlike their fathers will have a brand-new inner motorway and multi-storey carpark to play with. No doubt they will leave their mark on these new edifices as they grow up amongst them.

The routine, the living, the making do, the bad times, the good times, all continue. The Boys are changing their roles quickly, leaving the street as if to make way for the next generation. Now they have places of their own less susceptible to the policeman's attentions. But things haven't really changed. The flats have been tarted up, the youth club has some new equipment, more facilities are promised. Everyone is a little better off. It is the differentials both material and social that remain, as does the down-town man's relative isolation and powerlessness and lack of commitment to a society which ignores him until he tries to change his lot.

Glossary

Bevvy: An alcoholic drink.

Bird: Prison: 'doing bird' means undergoing a prison sentence.

Bondy: A warehouse, derived from bonded warehouse.

Busy: A policeman; 'the busies' are the police.

Catseyes: A very localised name for the main type of car radio sought in 'car attacks'. The shiny buttons at each end of the radio give rise to the name. A catseyes 3 and catseyes 5 refer to the number of push buttons the radio has.

Clobber: A generic term similar to 'gear'. As elsewhere usually means clothes, often used when the articles in question are stolen.

Clock: To catch sight of. To be 'clocked by a busy' is to be observed by a policeman.

Danny: A car.

Divvy: A 'nut', an idiot, someone unusual. If called a divvy The Girls often reply, 'A divvy is a nut, nuts grow on trees, trees are part of nature, nature is beautiful, thank you for the compliment.'

Dixy: To keep look-out or 'nicks'.

Dropsy: A backhander, a tip, a pay-off.

Gear: Similar to 'clobber'. Usually refers to stolen objects. Also a term for marijuana.

Grass: To 'stooley', to 'split', to tell Authority of a mis-demeanour, to break honour amongst thieves.

Jack: Policeman.

Judge: Judge, but most often magistrate.

Mooch: To 'go on the mooch' is to go on a theft expedition.

'Oller: From hollow, a piece of waste ground.

Pipe: Similar to 'clock', to pipe is to observe. 'Pipe-ing' usually refers to the practice of reconnoitring for a potentially profitable misdemeanour.

Plonkie: A wine drinker, usually to excess.

Poke: Money.

Punch: A tool, a spike, useful for opening car windows from the outside.

Scrubber: Used instead of 'tart' which has a non-derogatory meaning. 'A right scrubber' is a girl who's rough-looking, whorelike.

Scrubs: Attendance Centre.

Skint: Without money.

Skivvy: A slave, a servant, someone who does the dirty work.

Slag: To abuse, to bring down, 'slagging' is the practice of denunciation.

Tart: The girlfriend, not a derogatory term.

Whizzed: Stolen, robbed, taken surreptitiously.

Winey: A plonkie, or a wine lodge.

Appendix:
The Fieldwork Approach

As already pointed out I grew into, rather than systematically planned, this case study. It was the happy transactions at Sandhills which saw me moving towards The Boys. One of the requirements of the staff at Sandhills was that they should wherever possible be the same as, rather than different from, the visitors. The liaison was successful and it was in this highly favourable atmosphere that my credentials were checked out during the course of normal events. For my part and in retrospect Sandhills provided an almost perfect introduction into the specific style, dialect, dress, personal standards, humour, aggressions, etc, of The Boys and other Roundhouse youngsters.

I left Sandhills to take up a research post in the university, close to the city centre. Almost immediately I was encouraged to carry out my own project, and various commitments aside I found that the post provided the time and flexibility to try a participant-observation study. Since out of simple enjoyment I had continued my contact with Roundhouse anyway and since I was now living in the city, the opportunity to look in greater depth at a community which fascinated me was seized upon.

So by mid Year Two the study started in earnest, bolstered by many advantages including easy entry into the field.

At first I 'knocked around' the area and the local youth club during lunch breaks and in the evenings; initially it was the younger kids and The Girls who made me feel less uneasy. Of The Boys, Joey, Titch and Des were the friendliest with most others simply being civil and 'letting on' when they saw me. In fact getting started was the most anxiety-provoking period of the study. I no longer had a recognised role—Howard from Sandhills—and was without a *raison d'être*. Initially I simply said I was hanging around: I'd got a new job at the university but it wasn't really under way yet so I was just bumming around. Any more sophisticated explanations were left till later, not least because I myself was not altogether sure what I was doing either.

Although at the time it seemed laborious, entry into Roundhouse adolescents' 'normal society' was easy and rapid. That old faithful 'the pub' was of course the answer. At first I would only go for an evening drink when specifically asked to, and fortunately Joey and Des made a point in asking me whenever I was around.[1] Once in 'The Turk', Sandhills acquaintances were warm and friendly and always ready to recall the good laughs of the summer just past. Again the 'He's OK'[2] epithet was important. I was a drinker, a hanger-arounder, and had been tested in illegal 'business' matters and could be relied on to say nothing since I 'knew the score'.

So by appearing for a couple of hours in the day and most nights during the week, I gradually moved inwards and started to comprehend more fully the nature and extent of The Boys' network. I got friendly with Emo, Arno, Colly, Tommy and Streak fairly quickly, although Fosser, later to be a good friend, was totally indifferent towards me for several months. I still felt insecure if Joey or Des were not around. A lot of local people who knew me from Sandhills assumed I was on the dole: I always denied this and said I worked at the university. It was only with a few of The Boys that I mentioned research, and then in terms of studying the way the police and the Courts operated. The message was always 'I'm on your side boys'. As I settled in as a regular face, I was several times congratulated on having such a cushy number for a job. To be paid for hanging around and a few hours' teaching seemed to appeal to The Boys, who appeared to condone rather than resent my good fortune.

My first request made at opportune moments was that if anybody was going to Court would they let me know and I would come along with them, as I wanted to study the prosecution process and perhaps hear what they thought about it. This ritual became well established, not least because I had a car, could help out with technicalities and later was willing to stand bail if nobody else could. Sitting for a couple of hours as 'two mates' in an alien world was a great consolidator of my loyalty to The Boys, and I later followed the process even further by visiting any of them who eventually got 'stuck down'.

As mentioned in Chapter 3, my hanging around 'all the time' period came in the autumn (mid Year Two), when most of The Boys were unemployed and were spending their days knocking around the neighbourhood, standing on the Corner and following the routinised structure of the bumming days already discussed. Fitting into this set-up was not too difficult. Dress regulations were not unduly strict, and a dark pair of cord jeans and a leather jacket were as acceptable as all-blue denim or combinations of leather, cord and denim. I never attempted to copy dress style completely, adapting only to the extent of blunting differences. My own black shirt, black jeans, burgundy leather, style was always acceptable and indeed my leather (acquired locally at a very reasonable price!)became a bit of a joke and it was agreed that I most probably not only slept in it but copulated in it also. 'There's a leather going in the Block, Parker lad, 'bout time you went mad isn't it? They'll give you a needle at the Royal [hospital] to get that old one off.' (*Joey*.)

No doubt everyone was aware that I spoke differently and 'posher' than they did. This was not a problem. It was more important to be able to understand 'scouse' than speak it: the scouser is bilingual, the outsider can be understood. Since as a Merseysider I could understand the dialect, my own pronunciation, although occasionally 'skitted' at, caused little comment once I was known. As time went on, or when drunk, I found myself swearing a lot more and using local esoteric words and phrases—divvy, tart, gear, busies, come'ed, bevvy, etc.[3] This helped too.

More importantly, blending in was facilitated by certain basic skills. One of the most important involved being 'quick': although I was regarded as normally 'quiet' and socially marginal, this placidity is not always a good idea. Unless you are to be seen as something of a 'divvy' you must be able to look after yourself in the verbal quickfire of the Corner and the pub. Thus although I rarely suffered the barrage of friendly abuse that some of the network received I felt it necessary from time to time to counter any 'quickies'.

Joey Sideboards on you, it's Elvis the pelvis isn't it?
Self That's all right la', yours'll grow one day.
Joey Phh they better hadn't or there won't be room in our 'ouse.

Being able to kick and head a football reasonably accurately was also an important aspect of fitting into the scene. Again, whilst I was certainly 'no Kevin Keegan' and indeed occasionally induced abuse like 'back to Rugby Special', I was able to blend into a scene where kicking a ball around took up several hours of the week. I also followed The Boys' football team closely each week and went to 'the match' with them when I could. This helped greatly. Indeed when everyone realised I supported Preston (as well as Liverpool, of course) it was always a good joke since they were so often getting beaten. 'Why don't you play for them they couldn't do any worse?' 'Is there a blind school in Preston?' (*Danny.*)

During Year Two I made the usual block of minor mistakes

mentioned elsewhere, including commenting on the sexuality of a passing girl (as is the custom) who turned out to be some-one's sister.[4] Occasionally I would be confronted by a phrase which meant nothing to me and would reply incorrectly. Likewise I sometimes used words that no one else understood and received the deserved animadversion (see what I mean).

Looking back on the fieldwork I find it difficult to judge whether larger strategies were mistaken or not. The Flems affair discussed at the end of Chapter 5, for instance, was cer-tainly a cop-out from the participant-observation role, yet on the other hand it allowed me to function on The Boys' behalf and show where my loyalties were. It is arguable, therefore, that on other occasions such as routine police stops I should have 'spoken up', which I didn't.

During Year Two I carried out about thirty taped interviews (T), with most of The Boys and a few of The Ritz. I bided my time in setting these up, usually tentatively suggesting to some-body he might come up to my room for a chat about things, the area, work, school, the police, etc. I would arrange a day not far ahead and then be around ready to cancel: 'It'll do again, any-time, let me know.' Usually I 'interviewed' two people at once and found this discussion-type conversation much more fruitful than the more structured affair. I sometimes found myself em-barrassed by these occasions, however, and whilst the inter-viewees seemed to enjoy the novelty which broke up the day I was glad when they were all over. Again in retrospect it is hard to say whether interviews or taped conversations were a good idea. I tend to feel that most of the information would have come to me eventually anyway, but on the other hand the interviews did acquaint me better with the situation at the time and so help my comprehension progress more quickly. (I also had interviews with teachers, EWOs, health visitors, social workers, planners, the police and other officials during the fieldwork period.)

The end of Year Two had seen the catseye business evolve. My position in relation to theft was well established. I would receive 'knock off' and 'say nothing'. If necessary I would 'keep dixy' but I would not actually get my hands dirty. This stance was regarded as normal and surprised nobody; it coincided with the view of most adults in the neighbourhood. Further, given my job, relative affluence and 'middle-classness', it was also regarded as an expedient stance. I had things to lose by being caught. There were occasions when I in fact interfered with a car-radio theft and suggested to those about to get involved that given the situation and their strategy someone was likely to get caught. My advice was always taken. This reaction to anxiety[5] on my part can be seen as 'bad' participant observation since it was interfering with normal group behaviour. Yet on other occasions vetos came from other members of the network, for the same reasons, and were likewise considered. Thus in a sense my actions can also be seen as in harmony with the participant-observer role, depending on how one defines it, a point I will return to shortly.

Year Three saw me more relaxed, and for the most part I enjoyed my fieldwork, looking forward with everyone else to the regular nights out, camping holidays, trips off to Sandhills, etc, which broke up the more extensive periods of, for me at least, relative boredom. It was during the first half of Year Three that I found myself as accepted as I ever would be, in the thick of things and at my most functional. Due to my regular Court attendance I was being regarded as something of an expert in such matters and was able to give advice from time to time. I also found that people were asking me 'how so and so got on', what were his chances next time, etc.

One occupational hazard was drunkenness (and bankruptcy). The nights out achieved such a pitch at one time that I too became 'skint' by the end of the week. I survived most big drinking bouts as well as anybody, although on a couple of occasions I over-indulged. One evening in particular saw me 'rotten drunk' and slinging chairs across a club floor, demanding more of everything and generally making a fool of myself. The next day the feedback came in thick and fast: 'Who can't hold his ale then', 'Plonkie Parker', 'state of yous last night, lad'. These were the days when I was very nearly one of The Boys. My style, poise and humour were nearly there and I felt a genuine sense of belonging. It was a good feeling which dissipated only with the lessening of the network's solidarity towards the end of Year Three.

I made one big and indisputable mistake near the end of Year Three. It involved my mentioning a particular illegality and the name of its perpetrator to a man from Everomer I was friendly with, in the presence of Emo. Emo didn't know the outsider and for some reason found him untrustworthy. He thus interrupted our conversation to point out I had got my facts wrong. I hadn't, and since I didn't at the time understand Emo's motives I argued with him and added more 'incriminating' evidence to back my argument. Emo later told the 'offender' in question that I had been talking about his activities to an outsider who couldn't be trusted. This was fair enough, but having read the situation differently I knew the Everomer man could be trusted; I also knew he was in the same line of business. Nevertheless, I had made a mistake and had to suffer the consequences; for a couple of bad days I found myself much more upset than I wanted to be. Having always vowed that rather than dodge rumours and any confrontations I would face them, I made sure of finding 'him' before he found me, and asked him who he was calling a grass. I sorted things out with Emo and faced rumours head-on. It was a nerve-racking few days but things worked themselves out and I'm now probably the only person who still remembers the incident. I relate this affair because I think it makes an important point. The participant observer will almost certainly make mistakes and in the down-town situation this can well lead to him getting his head kicked in. If you intend to carry on the study your philosophy must be: better to have it kicked in today than next week. Unless you really have betrayed your subjects, you must ride your mistakes rather than retreat. Having made one big mistake, to have disappeared for a month would have been another. By then Mr X would have gone in every pub and asked everyone he saw where I was and told them an extreme version of why he was going to give me a hiding. If you confront Mr X on the same day the cloud bursts, he hasn't had time to tell anybody what a creep you are, nor can he be convinced by your disappearance that you really are guilty.

Dozens of other situations encountered and recorded by other (American) fieldworkers had to be faced: do you lend money, do you get involved in sexual escapades, do you act as a witness in Court? (For my part I felt acting as a witness in court would have jeopardised the project and I had to sit out police perjury without intervening.) There are no definite answers. It *all depends*, of course, and since the whole situation would be different for someone else, somewhere else, a long catalogue appears pointless.

Considering the study more generally, several points are pertinent. I have referred to 'participant observation', 'the third man' and 'the fieldwork' rather loosely throughout the book. Since in Britain at least we still await the 'obvious' example of a participant-observation study, there is a vagueness about what the method entails. Indeed it may well be misleading to regard participant observation as a single method at all. McCall and Simmons for instance talk of 'a characteristic blend or combination of methods and techniques that is employed in studying certain types of subject matter'.[6]

Although attempts are made at exact terminological definition of participant observation, for instance with regards the 'type' of participation, in this study at least, the mix has been too variable to allow such tidiness.[7] What I have aimed at throughout is to become an insignificant variable. That is whilst one can watch and/or take part in normal group activities and so contribute to the dialogue, one must not alter the group's processual direction. One may occasionally alter content, but never form. In these terms such events as, for example, my suggesting theft from a car be postponed because of strategic circumstances only, since it is part of *normal* behaviour by group members, altered the content of one particular evening but not the form taken by evenings during that period. This definition of participant observation is open to discussion, and since the whole research approach in question tends to be a personalised one, again I am merely elaborating on my own methodological approach. Thus whilst exactly what 'distortion' is may be somewhat ambiguous, I would not dispute Kluckhohn's very old maxim that as regards participant observation, 'The purpose is to obtain data about behaviour through direct contact and in terms of specific situations in which the distortion that results from the investigator's being an outside agent is reduced to a minimum.'[8]

Such a statement can of course be read on many levels. Research methodology is of course highly problematic, whatever technique is used. The sorts of doubts cast by the precision demanded from Schutz and the American ethnomethodologists for instance would demolish the validity of this little book with ease, with perhaps a consoling comment that it at least moved towards addressing itself to the commonsense meanings actors give to reality. But this is not the best of possible worlds and my view of sociology cannot allow the crippling limitations the ethnomethodologists demand. Sociology is also political and the sociologist needs to communicate to others outside his academic world. If he waits until he is absolutely sure about the truth of what he is saying, and works out in detail all the necessary qualifications and phenomenological brackets, he will never say anything but become like the Greek philosopher Cratylus who in the cause of such perfection was reduced to wagging his finger. What is more the ordinary man does not use such techniques and would find such an approach to writing about adolescence incomprehensible. For me the sociologist must become, in Alan Blum's terms, 'objective enough' to have something to say.

On the more practical level of gaining access to another's world, the problems of obtaining data are less complex. Each

researcher's individual personality, like each fieldwork situation, is different and the only real test of feasibility in the end
becomes 'suck it and see'. Although it is difficult to say exactly
I would guess The Boys are more amenable to the outsider than
some urban adolescent groups might be.[9] They seem willing to
tolerate a wide variety of outsiders as onlookers though obviously long-term entry into their network requires a more
sophisticated match. If I hadn't been young, hairy, boozy, etc,
etc, willing to keep long hours, accept 'permissive' standards,
the liaison would have failed. This project 'succeeded', at least
in personal terms, because the personality and style of the researcher and of The Boys were compatible. Other liaisons that
I might have attempted could well have failed. A nervous, very
'straight', guy has certain possibilities open to him which I
haven't, and vice-versa. Given the general match in terms of
age, style, etc, such a study is not as difficult as might at first
appear; basic factors such as time and energy are as important
as anything. Participant observation is not and should not be
rejected as impractical, as often as it is. McCall and Simmons
lead us in the right direction when they suggest: 'Virtually any
mature social scientist can, with good sense and close attention
to his methodology, carry out participant observation of, at
least, the less demanding varieties.'[10]

The problems do not of course finish once the fieldwork is
under way or completed. One has great difficulty knowing
what to record, how to record it and what to make of it anyway.
Again in retrospect I was too selective in recording data. I did
not take enough time in keeping my fieldwork diary, especially
in recording what I considered mundane events. Quite often I
would be obsessed with a small conversation piece to the exclusion of other events. Had I been more concerned with detailed
writing earlier on I would have probably hit upon on-going
social processes more rapidly than I did. My general conclusion
here therefore is that keeping a detailed and accurate diary *may*
be of great significance. Although it is probably a personal
idiosyncrasy I also suffered a great deal from insomnia during

Year Three. Thus even though I was coming in in the early hours and well plied with alcohol I still found the evening's events insisted on consideration before I could sleep. This sort of research is demanding right to the last.

The major problem in 'writing up' is an ethical one, however. The fieldwork data basically fell into three categories: that which I felt could definitely be published, that which could definitely not be published and that which I was unsure about. The third category was eventually broken up and distributed into the yes/no compartments through consultation with those involved and colleagues. Becker has pointed out in reviewing studies of this nature that publication will almost inevitably 'make somebody angry'.[11] This is probably true; my main concern is that no harm comes to The Boys. Thus what I have published is related to my knowledge of what Authority already knows about. The nature of The Boys' delinquency discussed is well known to Authority. The analysis blows no whistles but rather tries to explain what happens when whistles are blown. It is designed in this way and indeed suffers from it.

Finally, although I am unhappy with the finished product and a little depressed about having discovered such crippling limitations in my ability to 'getting things across', I am still satisfied the project was worth undertaking. It has impressed upon me and I hope it will on others how easy it is for sociological research to do grievous bodily harm to reality. How little we hear of reciprocity, dialectic, process, change, innovation, back-tracking, in relation to delinquency, although in this longitudinal study that is what it was all about. Yet did not William Whyte assure us over thirty years ago: 'Only as I began to see changes in these groups did I realise how extremely important it is to observe a group over an extended period of time.'[12]

Notes are on pp 232-3

Notes and References

Chapter *1* (pp 21–44)

1 See F. J. C. Amos, *Social Malaise in Liverpool*, City Planning Department, 1970. The survey shows statistical links between 14 core-group problems but cannot give reasons for these links. This study can hopefully forge a few of these links.
2 'The history of a delinquent area.' Paper given by Gail Armstrong and Mary Wilson to National Deviancy Symposium, York, 1970.
3 *Liverpool Echo*, 1935.
4 City of Liverpool Housing Committee, *Housing Progress 1864–1951*.
5 *The Walk up Flats*, City Housing Department, Liverpool, 1970.
6 Ibid.
7 Amos, op cit.
8 D. M. Muchnick, *Urban Renewal in Liverpool*, Social Administration Trust, 1970, p 107.
9 M. Young and P. Wilmott, *Family and Kinship in East London*, Routledge & Kegan Paul, 1957.
10 M. Kerr, *The People of Ship Street*, Routledge & Kegan Paul, 1958.
11 Ibid, pp 40–52.
12 R. M. McIver and C. H. Pope, *Society: An Introductory Analysis*, Macmillan, 1961, pp 8–10.
13 *Liverpool Echo*, 1962.
14 See Oscar Lewis, *La Vida*, Random House, New York, 1966, p xiv.
15 See R. A. Cloward and L. E. Ohlin, *Delinquency and Opportunity*, Free Press, Chicago, 1960.
16 G. D. Suttles, *The Social Order of the Slum*, Chicago Press, Chicago, 1968, p 232.

17   See also K. Coates and R. Silburn, *Poverty: The Forgotten Englishmen*, Penguin, Harmondsworth, 1970, pp 110–11. They point out that petty theft within a neighbourhood eats away at residents' communal sentiments and increases resentment about the area and each other. Roundhouse protects itself against this particular type of self-destruction.

18   'Our mothers used to think, "Well they are youngsters, that's why they go out every night." They didn't used to ask what we got up to. They cared but they never looked too deep.' *The Paint House: Words from an East End Gang*, Penguin, Harmondsworth, 1972, p 120.

Chapter 2 (pp 45–61)

1   For a critical comment on the 'career' concept see I. Taylor, P. Walton and J. Young, *The New Criminology*, Routledge & Kegan Paul, 1973, p 157.

2   See my article 'The joys of joyriding' in *New Society*, 3 January 1974.

3   This integration of age levels in a neighbourhood is also noted and discussed by James Patrick. See *A Glasgow Group Observed*, Eyre Methuen, 1973, pp 177–8

4   Roundhouse can be seen as a condoning or tolerant neighbourhood which has accommodated the dominant meaning system to fit in with its position in society. The street-corner milieu is a further extension of this accommodation which could perhaps be regarded as a 'subculture of delinquency'. What is important is the introduction of a conceptualisation which, unlike the cultural diversity perspective of the British subcultural school, allows for an overlap and cross-fertilisation between versions of social morality and normative order.

Chapter 3   (pp 62–116)

1   Jean-Paul Sartre, *Critique de la Raison Dialectique*, Paris, 1960, p 180. Sartre's 'petit bourgeois intellectuel' looking at men working in adjacent fields but separated by a fence and unaware of each other is no comfort to the sociologist as observer. This third man staring at the labourers took it upon himself to create meaning about them and yet his philosophising changes nothing.

2   Stanley Cohen, 'Vandalism, its Politics and Nature', *New Society*, 12 Dec 1968.

3   Elliot Liebow, *Tally's Corner*, Routledge & Kegan Paul, 1967, p 35.

4   See Malcolm W. Klein, 'On the Group Context of Delinquency', *Sociology and Social Research*, Vol 54 No 1, Oct 1968, pp 63–71. Klein also challenges the assumption that most delinquency is 'group' delinquency. Pointing to duos and trios as common 'groupings', Klein suggests 'companionate' delinquency might be a more fitting term, which is certainly true for The Boys' car-radio behaviour.

5 Walter Miller emphasises this transition also: see 'Theft Behaviour in City Gangs' in M. W. Klein (ed), *Juvenile Gangs in Context: Theory, Research and Action*, Prentice-Hall, 1967, pp 25–38.

6 The Collingwood, an East End gang, looked upon their successors in the same way. See *The Paint House*, Penguin, Harmondsworth, 1972, p 121.

7 J. B. Mays in *Growing Up in the City*, Liverpool University Press, 1954, makes the same point.

8 F. L. Strodbeck and J. F. Short, 'Aleatory Risks Versus Short-Run Hedonism', *Social Problems*, Fall, 1964, pp 127–40.

9 See Jock Young, 'The Role of the Police as Amplifiers of Deviancy' in Stanley Cohen (ed), *Images of Deviance*, Penguin, Harmondsworth, 1971, pp 27–61.

10 Albert K. Cohen, *Delinquent Boys*, Free Press, New York, 1955, p 88.

11 See K. Roberts, G. E. White and H. J. Parker, *The Character Training Industry*, David & Charles, Newton Abbot, 1974, for a full analysis of the ideologies held about the goals of adolescence by certain 'youth' organisations.

12 Erving Goffman's concept of man implicit in much of his work seems to stress the devious, calculative aspects of modern man; see *Strategic Interaction*, Basil Blackwell, Oxford, 1970.

13 Howard Becker, *Outsiders*, The Free Press, New York, 1963, pp 27–8.

14 See Erving Goffman, *The Presentation of Self in Everyday Life*, Allen Lane, 1969.

15 For a lively analysis of white-collar crime see Dennis Chapman, *Sociology and the Stereotype of the Criminal*, Tavistock, 1968.

16 James Patrick, *A Glasgow Gang Observed*, Eyre Methuen, 1973, p 178.

17 See Michael Duane, 'Freedom and the State System of Education' in P. Adams, *Children's Rights*, Elk Books, 1967, esp pp 205–7.

18 Frank Parkin suggests this socialisation is aimed towards furthering the dominant ideology; see his analysis of meaning systems, *Class Inequality and Political Order*, Paladin, 1972, pp 79–103.

19 David Downes, *The Delinquent Solution*, Routledge & Kegan Paul, 1966, p 258.

20 '... men who attempt to live by the value system are demoralised not simply by their *own* lack of means and their *own* failures, but also by witnessing that *others* may *succeed* even though they lack valued qualities'. Merton, quoted in A. W. Goulder, *The Coming Crisis of Western Sociology*, Heinemann, 1971, p 324.

21 'Some Notes on Delinquent Careers in a down town neighbourhood', paper given to National Deviancy Conference, York, Sept 1973.

22 The importance of different 'opportunity structures' for delinquency can be highlighted if Roundhouse is compared with another Liverpool neighbourhood close by. See my article on 'Joyriding' in *New Society*, January 1974.

23 Albert K. Cohen, *Delinquency and Control*, Prentice-Hall, Englewood Cliffs, 1966, p 65.

24 R. A. Cloward and L. E. Ohlin, *Delinquency and Opportunity*, Free Press, Chicago, 1960, p 32.

25 D. Downes, op cit, pp 257–8.

26 J. B. Mays, op cit, p 147.

27 J. B. Mays, *Crime and the Social Structure*, Faber, 1963, pp 88–9.

28 Mays simply avoids this issue—'Whether the falling away from delinquency in the early 'twenties and its increasing diminution with each subsequent decade is the result of growing ethical scruples or simple rational fear of the consequences of being found out cannot be decided and perhaps from a sociological point of view, is not very important.' *Juvenile Delinquency, The Family and the Social Group*, Longman, 1972, p 4.

29 Walter Miller, 'Lower Class Culture as a Generating Milieu of Gang Delinquency', *Journal of Social Issues*, XIV, No 3, 1958, pp 5–19.

30 See Charles Valentine, *Culture and Poverty*, University of Chicago Press, 1968, pp 43–5 and pp 135–8.

31 For an extended analysis of assumptions about delinquent motivation see Steven Box, *Deviance, Reality and Society*, Holt, Rinehart & Winston, 1971, pp 98–138.

32 Steven Box, op cit, pp 122–3.

33 I. Taylor, P. Walton and J. Young, *The New Criminology*, Routledge & Kegan Paul, 1973, pp 172–92.

34 David Matza, *Delinquency and Drift*, Wiley, New York, 1964.

35 Dennis H. Wrong, 'The Oversocialised Conception of Man in Modern Sociology', *American Sociological Review*, Vol 26, No 2, pp 183–93.

36 Ibid.

37 Taylor, Walton and Young, op cit, p 185.

38 M. J. Hindelang, 'The Commitment of Delinquents to their Misdeeds; Do Delinquents Drift?' *Social Problems*, 1970, Vol 17, No 4, pp 502–10.

39 Travis Hirschi, *Causes of Delinquency*, University of California, 1970, p 26.

40 E. Linden and J. C. Hackler, 'Affective Ties and Delinquency', *Pacific Sociological Review*, Vol 16, Jan 1973, pp 27–47.

41 Albert K. Cohen, 'The Sociology of the Deviant: anomie theory and beyond', *American Sociological Review*, 1965, 30 (1), pp 5–14.

42 Ibid.

43 Cloward and Ohlin, op cit, and Pat Mayo, *The Making of a Criminal*, Weidenfeld & Nicolson, 1969, emphasise the importance of opportunity structures in influencing delinquent styles.

44 See my 'Some Notes on Delinquent Careers in a down-town neighbourhood', paper given to National Deviancy Conference, York, September 1973. Here I try to relate the *context* represented by this study to a wider social theory of deviance; a theory which must be open-ended and flexible in order to allow for the significance of immediate context.

45 David Matza, op cit, p 26.

Chapter 4 (pp 117–56)

1   See Oscar Lewis, *La Vida*, Random House, 1966, p xiv, quoted in Charles Valentine, *Culture and Poverty*, University of Chicago Press, 1968.

2   Charles Valentine, op cit, and Elliot Liebow, *Tally's Corner*, Routledge & Kegan Paul, 1967, p 19.

3   Walter Miller, 'Lower Class Culture as a Generating Milieu of Gang Delinquency', *Journal of Social Issues*, No 3, 1958, pp 5–19.

4   See David Downes, *The Delinquent Solution*, Routledge & Kegan Paul, 1966, p 113.

5   Alexander D. Blumensteil, 'The Sociology of Good Times' in G. Psathas (ed), *Phenomenological Sociology: Issues and Applications*, Wiley, New York, 1973, pp 187–219.

6   'Interactional territories' are temporary in nature. Public territory includes 'those areas where the individual has freedom of access by virtue of his claim to citizenship'. 'Home territory' implies that 'regular participants have a relative freedom of behaviour and a sense of intimacy and control over the area'. From S. M. Lymon and M. B. Scott, 'Territoriality, a neglected sociological dimension' in *A Sociology of the Absurd*, Appleton-Century-Croft, New York, 1970.

7   See J. Davies and B. Stacey, *Teenagers and Alcohol*, HMSO, 1973. They suggest the heavy adolescent drinker sees himself as tough and rebellious.

8   What Sheila Yegar would call 'with problems in relation to their environment or in coming to terms with their own personal situation'. Yegar identified Terry (comparable to Voggy) in her description of pill parties in 'Greytown'. 'Weekend Junkies', *New Society*, 19 Feb 1970.

9   See M. Kerr, *The People of Ship Street*, Routledge & Kegan Paul, 1958. She points out that for the same sort of Catholic community in Liverpool, 'Sex training appears to be nil. Mothers express horror at the idea of telling their daughters even about menstruation' (p 73).

10 See also James Patrick, *A Glasgow Gang Observed*, Eyre Methuen, 1973, p 107.

11 Liebow, op cit, p 153.

12 Peter Wilmott identified this 'cult of toughness'—a respect for physical prowess—in his interviews with *Adolescent Boys of East London*, Routledge & Kegan Paul, 1966, pp 145–8.

13 See 'An Anatomy of the Liverpool 8 Riot', *New Society*, 17 Aug 1972.

14 R. R. Bell, *Social Deviance*, Dorsey Press, Illinois, 1971, see pp 306–29.

15 Patrick, op cit, p 190.

16 W. Miller, op cit, p 11.

17 Patrick calls this 'focal concern' the capacity to deliver 'brilliant patter', op cit, p 115.

18 W. Miller refers to this degradation contest as 'doin' the dozens', op cit, p 10.

19 David Matza, *Delinquency and Drift*, Wiley, New York, 1964, p 90.
20 Following Goffman, 'action' is found wherever the individual knowingly takes consequential chances perceived as avoidable.
21 Wan Sang Han, 'The Conflicting Themes: Common Values Versus Class Differential Values', *American Sociological Review*, 34, 1969, pp 679–90.
22 See Laurie Taylor, *Deviance and Society*, Michael Joseph, 1971, pp 183–4. Taylor in criticism of Miller also suggests 'focal concerns' must have a historical function.
23 Charles Valentine, op cit, p 136.
24 See David Matza, 'Subterranean traditions of Youth', *Annals of Political and Social Science*, 1961, pp 102–18. This study cannot of course prove the predominance of subterranean values in a middle-class society; it merely makes the assumption.
25 Liebow, op cit, p 227.
26 As Cloward and Ohlin, op cit, p 75, put it: 'The historical continuity theory of lower class values . . . ignores the extent to which lower class and delinquent cultures today are predictable responses to the conditions in our society rather than persisting patterns.'

Chapter 5 (pp 157–94)

1 See Leslie Wilkins, *Social Deviance*, Tavistock, 1964, for an explicit theoretical analysis of the amplification process.
2 I. Taylor, P. Walton and J. Young, *The New Criminology*, Routledge & Kegan Paul, 1973, p 161.
3 The other side can also be concentrated on. See Maureen Cain's study of the police, *Society and the Policeman's Role*, Routledge & Kegan Paul, 1973.
4 David Matza, *Delinquency and Drift*, Wiley, New York, 1964, p 102.
5 The 'individuality of the judge' is indeed relevant; see R. Hood and R. Sparks, *Key Issues in Criminology*, Weidenfeld & Nicolson, 1970, pp 152–4.
6 Gail Armstrong and Mary Wilson, 'The History of a Delinquent Area', paper given to National Deviancy Symposium, York, April 1970.
7 James Patrick, *A Glasgow Gang Observed*, Eyre Methuen, 1973, pp 126–30.
8 See their article in M. Rubington and E. Weinberg, *Deviance: The Interactionist Perspective*, Macmillan, 1968, pp 137–45.
9 Patrick, op cit, p 127.
10 Piliavin and Briar also note this distinction in Rubington and Weinberg, op cit, p 140.
11 Jock Young, 'The Role of the Police as Amplifiers of Deviancy', p 44 in Stanley Cohen (ed), *Images of Deviance*, Penguin, Harmondsworth, 1971.
12 Clive Davies found that 'it appears to be distinctly disadvantageous . . .

to be so detained' in custody, in his Liverpool study; see 'Pre-trial imprisonment' in *British Journal of Criminology*, 1971, pp 32–8.

13 For a full discussion of the importance of judging moral character see R. M. Emerson, *Judging Delinquents*, Aldine, Chicago, 1969, pp 81–172. Paul Rock suggests in *Deviant Behaviour*, Hutchinson, 1973, p 73, that courts are institutionalised attempts to dispel ambiguity: 'the authoritative casting of people and events into distinct categories represents a strenuous endeavour to make the practical business of making moral judgements somewhat less difficult'.

14 This distrust of probation officers has been noted elsewhere. See C. S. Smith, et al, *The Wincroft Youth Project*, Tavistock, 1972, p 96.

15 'We Live There', a detailed report by local men from Liverpool's Inner City, which I co-ordinated, has found this dissatisfaction with legal aid to be extensive. A small number of solicitors appear to have an oligarchy on providing the aid and are felt by some people perhaps to have sacrificed high standards for high returns.

16 R. M. Emerson, op cit, p 170.

17 *Report of The Chief Constable to the Liverpool and Bootle Police Authority*, 1971, p 11.

18 See Armstrong and Wilson, op cit.

19 From Liverpool and Bootle Constabulary Report, *Crime and Vandalism 1967–71*.

20 D. Matza, op cit, p 106.

21 For a concise discussion of these terms see M. Banton, 'Authority', *New Society*, 12 Oct 1972, pp 86–8.

22 R. D. Laing, *The Divided Self*, Penguin, Harmondsworth, 1965, p 62.

23 J.-P. Sartre, *Critique de la Raison Dialectique*, Paris, 1960 (trans Wilfred Desan).

24 'Legitimacy and authority never eliminate power—they merely defocalise it, make it latent. How could authority eliminate power when it becomes, in short, "normalised repression"?' *The Coming Crisis of Western Sociology*, Heinemann, 1970, p 295. Quoted in Taylor, Walton and Young, op cit, p 169.

25 L. Wilkins, op cit, pp 86–7.

26 David Downes and Paul Rock, 'Social Reaction to Deviance . . .', *British Journal of Sociology*, 1971, pp 351–64.

27 Taylor, Walton and Young, op cit, pp 139–72.

28 A. Strauss quoted in W. Carson and P. Wiles, *Crime and Delinquency in Britain*, Martin Robertson, 1971, p 172.

29 Rubington and Weinberg, op cit, p 318.

Chapter 6 (pp 195–207)

1 See also T. Hirschi and R. Stark, 'Hellfire and Delinquency', *Social Problems*, Fall, 1969, pp 207–13.

2 A similar 'shaking down' process was noted by John Mays in Liverpool

during the 1950s. See *Growing Up in The City*, Liverpool University Press, 1954.

3 See K. Coates and R. Silburn, *Poverty: The Forgotten Englishmen*, Penguin, Harmondsworth, 1970. They also note this apparent discrepancy for St Anne's residents who despite their actual low living standards *feel* they are not too badly off. It is perhaps only when slum dwellers have a chance to live elsewhere that their perceptions change radically.

4 See C. S. Smith, et al, *The Wincroft Youth Project*, Tavistock, 1972. They trace a youth-work programme's minimal effect related to expenditure, and conclude similarly.

5 'The greater the social distance between the typer and the person singled out for typing, the broader the type and the quicker it may be applied.' See E. Rubington and M. S. Weinberg, *Deviance: The Interactionist Perspective*, Macmillan, 1968, p 10.

6 J. B. Cortes and F. M. Gatti, *Delinquency and Crime*, Seminar Press, New York, 1972, pp 314–15.

7 American community-development projects have recognised the validity of this 'lack of practice' problem. See for instance 'Urban Poverty and Social Planning', Herbert Gans' chapter in *Uses of Sociology*, edited by P. F. Lazarfeld, et al, Weidenfeld & Nicolson, 1968, pp 437–76.

8 Elliot Liebow, *Tally's Corner*, Routledge & Kegan Paul, 1967, p 65. The present consumption versus deferred gratification discussion is a complex one. The dozens of colour television sets in Roundhouse, for instance, could be construed as a sign of affluence or as a symptom of financial mismanagement. Neither of these stock answers is adequate.

9 A similar process is noted by John Mack in 'Full time miscreants, delinquent neighbourhoods and criminal networks', *British Journal of Sociology*, 15, 1964, pp 42–5.

10 See M. D. Buffalo and J. W. Rodgers. 'Behavioural Norms, Moral Norms and Attachment. Problems of Deviance and Conformity', *Social Problems*, 1971, pp 101–14. They also note that, 'The delinquent is aware that his behaviour is non-conforming in relation to the dominant moral and legal norms of society and he takes steps to insure that his behaviour will not be detected and he will not be punished for his behaviour.'

11 From 'The Ideologies of Non-Skilled Industrial Workers', unpublished paper, by Michael Mann, Department of Applied Economics, Cambridge University, August 1972.

Appendix (pp 214–24)

1 William Whyte noted the importance of having the support of key individuals in any group studied ethnographically. *Street Corner Society*, University of Chicago Press, 1943, p 300.

2 'I found that my acceptance in the district depended on the personal

relationships I developed far more than upon any explanations I might give,' Whyte, ibid, p 300.

3   Elliot Liebow also found that blunting and 'dulling' differences in dress and language was more practical than attempting a complete copy. *Tally's Corner*, Routledge & Kegan Paul, 1967, p 255.

4   Whyte, op cit, p 302. He mentions such mistakes also.

5   See 'Anxiety as a Source of Distortion' by M. S. and C. G. Schwartz in G. J. McCall and J. L. Simmons, *Issues in Participant Observation*, Addison-Wesley, 1969, p 100.

6   Ibid, p 1.

7   Although the Schwartzes, for instance, distinguish between two ideal types, the 'passive' and 'active' participant observer as distinctive roles, such a dichotomy is untenable for this study. See their article in McCall and Simmons, op cit, pp 89–105.

8   Florence Kluckhohn, quoted in R. A. Berk and J. M. Adams, 'Establishing Rapport with Deviant Groups', *Social Problems*, vol 18, 1970–1, p 102.

9   James Patrick suggests a Glasgow gang of the 1960s was not very friendly, for instance. See *A Glasgow Gang Observed*, Eyre Methuen, 1973.

10   McCall and Simmons, op cit, p 28.

11   Howard Becker, 'Problems in the Publication of Field Studies', in A. J. Vidich, J. Bensman and M. R. Stein (eds), *Reflections on Community Studies*, Wiley, New York, 1964, pp 267–84.

12   William Whyte, op cit, p 309.

Acknowledgements

For their various forms of help I would like to thank the following: Gideon Ben-Tovim, David Downes, David Gairn, Owen Gill, Allan James, John Mays and Ken Roberts. For providing useful information, and permission to use it, Liverpool and Bootle Constabulary, the Social Services Department and the Education Department are thanked. For their typing efforts Dorothy Lewis, Margaret Grek, Erica Sheel, Linda Johnson, Dot Nelson and Phil Breen are gratefully acknowledged. Diana Parker, most of all, gave continuous support throughout. Although I cannot acknowledge all The Boys by their correct names, I thank them most sincerely for their friendship, and hope I haven't let them down.

Index

After references to items in the Notes and References section, the relevant pages in the text are shown in parentheses.

Amplification of deviance, 91–2, 157–8, 188–9, 192
Armstrong, G., 225 (22), 231 (182)

Banton, M., 185
Becker, H., 105, 224
Blumensteil, A., 121
Box, S., 112
Boys' network, The, 64–6
'Breaking out', 119, 156

Cameo Cinema Murders, 31–2
'Catseyes', definition of, 212
City Housing Dept, 24
City Planning Dept, 22, 25, 26
Cloward, R., 110, 228 (115), 230 (155)
Coates, K., 226 (40), 232 (202)
Cohen, A., 109, 115
Cohen, S., 226 (63)
Corner, the, 28, 121–2
Court, 87–8, 169–80, 187

Delinquent 'careers', 15, 46
'Down town', 12
Downes, D., 188, 227 (107)
Drug-use, 131–4

Emerson, R., 231 (170, 180)

Fighting, 139–47

Girls, The, 93–5, 125–6, 135–8
Goffman, E., 227 (105), 230 (152)
Gouldner, A., 186

235

Hackler, J., 114
'Hanging around', 72, 121–2
Hindelang, M., 114
Hirschi, T., 114

Jobs, 68–74, 122–3, 154, 205
Joyriding, 52–3

Kerr, M., 27, 229 (135)
Klein, M. 226 (78)

Lewis, O., 37, 229 (119)
Liebow, E., 71, 155, 233 (217)
Linden, E., 114
Liverpool Corporation, 24–5
Liverpool Echo, 12, 32, 33
Liverpool Review, 23
Liverpool Post and Mercury, 23

McCall, G., 221, 223
Mann, M., 206
Marriage, 96–8
Matza, D., 14, 112, 116, 150, 184, 230 (160)
Mays, J., 110–11
Merton, R., 109, 227 (107)
Miller, W., 111, 120, 150–1

Ohlin, L., 110, 155, 228 (115)

Parents, 37–8, 40–6, 60
Participant observation, 221–3
Patrick, J., 226 (53), 227 (106), 229 (137), 230 (162, 163)
Police, 57–8, 86–7, 125, 159–69, 181–4

Religion, 30, 199
'Repartee', examples of, 129, 147–9, 217
Ritz, The, 55–61, 91
Rock, P., 188, 231 (170)

'Sandhills', 15, 103–4, 214–15
Sartre, J.-P., 105, 186, 226 (63)
School, 42, 47, 67, 196–200
Sex, *see* Girls
Silburn, R., 226 (40), 232 (202)
Simmons, J., 221, 223
Smith, C. S., 232 (203)
Social work, 173, 202
Street corner milieu, 108
Suttles, G., 38

Task Force, 80, 182
Taylor, I., 158, 228 (112), 231 (114)
Taylor, L., 153

Vandalism, 39

Walton, P., 158, 228 (112, 114), 231 (189)
Whyte, W., 224, 232 (215), 233 (215)

Wilkins, L., 188
Wilmott, P., 27, 229 (141)
Wilson, M., 225 (22), 231 (182)
Work, *see* Jobs
Wrong, D., 113

Young, J., 158, 228 (112, 114), 230 (169), 231 (189)
Young, M., 27